The Open Door

A History of the Order of Women Freemasons

Most Worshipful Brother Brenda Irene Fleming-Taylor, Grand Master of the Order of Women Freemasons from 1989 to 2010.

THE OPEN DOOR

The History of the
Order of Women Freemasons
1908 - 2008

Ann Pilcher-Dayton

The Order of Women Freemasons

4

Published by the
Order of Women Freemasons
27 Pembridge Gardens
London W2 4EF
2008, 2012

Printed and finished by
The Repro Studio

ISBN 978-0-9558598-0-9

Preface by the Grand Master

M.W.Bro. Brenda I. Fleming-Taylor

This year we celebrate the 100th anniversary of the formation of the Honourable Fraternity of Antient Masonry. The Grand Lodge of this organisation met for the first time on 20th June 1908, when the first three Lodges were consecrated. The research and compilation of a full and detailed history, recording and reviewing those beginnings and the subsequent remarkable development of our Order - which since 1958 has carried the subtitle of *The Order of Women Freemasons* - is long overdue, and I am both excited and delighted by the fact that it has now been written and that it is being published in this, our Centenary Year.

Throughout our one hundred years of history as an Order, there have been many momentous occasions, events and achievements. This book recounts these, often in the words of the time, and uses many illustrations from the past, most of which first appeared in our journal *The Gavel*. This material has hitherto been unavailable to readers and researchers.

The United Grand Lodge of England, in their statement of February 1999, has formally acknowledged the existence of female Freemasons - how pleased and proud our Founders would have been to know it!

This volume makes an unprecedented and invaluable contribution to our knowledge and understanding of the history and development of the Order of Women Freemasons. A great deal of work and care has been undertaken over several years by the Grand Registrar and Librarian of the Order, R.W.Bro. Ann Pilcher-Dayton, P.J.G.W., Grand Registrar, G.M's.G.S., which has now culminated in the publication of this book. I commend it not only to all members of our Order but also to Masonic historians and to the many readers interested in the social history of the last century.

Brenda I. Fleming-Taylor
Grand Master

Author's Preface

This book is not intended to be a critical history of the Order of Women Freemasons, but it is hoped that it is as objective as possible. *The Open Door* was written for members of the Order and interested outsiders. It therefore assumes some knowledge of Freemasonry, which is readily found in this information age. The Order of Women Freemasons has always kept a low profile and consequently up to now an accurate record of its history has never been freely available.

The title *The Open Door* refers to the admission of women to Freemasonry, as described by the pioneer woman Mason Maria Deraismes in 1882. The Order's Banner shows the door as it is today - partly open.

It was decided to adopt a generally chronological arrangement. Both a subject and a chronological approach would necessitate some material out of sequence, but it was felt that the latter would be less disruptive. Individual Lodge Consecrations are recorded in the page margin.

Two concerns in writing have been firstly the lack of archive material and secondly the citation of documentary support for statements of fact. The sources used in compiling this history are primarily the Minute Books of the Quarterly Communications of Grand Lodge from 1908 onwards and past issues of *The Gavel*. To this has been added the four history booklets issued between 1938 and 1963 and the record of the Diamond Jubilee pageant at the Albert Hall in 1968.

It would be inappropriate for a book of this nature to have copious footnotes and so it is hoped that this explanation of sources will suffice. Any important additional sources used are cited at the end of the relevant chapter.

The choice of illustrations was entirely dictated by the material available. It was thought important to reproduce as many early pictures as possible - mainly from past issues of *The Gavel* - so that they would become more widely available.

A. P-D.

Table of Contents

Prologue

On 5th June 1908 eleven men and women met together in London to found a new Grand Lodge and a new Masonic Order. The Honourable Fraternity of Antient Masonry was set up to emphasise the spiritual basis of Freemasonry and to give women their proper place in the Brotherhood. Two weeks later the first three Lodges were consecrated, the entire Order consisting of only thirty nine people.

So it all began one hundred years ago
- and this is our story.

Chapter One - *How did it all begin?*

The Development of mixed Masonry in France

Speculative Masonry for men, which developed during the 17th century in England and expanded on an organised basis following the establishment of the first Grand Lodge in 1717, is generally thought to have been carried to France in the 18th century.

There, in 1882, the first step towards the founding of an organisation open to both men and women was taken. Under one of several independent Masonic authorities in France, very liberal control had been granted to daughter Lodges. One of these - *Les Libres Penseurs*, which met at Pecq near Paris and which worked under the charter of the Ancient and Accepted Rite of *La Grande Loge Symbolique de France*, resolved that the time had come when women who had proved themselves free and of mature mind and understanding should receive initiation into Masonry. One of their principles was 'a free mason in a free lodge'.

Mlle. Maria Deraismes was initiated into the Lodge in 1882. She was a distinguished author and lecturer, noted for her devotion to the cause of feminism, suffrage and to humanitarian and democratic political ideals. At her initiation, the Master of the Lodge, R.W.Bro. Houbron, said "We are about to consecrate one of the greatest humanitarian principles, that of Equality. By admitting a woman

Mlle. Maria Deraismes, initiated into Freemasonry in France in 1882.

into our Mysteries, we proclaim the Equality of the two human beings who together incur in the propagation of the human race ... [since woman is the child's first leader] to do away with her prejudices by the moral teachings and the light of Masonry would be to bring about by peaceful means true social emancipation." Part of her address to the

Lodge following the ceremony was a rallying call indeed: "If the feeble support that I may be able to render you cannot be effective, that fact in itself is small and of little import, but it well has another importance. The door that you have opened to me will not be closed upon me and all the legion that follows me."

The initiation of women met with considerable opposition and it was not until 1893 that, encouraged by Dr. Georges Martin, a member of the French Senate and of the Lodge *Les Libres Penseurs*, Mlle. Deraismes was able to initiate seventeen more women. On that day a new Grand Lodge was established with the title *Le Droit Humain*. This became the Grand Lodge of the mixed Co-Masonic Order. Their first Craft Lodge in Paris was called Lodge Maria Deraismes No.1. At first only the three Craft Degrees were worked, but in May 1899 the decision was taken to work the full thirty three Degrees of the Ancient and Accepted Scottish Rite.

The Spread of Co-Masonry to England

The first Englishwoman to join the French Lodge was Mme. Maria Martin (no relation to Dr. Georges Martin) who had married a Frenchman. She was the sister of Francesca Arundale, close friend and co-worker of Annie Besant, who was a well-known speaker and worker for social justice in England. Francesca joined the French Lodge in July 1895 and took the Degree of a Master Mason in August 1896. She gave her reasons for joining:

Georges Martin and Maria Martin of Le Droit Humain.

"My sister was an ardent feminist, and I sympathised most strongly with her views, and the fact that in this movement men and women could work together and that once again women could triumph in a disability removed, was sufficient to draw me within the Order. There was certainly apart from this nothing very attractive in the meetings, the ritual of which was the most meagre because our brothers there objected to ritual. But they were men and women earnestly working together to give a nobler ideal of brotherhood to humanity, and their discussions and papers were very interesting."

Francesca Arundale related later how an apparently casual remark of Annie Besant's led to the establishment of the Co-Masonic movement in England. "I was travelling with her on the District Railway between Ealing and London when she said 'I have been told to join the Masonic Order. I know

Annie Besant.

there is a section that admits women, but I do not know where it is to be found'. That information I was able to give her...". Mrs. Besant had become convinced that a system of Masonry admitting men and women on an equal footing could have great value and help many people on their spiritual progress. It is possible that she had become aware of the principles of Freemasonry through Charles Bradlaugh, who was a Freemason at one stage of his life and with whom she had worked so closely on secularist matters and controversial social issues such as birth control.

As one of Annie Besant's contemporary lady Masons wrote: "With her tireless energy, and her characteristic devotion to a Cause, which she had reason to believe was considered important by some of those great Agents of the G.A.O.T.U., to whose service she was utterly dedicated, Sister Annie Besant had set to work to interest [others] in the new project, and by degrees to draw into the Order, those who might be able to respond to its ideals. Those ideals were pre-eminently the furthering of the Brotherhood of Man, and the restoration to what had been their place in the ancient Mysteries of that half of Humanity which up to quite recently has been and still in most countries is excluded from Masonry."

In the summer of 1902, Annie Besant was living in the home of Ursula Bright and her daughter Esther at 31 St. James' Place, London. The Brights were a prominent Quaker family and active in feminist causes.

Esther Bright wrote in 1947:

"Doctor Annie Besant became deeply interested in the possibility of starting a Co-Masonic movement in England in the summer of 1902 … she asked us if we would be willing to co-operate with her in the formation of such a movement. We were of course only too willing to stand by her and do all we could to help. I well remember those early days when she chose those whom she thought suitable to be the founders of the new movement, workers whom she trusted and who had been in close touch with her for many years. So we, whom she had chosen, all travelled to Paris - Dr. Besant, Captain and Mrs. Lauder, Miss Arundale, George Arundale *[Francesca's nephew]*, my mother Ursula M. Bright and myself, Esther Bright. We were initiated, passed and raised into the *Ordre Maconnique Mixte International*." The particular Lodge was Maria Deraismes Lodge No.1 and it was on 27th July 1902.

To extend the movement to Britain, it was decided to set up a provisional Lodge at the Bright's home in London, to prepare for the founding of the first British Lodge. It is reported that a Provisional Lodge Meeting was held on 29th July 1902 when the seven founding members (those who had travelled to Paris) drew up and signed a Petition for the Lodge to the Supreme Council. The name of the Lodge was to be *The Scotch Symbolical Worshipful Lodge of England: Droit Humain, No.6 Human Duty.* The issue of the title to be given to lady Masons arose, but after discussion "It is decided to use the terms Bro. and Sis. in speaking of members thereby maintaining the distinction of sex."

On 22nd September a special Delegation from Paris visited the Lodge. This included Bro. Georges Martin, the Founder Orator of Lodge Maria Deraismes No.1, and Sister Maria Martin, the Grand Secretary of the Supreme Council. It was to arrange preparation for the great day of the Inauguration and Installation, fixed for September 26th 1902.

Esther Bright tells us that "Dr. Georges Martin and his charming wife came to stay with us at 31 St. James' Place for some days to attend Masonic Meetings … Many Meetings and rehearsals were held in our home ... and when the great day came for our first real Lodge meeting in a big hall we were all slightly nervous, anxious to play our parts as well as possible. I drove in a hansom cab with Dr. Annie Besant and for the first time she was going to do without her ritual book! It was a great occasion, but all went well!."

The formal Consecration of Lodge Human Duty No.6 took place in the Lecture Hall of the Theosophical Society in London. There was a close connection between Co-Masonry and this Society. The Theosophical movement was a feature of the last quarter of the 19th century, when its eclectic philosophy of a mixture of Eastern religions, mysticism and the occult appealed to those whose Biblical faith had been shaken by advances in physics and biology, particularly Darwin's theory of evolution. The Theosophical Society, founded in 1875 by the Russian psychic Helena Blavatsky, strongly believed in the universal brotherhood of humanity and the necessity for social reform to achieve this and it aimed to combat ignorance in all its forms, imposing no restrictions on the free search after truth.

Annie Besant was a senior member of the Theosophical Society (she became President later in 1907) and at the turn of the century women were beginning to out-number men in the membership. While not officially a theosophical activity, Co-Masonry in England was from the beginning dominated by

Founders of L. Human Duty No.6, the first British Lodge of Le Droit Humain, with Annie Besant and William Lauder (centre) and Esther Bright on his left.

theosophists, especially when Annie Besant was created Vice President Grand Master of the Supreme Council and Deputy for Great Britain and Its Dependencies, and the membership of the two organisations overlapped to a considerable extent. Universal Co-Masonry claimed to be returning to the ancient practice from which true Masonic orders derived, and argued that a movement which professed to be the Brotherhood of Humanity could not accomplish its object if it refused entry to one half of the human family - women. It was also strongly linked to the women's suffrage movement.

Annie Besant was to be installed as the first Right Worshipful Master of Lodge Human Duty No.6. In her speech of welcome to the French delegation she said that if the impulse of Speculative Masonry was carried from England to France in the 18th century, it was the French who had that day brought it back, completed and strengthened by the admission of women on equal terms with men. The Delegation from France took over the offices of the Lodge, and four candidates were initiated. The French Grand Master, having given an account of the formation of the first Lodge in France, then proceeded to the constitution ceremony of the new Lodge. The Master Elect Annie Besant took the Obligation, as did the Senior and Junior Wardens, Francesca Arundale and William Lauder. Evelyn Lauder, as Senior Deacon, surrounded by the other officers of the new Lodge, then took an Obligation on their behalf. The Grand Master handed Annie Besant the Warrant of the Lodge and "declared the Lodge duly constituted, establishing to it the right of initiating, passing and raising to the three Degrees of Masonry men and women who were deemed suitable."

Annie Besant in regalia.

Problems in England

The mixed Masonic movement expanded in England. Annie Besant, although the chief English official, spent most of her time in India, which made administration difficult. Other Lodges were founded, including one in Edinburgh.

In 1907 and 1908 there were rumblings of discontent within the hierarchy of Co-Masonry. Some members wanted to return to the spiritual values which they felt were lacking in mainstream Freemasonry; to return to the 'purer' form of ceremonial working which consisted of the three Degrees of the so-called York Rite, as opposed to the thirty-three Degrees of the Ancient and Accepted Rite worked by the Co-Masons; to no longer be governed by a Supreme Council that worked in Paris; but above all to distance themselves from the Theosophical bias of Co-Masonry and to admit men and women on equal terms.

Foremost among the dissidents was the Rev. Dr. William Cobb, Rector of St. Ethelburga's Church in the City of London, a member of the Human Duty Lodge No.6. He had crossed swords with Annie Besant and other members of the ruling body because he wanted to change the constitution of Co-Masonry in England and set up a governing council separate from that in Paris.

Peter Birchall, a fellow Co-Mason who later became Deputy Grand Master of our Order and editor of *The Gavel*, wrote some years afterwards:

"To Dr. Cobb, more than to any other individual, the praise and gratitude of our Order is due for his courage, wisdom and prevision in breaking with Co-Masonry and leading a small but determined company into the spacious world of 'Free' Masonry proper, *i.e.*, Masonry unattached to any eclectic system of philosophy, Freemasonry based upon age-long principles and landmarks as enunciated through the rites and ceremonies of such a body as the United Grand Lodge of England."

Eventually it became obvious that compromise between the dissidents and their governing body was impossible. Dr. Cobb and his group resigned from Lodge Human Duty No.6 and the Co-Masons in November 1907.

They immediately took steps to set up a new Order in Freemasonry for both "men and women, following the ancient Masonic teaching and taking as a model the United Grand Lodge of England." By mid 1908 plans had matured sufficiently for a 'Meeting of Masons' to be held on

5th June at 1 The Mall, Notting Hill Gate in London, when Dr. Cobb and ten other Brethren agreed the following Resolution:

"The following Masons being desirous of forwarding the purpose of Freemasonry by the free association of men and women do hereby form themselves into a Masonic Order to be termed the Order of Ancient Masonry and also do hereby elect Brother Dr. W.F. Cobb, Brother John A. Johns and Brother H.P. Geddes to be Master, Senior Warden and Junior Warden respectively of a Lodge to be called GOLDEN RULE; Brother J.W. Sidley, Brother P. Birchall and Brother S.H. Old of a Lodge to be called EMULATION; and Sister F. Faulding, Brother E. Greenfield and Brother Lacey of a Lodge to be called UNITY."

These names were taken from those of Co-Masonic Lodges - Golden Rule was their No. 21 in London, Emulation was No. 24 in London and Unity was No. 35 in Bournemouth.

Brother Rev. Dr. William Frederick Cobb, inspiration and mainstay of the new Masonic movement, was elected Grand Master. The next Chapter will describe the background of this charismatic character.

Additional Sources

A. Pilcher-Dayton, *The Social Impact of Women's Freemasonry in England to 1935.* Ph.D. thesis, University of Sheffield.

Material from the archives of Co-Freemasonry is reproduced by kind permission of the Most Puissant Grand Commander, V.Ill.Bro. Brian Roberts and the British Federation of the International Order of Co-Freemasonry *Le Droit Humain*.

Chapter Two

The Rev. Dr. William Cobb and the early years of the new Order

The Rev. Dr. Cobb lived for eighty four years. He became our first Grand Master in 1908, when he was 51 and, like a shooting star crossing the heavens, disappeared from the Order after four brief years, in 1912. In that short time he made an indelible impression. In the newspaper the *City Press* of 19th December 1941, his obituary commenced "In the death of Dr. W.F. Geikie-Cobb ... the City has lost an outstanding figure and the Church an original thinker ..." and it ended " ... he was a mystic and a scholar and a very human fellow."

William Frederick Cobb was born in Danbury, Essex, in 1857, the son of George Cobb, a land steward on one of the local big estates. Educated at Chelmsford Grammar School and Trinity College Dublin, he was ordained in 1882 and served as Curate at parishes in Surrey, Winchester and London's Kentish Town. At the age of 41 in 1898 he became Curate-in-Charge of St. Ethelburga-the-Virgin within Bishopsgate, a small Henry VIII church in the City of London, and two years later was appointed Rector, a position he held until his death in 1941.

He was an Anglo-Catholic and as such the principles of natural law and equality influenced his life and actions. His belief in mysticism - achieving an identity with God through insight and holding this communion to be a source of wisdom - led to an interest in the spiritual side of Freemasonry. His concern for the equality of women, as shown both

The Rev. Dr. William Frederick Cobb.

The rebuilt church of St. Ethelburga-the-Virgin within Bishopsgate, City of London, parish of Rev. Dr. Cobb from 1900 to 1941. The church was bombed by the I.R.A. in 1993.

in his activity on behalf of the women's suffrage movement at the beginning of the twentieth century and his important work in the field of marriage and divorce law reform, naturally extended his Masonic thinking towards a form of Freemasonry which would include women. We know that he had become a Co-Mason by 1905.

Dr. Cobb was critical of the exclusion of women by the male establishment of the United Grand Lodge of England. He believed that for women to be in Freemasonry was no more than a restitution of their rights. "Not only does Masonry appear to have lost its original spirit, but it has done what no religion of antiquity ever did: it has excluded women from its mysteries. That is, it professes to be the basis of a universal brotherhood, but excludes women, which is a contradiction in terms."

In the Order's periodical *The Gavel* he wrote in 1909:
"The admission of women is not so much an innovation as a recovery. It is but one recognition of the right of women to share in the labours of men, and to give them that training in common work which has taught men most of the virtue they possess". In 1910 he again pursued the same theme:
"Now at this present moment particularly one movement amongst many others stands out pre-eminently as characteristic of our age. It is what may be called tersely the Woman Movement. Whatever may be the reasons alleged for or against the emancipation of women, no thoughtful observer can fail to see that a cosmic process is at work in

bringing them from the background, and putting them into a place side by side with man.

In social movements, in education, in municipal affairs, in politics and the economic realm women are assuming a new importance. We may applaud their appearance on equal terms with men, or we may decry it as monstrous and dangerous, but it is there and has to be dealt with. English Masonry has so far shown no signs that it at all appreciates the enormous importance of this movement. It has been left for other Masonic bodies to step into the breach and to assume the duty which English Masonry has not cared to undertake."

As a clergyman, he did not shy away from religious controversy and during his tenure as Rector often acted with characteristic boldness. The 1662 Prayer Book was revised for the first time in 1928, to considerable opposition. The Rector held experimental services based on the revised version, at which, as the *City Press* rather laconically remarked "the proceedings were disturbed." He also conducted marriage services which omitted the words "obey" and "serve", and was well-known as one of the few clergymen willing to marry divorced people, providing they were the innocent party.

Dr. Cobb died in December 1941 and at a Thanksgiving Service the same month the address was given by the Rev. Walter Muirhead Hope, a member of the United Grand Lodge of England, and a frequent visitor in the early days to our Lodges. Both the Rev. Hope's daughters and his wife were members of our Order and one daughter - Mary Gordon Muirhead Hope - became Grand Master in 1948.

The Early Years of the New Order

At the 'Meeting of Masons' held on 5th June 1908, the assembled eleven Brethren constituted themselves as a Grand Lodge, with Dr. Cobb at their head. Two weeks later, the first meeting of the Grand Lodge of England of the Honourable Order of Antient Masonry was held at 1 The Mall, Notting Hill Gate (since demolished) on 20th June 1908. The founding members were Dr. Cobb, John W. Sidley, Alfred and Florence Faulding, Horace P. Geddes, John A. Johns, T. Anderson Marks, F.W. Schon, Frederick W. Lacey, Edward Greenfield and Peter

Birchall. Grand Officers were appointed. Three petitions to warrant the first three Lodges were presented and a draft Declaration of Principles agreed, together with draft *Instructions for Candidates* which had a strong spiritual bias: "Since Ancient Masonry aims at filling the traditional forms of Masonry with a spiritual content, no one should offer himself as a Candidate who is not striving sincerely to spiritualise his own life."

Lodge Golden Rule No.1 in June 1908

Lodge Emulation No.2 in June 1908

Lodge of Unity No.3 in June 1908

At the same lengthy session, the three founding Lodges were consecrated. The founders of Lodge Golden Rule No.1 were Rev. Dr. William and Mrs. Hettie Cobb, Horace and Emma Geddes, E.C. Ryan, John Johns and Millicent Mackenzie. Lodges No.2 and No.3 similarly included married couples - John and Ethel Purcell Quinton were founders in No.2 and Alfred and Florence Faulding in No.3. There was confusion over the title of lady members - Brother or Sister? It was quickly decided after the first few Lodge meetings that everyone should be called Brother.

The Cobbs' second son Ivo and daughter Monica also joined the Order from the Co-Masons - both were Fellowcrafts, and a Dispensation had to be requested from Grand Lodge for Monica, as she was only 18.

A modern copy of the banner of Lodge Golden Rule No.1.

The draft Declaration of Principles was explicit in describing its aims:

"The Order of Antient Masonry exists for the purpose of emphasising the spiritual end of Masonry and of demonstrating the spiritual meaning of its traditional rites and ceremonies. It does not seek to oppose but to supplement Masonry as practised under the United Grand Lodge of England."

"The aims of the new Fraternity then are briefly:

(1) To spiritualise Masonry;

(2) To give women their proper place in the Brotherhood of Masonry."

Following much protracted discussion over the course of two Grand Lodge meetings, on 10th October 1908 nineteen Rules were adopted as a Constitution, setting fees (one guinea for each of the ceremonies; three guineas for the Consecration of a Lodge); establishing a Benevolent Fund and setting regulations for the admission of members. Clause 15 stipulates: "Lodges shall not allow the ratio of the numbers of the two sexes each to each, to exceed that of 3:2, except by special dispensation from Grand Lodge."

The Ritual Book to be used was Taylor's *Handbook of Craft Masonry*, well-known in United Grand Lodge, as opposed to the Dharma (Indian) working of the Co-Masonic Order or their more mystical Lauderdale ritual, although within the next few months petitions were presented to Grand Lodge to allow some of the Co-Masonic ceremonial and ritual to be used. The new society became known as the Honourable Fraternity of Antient Masonry - a title still to be seen on our emblem.

A room was booked for meetings at the Eustace Miles Restaurant, Chandos Street, Charing Cross for one guinea a night. Eustace Miles and his wife Hattie had been Co-Masons and had left that Order with Dr. Cobb. The restaurant was vegetarian and the Miles' were prominent in the

Banner of Lodge Emulation No.2.

*Banner of the
Lodge of Unity No.3.*

The cover of The Gavel *in April 1909*

socialist-suffrage-radical society of the time, hosting meetings of the militant women's suffrage movements and the Men's League for Women's Suffrage. They both became members of our Lodge Emulation No.2 at the first meeting in June 1908.

In the course of his parochial work, Dr. Cobb had been taught the craft of printing by one of the parishioners at his church of St. Ethelburga and he set up a printing press in the Vestry to print his parish magazine. Less than a year after the founding of the Honourable Fraternity of Antient Masonry, in April 1909, he decided that the new Order needed a journal to act both as a means of communication between Grand Lodge and the ninety-nine members of the three Lodges then existing, and as a source of information about the Order for other Masons.

Called *The Gavel*, the first issue was a single sheet folded into four, in a blue cover with a drawing of a gavel on the front. Entirely written by Grand Master Cobb, it gave the meeting dates of the three Lodges, listed the 'more important' Landmarks of Masonry, the desirable qualifications of a Candidate and the objects of the Honourable Fraternity. The subscription was one shilling a year for four issues.

The Gavel temporarily ceased publication on Dr. Cobb's resignation from the Order in 1912. Most of the content reflected his own strong opinions, particularly on the subject of women in Freemasonry and the lack of official recognition of them. Some was contentious, even inflammatory. Peter Birchall, who took over the editorship when publication resumed in 1929, wrote: "It had a short but brilliant existence, not bringing peace but a sword. It was a weapon of offence, polemical, trenchant and utterly unafraid…" In 1929 it was very different - strictly a means of instruction and education.

In early 1909 J.W. Sidley and Alfred Faulding were empowered by Grand Lodge to consecrate Lodges, make Masons and grant provisional Charters in the United States of America - an unusual resolution but made at a time when America was the land of the future. A petition was presented by Lodge Golden Rule No.1 to form a Lodge to be called Harmony No.4, which was duly consecrated on 19th February 1910. At the same time the Lodge of Unity No.3 desired to found a daughter Lodge called Stability No.5.

Lodge Harmony No.4 in February 1910

Lodge Stability No.5 in April 1910

Members of Grand Lodge thought that it would be a good idea if a small committee be set up from amongst themselves to regulate the affairs of the Order in the intervening periods between the Quarterly Communications of Grand Lodge. In June 1909 the Senior Grand Warden Alfred Faulding proposed that a Board of General Purposes be set up, consisting of five members of Grand Lodge, for this purpose. Ever since, the Board concerns itself with "whatever it may deem conducive to the welfare and good government of the Craft", recommending certain courses of action to Grand Lodge for its approval and ratification.

The Eustace Miles Restaurant being only a temporary venue, eventually in 1911 a meeting room was rented at the Baptist Union Chapel at 4 Southampton Row, Holborn for £25 per annum or £2/10/0 (£2.50) per night. With the later addition of administrative offices, these premises served the Order until 1925. Grand Lodge also decided to form a lending and reference Library for the use of the Order. Bro. Hilda Haslam, Senior Warden of Lodge Golden Rule No.1, was appointed Librarian and an appeal was made for books and funds to be donated.

The initial brief of the 'Library of Masonic and kindred literature' is interesting. Dr. Cobb wrote "We should suggest that a three-fold division of the Library should be made corresponding to our three Degrees. In the first would be placed works on ethics; in the second, works on philosophy and especially psychology; and in the third, books on religion in its purest form." His list of examples included

Aristotle's *Ethics* and Plato's *Republic*, psychology textbooks of the time such as William James' *Principles of Psychology*, and works on comparative religion, mysticism and Gnosticism. Vestiges of the original plan - in particular, an emphasis on aspects of mysticism - can still be detected, but we have to remember here that one of the aims of our Order was to increase awareness of the spiritual basis of Freemasonry, and that our Founders worked on a high intellectual plane. By early 1912 a Circulating Library was ready, with Bro. Alice Stow of Lodge Stability No.5 to assist the Librarian in its administration.

Banner of Lodge Harmony No.4,
consecrated in February 1910.

The Resignation of Dr. Cobb

The first suggestion of opposition to Dr. Cobb within the new Order comes in criticism of *The Gavel*. At the beginning of 1911 it was proposed by Cobb as Grand Master, in Grand Lodge, that 1/6d (7.5p) be added to members' subscriptions to pay for an obligatory copy of *The Gavel*. The motion was not carried, but referred to the Lodges. In Lodge of Unity No.3 this was opposed, on the grounds that *The Gavel* was not the official organ of the Order and therefore members should not be compelled to subscribe to it; that "the existence of *The Gavel* is undesirable in as much as it has touched upon the secrets of Freemasonry and antagonised the Grand Lodge of England" and that in it an attempt had been made to destroy the allegiance of male English Masons to their Grand Lodge. From correspondence it is clear that other members of Grand Lodge felt the same.

In the following April Dr. Cobb wrote to Grand Lodge resigning from the editorship of *The Gavel* "which I feel unable to hold longer in view of the irregular and irresponsible criticism passed on my conduct of their organ by members of Grand Lodge out of Grand Lodge." Two weeks later he sent his apologies to Peter Birchall for being absent from the forthcoming Grand Lodge meeting and said:
"On the question of *The Gavel* itself I would remind Grand Lodge that the paper was started to be both a means of information for members of our Order, and still more to act as a medium for influencing members of other bodies. It has failed in the former, but done useful work for the latter object. Should Grand Lodge decide to discontinue the issue of the *Gavel* the decision will carry with it necessarily a note of failure. If, on the other hand, G.L. should decide to continue the *Gavel* an appeal should be made strongly for more support from our members. I could not always secure from all the Lodges so small a thing even as a note of their doings."

Matters obviously went from bad to worse, for nearly a year later - 17th March 1912 - Dr. Cobb resigned his membership of Lodge Golden Rule No.1, his Mother Lodge, and therefore his membership of the Order. The Worshipful Master was Marion Lindsay Halsey. In his letter he said to Bro. Secretary, the Rev. Walter Secker:

"Your W.M. is aware that for some time past the conviction has been maturing in my mind that I could not consent much longer to hold the office of Grand Master, with which I have been honoured for the past four years. From the foundation of the Order I have had to withstand certain sinister tendencies within the Order to revert to the Order of Universal Co-Masonry out of which our Order took its rise, and against which it was founded to protest. So long as my efforts to resist those tendencies were supported by the general approbation of the Order, I was content to go on discharging the duty of keeping the Order true to its principles.

Recent events, however, have convinced me that I cannot rely on the support of the Order, and as I can neither stoop to nor condone the methods by which my authority has been in some quarters undermined, I have come to the conclusion that I could neither continue to be in any degree responsible for the Order as Grand Master, nor even continue in an Order which, in my humble judgement, has ceased to follow the object for which it was founded."

He ended "Although I shall lay down the Grand Mastership with relief, I leave your Lodge with deep and unfeigned sorrow, and it has cost me much to come to this decision."

Marion Lindsay Halsey had been appointed Deputy Grand Master in November 1911, in succession to J.W. Sidley, whilst she was still a 'light blue' and had only been a member of the Order for two years. A meeting of Grand Lodge was called for 27th March 1912 at her house in Portman Square for the express purpose of receiving Dr. Cobb's resignation as Grand Master of the Order. The record of the meeting reveals considerable antipathy towards Dr. Cobb, with very strong feelings all round. Deputy Grand Master Marion Halsey explained that there had been a meeting the previous evening when Dr. Cobb withdrew his resignation and asked for leave of absence from his own Lodge Golden Rule No.1, for twelve months from the coming June. However, she knew that Dr. Cobb really wanted his resignation accepted, and put forward a resolution: "This Grand Lodge accepts with great regret the resignation of W.Bro. Cobb from the office of Grand Master and only so accepts his resignation because they understand it to be final and irrevocable. They beg to express their sincere gratitude to W.Bro. Cobb for his arduous work of the last four years on their behalf." The motion was carried by ten votes to four, with four abstaining.

Apparently at the meeting the previous night Dr. Cobb had made a strong personal attack on Alfred Faulding, who was not present. At the same time he made allegations against other Grand Lodge Officers, suggested the abolition of the Board of General Purposes and demanded the resignation of four well-known Brethren. It was felt that this was not Masonic behaviour, in that we promise to defend the honour of other Brethren, and that Dr. Cobb should carry out his Obligation. It was suggested that he put his charges on paper, covering Co-Masonry, Theosophical teachings, the resignation of the four members and the explanation of the words "sinister tendencies" used by him. Alfred Faulding would then have the opportunity to answer the charges made against him.

Amidst charge and countercharge, with several resignations being made and withdrawn, the Grand Senior Warden then proposed that Marion Halsey be voted "as acting Grand Master of this Grand Lodge. Unanimously carried with acclamation."

A series of letters at the beginning of April between Dr. Cobb and Walter Secker of Lodge Golden Rule further inflamed the situation, with Cobb asserting "… it is clear from what has been done since March 26th that Grand Lodge is incapable of reform…" and Secker countering "She *[Marion Linsday Halsey]* is very much hurt and upset by the suggestion … that she might have been contemplating doing anything inconsistent with honour." Lodge Golden Rule, loyal to Cobb, considered suspending their workings and handing in their Charter until Grand Lodge implemented Dr. Cobb's reforms, but in the end decided against it. They did, however, propose that a general assembly of the whole Order be called so that Dr. Cobb could state publicly his reasons for resigning. In all, twenty-five of the sixty-three members of Lodge Golden Rule resigned, including the other members of the Cobb family - Hettie, Monica and Ivo - Secretary Secker and several of the officers.

So just why did Dr. Cobb resign from the Order he had founded, after four short years? Firstly, one of the reasons for creating a new Masonic organisation in 1908 had been to move away from the Theosophical teachings which were so dominant in the ritual and ceremonies of Co-Masonry. These probably centred on the occult, such as the belief in the occult 'Masters of Wisdom', one of whom - the Comte de St. Germain (previously re-incarnated as, amongst others, Christian Rosenkreutz and Francis Bacon) - was held to preserve and direct all ritual and ceremony as the 'Head of all True Freemasons'. It was such supernatural influences which Dr. Cobb described as "sinister tendencies." As all the founders of the Honourable Fraternity had been Co-Masons, it would not be surprising if there were still those who wished to retain some of the occult elements, in opposition to their Grand Master.

Secondly, Dr. Cobb was a forceful and dominant character. He left Co-Masonry partly because he was stopped by Annie Besant and the ruling council from introducing a more democratic structure to the organisation; in other areas of his life he left groups such as the Indian Church Aid Association and the Divorce Law Reform Union whenever he was baulked in introducing changes. If he could not get his way, he left and went on to pastures new and there is no reason to suppose that his departure from the Honourable Fraternity of Antient Masonry was any different.

A Good Story

As a footnote to history, the grandson of the Rev. Dr. Cobb relates the following anecdote about a much later period, near to the end of his grandfather's life:

Edward VIII succeeded his father George V as King on 20th January 1936. Edward was very anxious to marry the twice-divorced American, Wallis Simpson. To most of the country, that would have neither been compatible with his position as Head of the Church of England, nor would it have been socially or politically acceptable. But Edward was adamant, so the search was on to find an accommodating clergyman who would be willing to marry them in an attempt to regularise the position.

Dr. Cobb's reforming views on marriage and divorce law, together with his high profile as Rector of St. Ethelburga's church in the City of London, resulted in quite a number of public figures approaching him where their matrimonial needs were concerned.

That winter, Dr. Cobb was staying at the country house of his doctor son Ivo and family at Burnham Beeches in Buckinghamshire. One of

H.R.H. the Duke of Windsor and Wallis Simpson on their marriage in 1936.

his favourite jobs was tree pruning, collecting leaves and making bonfires on the estate. Suddenly there was a big fuss (or so it seemed to the ten year old grandson) because of the arrival of an important visitor, Sir Walter Monckton, the Private Secretary to the King. Dr. Cobb was called out of his wood and he and Sir Walter disappeared into the study for a couple of hours. The purpose of the visit was of course to see if the Rector would marry Edward and Mrs. Simpson.

Dr. Cobb suggested an audience with Queen Mary, the King's mother, before he would reply to the King's request. The Audience duly took place and the Queen Mother, extending her hand, opened the conversation with the greeting "Well, Dr. Geikie-Cobb, this is a pretty kettle of fish!"

In the event, he declined to marry them, on the ground that "both were far from innocent in their earlier lives." Although liberal in his views, the Rector only ever agreed to re-marry truly innocent parties in divorce cases.

Chapter Three

The Reaction of United Grand Lodge

It was not long before the United Grand Lodge of England was alerted to the fact that some of its members were attending meetings of the Honourable Fraternity of Antient Masonry. This fraternisation with an irregular Masonic body was contrary to the fundamental precepts and the Constitutions of their Order. In March 1910 their Grand Lodge issued a directive to all Lodges forbidding such visiting and giving the sanctions that would be invoked for non-compliance:

"DEAR SIR AND WORSHIPFUL MASTER,
    It having been brought to the attention of the Board of General Purposes that certain irregular bodies are in the habit of holding meetings - within the jurisdiction of the Grand Lodge - professing to be Masonic meetings, for working ceremonies of an alleged Masonic nature, and called by summons copying the summonses of regular Lodges, I am directed to remind you and all the Brethren of our Order, that such bodies have no authority or warrant from the Most Worshipful the Grand Master or the United Grand Lodge of Antient Free and Accepted Masons of England, which latter Body has the sole jurisdiction in matters relating to the Craft in this country; and further, I have to remind you that any members of our Order who take part in or visit such spurious and irregular bodies, are, by Rule 204 of our Book of Constitutions, precluded from being admitted as

Sir Edward Letchworth, Grand Secretary of the United Grand Lodge of England from 1892 to 1917.

members, or even as visitors, into any regular Lodge, or from being entitled to relief from the Fund of Benevolence, or to any other Masonic privilege and by other of our laws, in cases of wilful persistence, they are liable to suspension, and even expulsion by Grand Lodge.

You will see, by reference to Grand Lodge Reports for 1908, that in May the Grand Lodge unanimously confirmed a sentence of suspension passed upon a Brother in India for having taken part in one of the irregular meetings referred to. I am further to ask that you and your successors in office will use the greatest caution with respect to the admission of visitors to your Lodge, drawing your attention to the Antient Charges and Regulations which every Master has promised to submit to and support … and that you will enjoin upon all your members the absolute necessity of each being extremely careful not to enter upon any discussion of internal Masonic matters with any person, unless one whom he already knows to be a Freemason regularly admitted into a regular Lodge, so that, in the words of one of our Antient Charges, "the most penetrating stranger shall not be able to discover or find out what is not proper to be intimated."

It must be distinctly understood that in case of any infraction of what has been laid down, as intimated above, the Board will not hesitate to use the powers with which it is clothed. You are, at the first Meeting of your Lodge after the receipt of this circular, to cause it to be read in open Lodge, together with the Rules and Charge specially referred to, and the circular to be entered upon or attached to the minutes for easy reference. Also, to take care that your Tyler's attention shall be particularly directed to the requirements as to Visitors, and reminded that no certificate of membership is valid in case of English Masons, unless granted by our own Grand Lodge … In any case of doubt, a full examination must be conducted by the Junior Warden as provided.

I am, Dear Sir and Worshipful Brother,
Yours faithfully and fraternally,

> E. Letchworth
> G*[rand]* S*[ecretary]*"

Principles

Dr. Cobb proposed that the Board of General Purposes should meet to revise the Declaration of Principles and that this, together with the March directive and his own address *A Word for Peace* should be published in *The Gavel* of July 1910 and issued as a response to United Grand Lodge.

The Declaration of Principles affirms the importance of truth and tolerance:

The Order of Ancient Masonry exists for the purpose of emphasising the spiritual end of Masonry and of demonstrating the spiritual meaning of its traditional rites and ceremonies. It does not seek to oppose but to supplement Masonry as practiced under the United Grand Lodge of England.

It asserts the right to exercise the ancient privilege of assembling as Masons which rests in the power of the Fraternity generally - a right which has not been abrogated by the establishment of the United Grand Lodge of England. It regards that Grand Lodge with reverence, but does not, therefore, regard itself as precluded from organising itself for work which at present that Lodge does not undertake.

It venerates one Creative Principle, and regards the Universe as His Self-revealing Word.

It claims as its own all Truth, whether preserved in Religious Mysteries; in the hidden lore of Secret Societies; in the systems of established institutions; in the speculations of Philosophy; in the conclusions of Science; or in the creations of Art.

It maintains all the Landmarks of Freemasonry, and preserves all its ancient usages and established customs.

It repudiates all autocratic government as the fore-runner of tyranny; asserts the right of self-government as the guarantee of freedom; and upholds freedom as the necessary pre-condition of growth in wisdom.

It admits women on equal terms with men.

It allows the fullest discussion of all topics of religion and politics. It recognises all religious truth, and tolerates, but does not accept sectarian dogmas. It is not lawful to use its organisation for sectarian or party purposes.

Its jurisdiction extends to the three Craft Degrees, the Degree of the Mark Mason, of the Royal Arch, and none other.

Peace

A Word for Peace - written by Dr. Cobb at his most trenchant - belied
its title in the fierceness of its oratory:

"We understand that the minds of some Masons of the English
Obedience have been somewhat exercised of late by the appearance
in their midst of a mode of Masonry which encourages suspicion of
its genuineness. It is said that the Masonry in question is tainted at
its origin by deriving from a French jurisdiction; that, moreover, it is
permeated by a philosophy of doubtful validity, and that it is
somewhat careless in the performance of Masonic ceremonies. It is
also charged with having made considerable innovations in the
substance of the ritual in use. That English Masons trained in habits
of strict regularity, and owing obedience to long established
authority, should view with disfavour so troublesome an intruder
upon its domain is but natural. It was equally natural also, therefore,
that authority should be invoked for the purpose of safeguarding the
virgin purity of English Masonry. We understand that its Lodges
have been warned against permitting visits from Masons of this
strange and doubtful character. To this of course no exception can be
taken, for it is one of the primary duties of Masonic authority to see
that Masonry is maintained in all its purity and vigour.

Unfortunately, however, as often happens when the net is thrown
by authority, it gathers in its meshes more than it intended. It has
been thought that the action of our English brethren covers, and was
intended to cover, the *Honourable Fraternity of Ancient Masonry*.
This, however, as we hope to show, is founded on a mistake. For our
Fraternity does not derive from any Foreign jurisdiction, it has not
innovated and it does not intend to innovate on the body of Masonry,
it is not careless in the performance of traditional Masonic ritual, and
it does not import into that ritual any interpretations but what are
suggested by the ritual itself.

A little consideration of the nature of the two Obediences will
serve to make the ground quite clear. As is well known some ancient
Brethren in February, 1717, met at the Apple-tree Tavern in Charles
Street, Covent Garden, and having voted the oldest Master Mason
then present into the Chair, constituted themselves a Grand Lodge.
In other words they acted upon the ancient right of Masons to

assemble as they pleased and where they pleased, to organise themselves at their own will and pleasure, to make Masons and to discharge all the duties of Masonry without any Warrant or Constitution. That this right was fully recognised and acted upon is made clear by a resolution which appears to have been taken, in 1723, by which this ancient right was restricted so far as the newly-constituted body was concerned ...

From the humble beginning of Masonry in 1717, there has sprung the movement which is now found in the four quarters of the globe, and looks to the United Grand Lodge of England as its mother. Its influence on the whole has been on the side of law and order, and virtue, kindly feeling and human progress. Of course, it is but natural that something of the same fate should have befallen it as falls to all successful and long established bodies; it has become prosperous, and therefore has yielded to the temptation to ignore the ideal. Its history runs on parallel lines to that of all established bodies. It has become respectable, and has been content with the virtues of respectability. It is cursed, unfortunately, by that spirit of legalism which is fatal to all spiritual vitality. Hence it has settled down into a conservative body with all the virtues (and they are many) of conservative institutions, but it has failed to satisfy the higher aspirations of a minority amongst its members. Content to live on the past and to reproduce the past it has marked time, and failed to march with the times."

Dr. Cobb then introduces the subject of the 'Woman Movement' and the increasing part played by women in all aspects of society, continuing:

"We may applaud their appearance on equal terms with men, or we may decry it as monstrous and dangerous, but it is there and has to be dealt with. English Masonry so far has shown no signs that it at all appreciates the enormous importance of this movement. It has been left for other Masonic bodies to step into the breach and to assume the duty which English Masonry has not cared to undertake."
In talking of the relations between the new Grand Lodge and U.G.L.E., the Honourable Fraternity "... only asks, and it thinks it has a perfect right to ask, that the older body shall not show any jealous or exclusive spirit but shall hold out the right hand of

fellowship and welcome any attempt legitimately made to further the cause which all true Masons have at heart. It has been careful to do nothing, and to admit nothing which may lawfully prevent recognition by the older body. Its own Grand Lodge was formed precisely as the first Grand Lodge of England was formed. Its members are all duly-made Masons; its Lodges are carefully tyled, and the credentials of all visitors duly scrutinised; its rites are those practiced under the Jurisdiction of the United Grand

The arms of United Grand Lodge.

Lodge of England; its Lodges are all as just, perfect and regular as are English Lodges; its workings in no way fall short of the precision attained by their brethren, while they are animated by a spirit which is seldom to be found in the older Lodges."

War

The Gavel article continues with a section entitled *War*: *'When I spake unto them of peace they made themselves ready for battle'.* On 25th April 1910 our Lodge Stability No.5 was consecrated at a public venue, the Holborn Restaurant in London. As a result of participating in this ceremony, word got back to the Older Obedience that J.W. Sidley of Lodge Emulation No.2 and F.W. Lacey of Lodge of Unity No.3 had been present. Sidley belonged to Clarendon Lodge No.1769 of U.G.L.E. and Lacey to Valentia Lodge No.3097. They were summoned to appear before their own Board of General Purposes, which they refused to do. They were therefore suspended from all Masonic privileges under United Grand Lodge - in other words, expelled.

The replies of the two male Masons (neither mentioned by name) to their Grand Secretary were included in the retaliation printed in *The Gavel.* J.W. Sidley wrote:

"… From [the general position of the Honourable Fraternity of Ancient Masonry] you will see that no charge can be brought against that Fraternity on the ground of origin, authority, Masonic fidelity, or respect for Landmarks. Its Lodges are in all respects as just, perfect, and regular as those under the United Grand Lodge of England. Moreover, that Fraternity does not derive from any French jurisdiction.

I would venture with all respect to urge, since the Honourable Fraternity of *Ancient Masonry* contains nothing in its origin, constitution, or workings which forbids recognition by the United Grand Lodge of England, that it is both premature and inexpedient for your Board to take any action which would make friendly communion unlawful between members of the two jurisdictions. The Honourable Fraternity of *Ancient Masonry* is already so well founded that it will flourish with or without recognition by the United Grand Lodge of England, but it would deprecate any premature barring of the way to brotherly relationship between the two bodies."

F.W. Lacey, in his defence, wrote: "… I understand that the purpose of the summons *[to the Board of General Purposes]* is to enable me to state the position of the Honourable Fraternity of *Ancient Masonry*, and to give my reasons for belonging to it, while retaining my position as a member of one of your Lodges.

My connection with *Ancient Masonry* does not in any way conflict with the discharge of my Masonic duties. On the contrary, I am a better Mason for belonging to the new movement; and but for it in all probability I should have relinquished my membership of the Valentia Lodge, in which I have been an officer, shortly after its consecration.

The working of the ceremonies in the Lodges of *Ancient Masonry* is carefully and reverently performed, and the Ancient Landmarks are scrupulously preserved. The admission of Women into Masonry cannot be prevented, and is now absolutely essential if our Order is to retain and extend its influence.

Ancient Masonry is attracting the more thoughtful and earnest men from the Craft Lodges, and by careful selection of the fit, and rigorous exclusion of the unworthy, a body of men and women is being gathered, worthy to be a nucleus of the Universal Brotherhood.

The new movement stands for the realisation of the true ideals of

Masonry, which do not end with the practice of the virtues of Benevolence and Charity.

Ancient Masonry "instructs" as well as employs its members. This is part of the "Master's" duties which is almost entirely neglected by the Lodges which work under your Charters; this duty is systematically discharged by the Masters of all the Lodges of *Ancient Masonry.*

The new movement has not injured, but rather helped, the older Craft Lodges, and has infused a new spirit into the workings of some of your Lodges, where the performance of the ceremonies left much to be desired.

… The question for your Board, and possibly for Grand Lodge to consider is, whether you will or will not recognise the *Honourable Fraternity of Ancient Masonry.* It is certain that no power will be able to stop the new movement, for it is founded on right, and therefore must go forward."

Dr. Cobb commented in characteristically forthright and colourful prose:

"… The charge is this. The United Grand Lodge has money, prestige, worldly power and pomp behind it. But it lacks the one thing needful. It lacks Life. We say only what every Mason knows well when we affirm that ostentatious charity - we are compelled sorrowfully to use the adjective - the perfunctory performance of rites and ceremonies (whether punctiliously or with slovenliness makes no difference), the proud parade of rank and fortune, and swollen coffers are no substitutes for Life. To the prophetic eye such Masonry has a name that it liveth, but it is dead.

That is the position, and we commend it to our brethren of the older Obedience. We are at least as valid Masons as they; our Lodges are as just, perfect and regular as theirs; our Grand Lodge is as well-founded as theirs; and our proceedings throughout are as regular as any in orthodox Masonry. Our sole offence is that we are putting life and reality into Masonry, and have not humbly sued for permission for our proceedings from the lawyers and officials who have turned a Brotherhood into a business concern. It will be observed that our criticisms are not directed against Masons themselves of the older Obedience, or against their Lodges, but against the authority which we are persuaded does *not* represent them. That the Constitution of the United Grand Lodge wants reforming is the opinion of many besides ourselves."

A further and more explicit directive was sent by United Grand Lodge to all its Brethren in October of 1910:

"… Brethren are therefore warned that their association in any way with such Bodies would not only be a violation of their solemn pledges, but would subject them to the penalties imposed by the Constitution, the provisions of which are binding on every Brother owing allegiance to the Grand Lodge of England.

Masters of Lodges must make it their duty to see that every Brother in their Lodge clearly understands that it is not permissible for any member of our order even to visit any Lodge styling itself a Masonic Lodge which is not recognised by the Grand Lodge of England."

Conflicts of Loyalty

The Rev. F.W. Gilby was at that time both our Grand Chaplain and a member of Lodge Emulation No.2, but also the Past Provincial Grand Chaplain for Warwickshire under United Grand Lodge. By the end of 1910 his connection with the Order had been reported to his Grand Lodge and he had been called upon to resign from us. In spite of the criticism and sanctions, he did not resign from our Order until November 1918, when he left his Mother Lodge and also Lodge of Unity No.3, of which he was an honorary member.

Nevertheless he still had a loyalty to H.F.A.M. and read a paper to the *[men's]* Lodge of Installed Masters at Birmingham in 1925, which was subsequently printed in *The Freemason*, entitled *Women and Freemasonry in the past and present*. It deals with Adoptive Masonry and the restitution of a Landmark, in that women shared in the ancient Mysteries and should continue to do so in Freemasonry:

" When Dr. Cobb seceded from the Co-Masons I joined the new Order of 'The Honourable Fraternity of Ancient Masonry'. This, but for the fact that men and women meet in that Order, is a pure and well-worked Masonry. I was Grand Chaplain of the Order for some years and learned much. Papers were constantly being read and lodge meetings were opened with silent prayer. A prayer was always said with the initiate outside the lodge room before his entrance. The initiate wore a white Monkish gown, but was otherwise prepared as our candidates. ...This Order has nothing whatever to do with Co-Masonry.

The working of that Order was practically identical with our own. It possesses all the workings of the Craft. One great difficulty in the minds of English Masons seems to be the preparation of candidates for initiation. It must be patent to everyone who has seen his wife or daughter in evening dress that there is no great difficulty in carrying out the symbolism of admission with perfect decency. I should not think it worth while to explain this, but that the point is so often raised. The Order to which I allude has only five lodges, in addition to its Grand Lodge and Installed Masters' Lodge. It is about to have lodges in the provinces. Its members are of all sorts - titled women are found in its ranks. I remember the names of several intellectual writers of books, novelists, and many others with whom it was a pleasure to be regularly associated. Grand Officers *[of the Older Obedience]*, whom I shall not name, were sometimes among the visitors in my day, and encouraged the Order to go ahead."

The paper ends: "We cannot stem the movement. What are we going to do about it ? When the numbers run into hundreds of thousands then some of us will be rising up to reproach our rulers with having missed a very great opportunity."

Another casualty of the gender conflict was Alfred Faulding. A Founder Member of the Order, he was Director of Ceremonies of Lodge of Unity No.3 of H.F.A.M. but also belonged to Unity Lodge No.183 and Clarendon Lodge No.1769 of the Older Obedience. In connection with the edicts sent out by U.G.L.E. to its members, Faulding had apparently stated in writing that, on his honour, he had no connection with an Order which had anything to do with women. However, in early 1912 he was present at a meeting at 4 Southampton Row, the headquarters of the Honourable Fraternity, together with R.W.Bro. John Sidley, Past D.G.M., who also had loyalty to both sides. During the meeting there was an alarm, and Brethren of the men's Clarendon Lodge were at the door. Alfred Faulding thought that Sidley had invited them in order to catch him attending a meeting of an "irregular body" and so incriminate him. This would have caused quite a problem for Alfred, as he had already been summoned to appear before his own Board of General Purposes on 15th April to answer the charge of unlawfully associating with a ladies' Lodge.

He took great pains to establish the fact that he had resigned from the mixed Lodge of Unity No.3 some time earlier - in fact he may possibly even have back-dated his letter of resignation to December 1911. He seems to have got away with it and even asked our Grand Lodge to write a letter confirming that he was no longer a member of our Order "so that I might put myself right with the English Order." His wife Florence, the first Worshipful Master of Lodge of Unity No.3, resigned not long afterwards and went back to the Co-Masonic Order.

Additional sources

Acknowledgment is made to the Councils of Lodge Golden Rule No.1, Lodge Emulation No.2 and Lodge of Unity No.3 for permission to use material from their Minute Books 1908-1912.

Chapter Four

Marion Halsey, the Stability scandal and War Work

A New Grand Master

Marion Lindsay Leigh had been proposed as a candidate for initiation into Lodge Golden Rule No.1 by Dr. Cobb in April 1909. At the same meeting, Reginald Halsey was proposed as a candidate by affiliation - he was therefore either a member of United Grand Lodge or a Co-Mason. In April 1910 Mrs. Leigh, a widow, became the Honourable Mrs. Reginald Halsey, her husband being a younger son of Sir Thomas Halsey, Baronet, and Deputy Grand Master of United Grand Lodge from 1903 to 1927. She was married by the Rev. Dr. Cobb at St. Ethelburga's, when she wore a dress of pale heliotrope satin, with an overskirt bordered with gold embroidery and an ostrich-feather toque to match. A member of high society - the 'coming-out' dance she gave for her debutante daughter Diana was reported in the Court Circular - she epitomised the aristocratic and intellectual ladies who entered Freemasonry in the first decade of the twentieth century. In October 1911 she was installed in the Chair of Lodge Golden Rule No.1 and the same year - still a 'light blue' - became Deputy Grand Master of the Order.

Marion Lindsay Halsey, Grand Master of the Order from 1912 to 1927.

Highly educated, she was very much inclined towards mystical and esoteric traditions, as demonstrated by the range of books she donated to the Library at Headquarters on Christian mysticism, the Kabbalah, the Tarot, the works of Plotinus and the Ancient Mysteries. As well as being a Freemason she belonged to the *Stella Matutina*, an offshoot of the Hermetic Order of the Golden Dawn. This was one of several secret magical societies in existence at the time and was concerned with the preservation of that body of knowledge called Hermeticism or the Western Esoteric Tradition, dedicated to the philosophical, spiritual and psychic evolution of humanity. Members learnt the principles of occult science and elements of western philosophy and magic. Like mixed Masonry, the Golden Dawn and similar societies gave women complete equality in their activities.

We have seen that Dr. Cobb's resignation from the H.F.A.M. was accepted in March 1912 and Marion Halsey was elected Acting Grand Master. At the Quarterly Communication in the following June "a ballot of Grand Lodge was taken to decide the name of the occupant

for the Grand Mastership." The Acting Grand Secretary declared the vote to be unanimously in favour of R.W.Bro. Marion Lindsay Halsey. The account reads very simply - the Grand Secretary moved "that the heartiest congratulations of the Grand Lodge be offered to our Grand Master Elect. This was carried with enthusiasm. The Grand Master Elect replied suitably."

In October 1912 Marion Lindsay Halsey was placed with very little ceremony in the Chair of King Solomon as Grand Master, presumably by Peter Birchall as Deputy Grand Master designate.

In 1938, her successor Adelaide Litten wrote of her:
"[Her initiation] although possibly not then realised, was an epoch-making event in the history of our Order, for it

attached to us one who was destined to become a pillar of great strength and whose work for the Order was incomparable and far-reaching. She devoted her life henceforth to furthering the interests of Freemasonry for women, and, notwithstanding her many activities and responsibilities, she was always working strenuously for the advancement of the Cause she had so dearly at heart.

There has rarely been combined in one individual, in the same degree, all the qualities of 'a great lady'. Nobility of character, simplicity, independence, quiet insight, understanding, high ideals, wide culture and great qualities of leadership, which won for her the affection, admiration and respect of all those who had the privilege of knowing her. She remains a beautiful, gracious and inspiring memory in the hearts of the members of the Order, which she served for so long with such conspicuous fidelity, zeal and ability."

In May M.W.Bro. Lindsay Halsey put some suggestions by letter to the Board of General Purposes as to changes in administration. Amongst these were the revision of the Constitution and the introduction of a Central Lodge of Instruction, both of which were agreed.

The first Installed Masters' Lodge

The first Lodge of Installed Masters - No.6 on the register - was consecrated in June 1912 at Southampton Row by M.W.Bro. Marion Lindsay Halsey. Peter Birchall was installed as the first Worshipful Master, and he invested Marion Halsey as his Senior Warden. Although the Order was still very small, with only five Lodges, Marion Halsey with great foresight had decided on the establishment of this Lodge to be a centre of learning and exploration. It would be able to use the experience of all the Past Masters of the Order; it would maintain high standards of ritual and assist new Lodges. As R.W.Bro. Olwen Lloyd said much later on taking the Chair of No.6 in 1935, "The true road forward will be the spiritual road - No.6 should always serve as a source of inspiration to the whole Order."

Lodge of Installed Masters No.6 in June 1912

M.W.Bro. Halsey presented No.6 with a Master's Jewel - a sixteen-pointed star inlaid with cut crystals, with a central handpainted disk showing a female figure holding a sword. The motto of the Lodge -

Est Concordia Fratrum (Brotherhood is Harmony) - is above it. This refers to the symbolism of the trowel as an emblem of brotherly affection, as is explained in the Working Tools of the Extended Ritual. Up until 1944 the ceremonial work of No.6 consisted only of Opening and Closing in the three Degrees and the Board of Installed Masters, with the presentation of papers and discussion of them afterwards. In 1944 Lodge Stone of Foundation (Installed Masters) No.22 was consecrated in Manchester and started to work the Extended Ritual of an Installed Master. Unfortunately the early Minute Books of this Lodge are missing, and so we can only guess how and why the new working was adopted. Three years later the Manchester Brethren came to London to demonstrate this Working to the members of No.6, and it was adopted by them in April 1947.

The Master's jewel of
Lodge of Installed Masters No.6.

The Extended Ritual consists of the opening and closing of a Board of Installed Masters, with additional signs to those in an ordinary Installation, the reception of a Candidate to receive the Extended Ritual and a description of Adoniram and the building of the Temple. Before the middle of the 18th Century the usual procedure in Lodges for installing a Master was simply to put him in the Chair, provided the reigning Master and his Wardens were satisfied as to his suitability.

The Antients, or Atholl Masons, were probably the first to put Masters in the Chair with some ceremony, and it is possible that the ceremony worked by the Antients was that which we now know as the 'Extended Working'. In 1926 the ceremony was banned by the United Grand Lodge of England as far as the men's Lodges were concerned, but later that same year they lifted the ban, on the condition that the Installing

Master made clear that "the signs, tokens and words given in the Extended portion are not known to or required of Installed Masters generally, and that no new Degree in Masonry has been conferred" - a condition that is still emphasised in the ceremony today. A ritual published in 1888 by an American, Franklin Thomas, includes the Extended Working in the actual Installation of a Master, and is very similar to our practice. The Opening of the Board of Installed Masters is used today by a few of the men's Lodges as part of their usual Installation ceremony.

The early meetings of the Lodge of Installed Masters

Banner of the Lodge of Installed Masters No.6

No.6 were held at 4 Southampton Row, but the outbreak of war in 1914 and the demands of war service on its members resulted in irregular meetings. In addition, the loss of five members from Lodge Stability No.5 *(see below)* depleted the membership so that it was impossible to fill all the offices. From 1916 to 1932 no meetings were held at all. In the latter year regular meetings were resumed at 27 Pembridge Gardens, with Peter Birchall again in the Chair until 1934.

The Stability Scandal 1913-1914

At the beginning of 1913, the total membership of the Order stood at one hundred and sixty four. Grand Lodge then consisted only of the Grand Officers and the Masters and Wardens of the five existing Lodges, twenty eight people in all. The fifth Lodge of the Order - Stability - had been consecrated on 25th April 1910 at the Holborn

Janet Elizabeth Boswell-Reid.

Restaurant in London. Its Worshipful Master in 1913 was Seton Boswell-Reid Challen, and both her mother Janet Elizabeth Boswell-Reid and her husband Howard Challen were members.

At Grand Lodge in June 1913, without having given any prior notice to the Grand Secretary or anybody else, W.Bro. Boswell-Reid rose and, on behalf of herself, her daughter and W.Bro. Annie Symonds (who was Junior Grand Deacon) of Lodge Emulation No.2, applied to the Grand Master for a Charter to open a Royal Arch Chapter as soon as possible. Imagine the shock and consternation! The Order in the five years of its existence had only worked the three Craft Degrees and the Constitutions had been amended to delete the Holy Royal Arch from Clause 1: "Antient Masonry consists of the three Degrees and no more … "

Grand Master Halsey immediately asked how they would prove themselves Holy Royal Arch Masons, to which W.Bro. Seton Challen replied that they refused to give their source for the secrets " ... but admitted they were confirmed in a Chapter now out of existence, and that they held no certificates from such Chapter, which had been hastily convened for the purpose of conferring such secrets". The Grand Master and Grand Secretary pointed out that the introduction of a new item onto the agenda was out-of-order and suggested that a Committee be formed to hear further from those Brethren. Grand Lodge appointed the Grand Master, her Deputy Peter Birchall,

R.W.Bro. Florence Faulding, Bro. Adelaide Litten, Grand Registrar and Grand Secretary Peter Slingsby to the Committee.

The Committee reported back at October Grand Lodge. The four protagonists disputed some of the wording in the Minutes for June, but confronted by the fact that the wording had been approved by the Board of General Purposes and that the Grand Secretary took a shorthand record of all that was said at Grand Lodge, they capitulated. The report of the Special Committee was read by Peter Slingsby.

The Grand Secretary then read an extraordinary letter that he had received in July from W.Bro. Annie Symonds, one of the group. Its content was of less significance than the heading and salutation - the typewritten heading on the letter read 'The Supreme Order of Holy Royal Arch' 'The Grand Holy Royal Arch Chapter of English Antient Masonry', and it was signed 'On behalf of the Grand Sanhedrim'. It appeared that the Stability group had set themselves up as an independent Chapter governing body, in response to the Grand Master's assertion that she had no authority to grant a Charter for a Chapter. Grand Master Halsey felt strongly that until she herself had gained the secrets of the Holy Royal Arch in a regular manner, she was in no position to give such information to others.

The Grand Master had previously undertaken to obtain the opinion (in confidence) of some senior members of the Older Obedience as to the correct procedure and course of action. She read letters from three anonymous but distinguished Brethren. These letters and the interviews which she had had confirmed her in the opinion that Grand Lodge could not recognise the so-called Chapter reported to be in being. She begged the Brethren concerned to stop immediately working in this irregular manner because, apart from the disloyalty of their conduct, it would prejudice possible future recognition of our Order by United Grand Lodge of England.

Deputy Grand Master Peter Birchall was asked to speak on the legality of the matter. He had obviously become increasingly angry and upset as proceedings went on. He referred "with some heat" to the conduct of some Brethren being a violation of the sanctitude of the Temple and that the Brethren had spoken of receiving these things *[the secrets]* but to his mind the matter was practically one of theft. The Grand Master told him that however strongly he might feel he should abstain from harsh language (he later apologised). The Grand Chaplain, V.W.Bro. the Rev. F.W. Gilby, summed up the feeling of the meeting when he said that the Grand Master should have been consulted by the Brethren during their research and before the situation reached such an advanced stage. The matter had been sprung upon Grand Lodge with undue haste and rushed along without any consideration, and under our Constitutions the so-called Chapter could not be regarded as legal. The Brethren should now submit and abandon the undertaking.

Peter Slingsby - less volatile than Birchall, more considered in speech and realistic - in reviewing the situation emphasised that the primary loyalty of all Brethren was to the Grand Master and to Grand Lodge. The Brethren concerned had, in refusing to give the source of the secrets, rejected all the efforts to see if recognition could be granted. As part of these efforts the Grand Master had invited W.Bro. Boswell-Reid to her London home in Mount Street in order to discuss the situation. In reply to a warning of the dangers of pursuing their line of action, W.Bro. Boswell-Reid replied that she would be very sorry to break up any part of the Order and would rather give up the Chapter than let this happen. W.Bro. Boswell-Reid later said she had no memory of this conversation.

The climax came when the Grand Master asked Elizabeth Boswell-Reid "Is your Charter self-given?", to be told "Our reply is silence". To add insult to injury, the Grand Master went on to relate to Grand Lodge how, on a recent official visit to Lodge Stability No.5 "she found all around her Brethren wearing in open Lodge the decorations of a body which had neither the approval nor recognition of Grand Lodge and against the formation of which she had expressed herself most strongly. She also realised for the first time that her Senior Grand Warden *[W.Bro. F.W. Lacey, who had been the first Worshipful Master of Lodge Stabilty]* had cast his lot in with the Brethren whose action she deplored".

A Resolution was then proposed - not without opposition to the wording - to the effect that Grand Lodge could only recognise Higher Degrees formed in a just, perfect and regular way, and that it would be against the best interests of the Order to grant the Charter originally applied for. It was hoped that the Brethren would "in the interests of unity and peace" submit to the decision of Grand Lodge, would dissolve their irregular Chapter and "return to work as loyal members of Antient Masonry". The Resolution was carried by thirteen to five.

The dissenting Brethren were asked where their loyalty lay? With the irregular Chapter formed that summer or with the Order for which they had worked so well for years? Elizabeth Boswell-Reid asked if they could give their reply at an adjourned meeting of Grand Lodge and this was approved. In the meantime, the Grand Master requested a pledge that the irregular working should be suspended. This was refused point blank, which made the situation even worse and the Grand Master's wrath was barely kept in check - she "expressed her disappointment and entire disapproval of such an attitude and that only her sincere desire to afford the Brethren every opportunity to consider their position prevented her dealing with the matter at once". An Emergency Meeting of Grand Lodge was called for 12th November 1913.

In the meantime, Marion Lindsay Halsey sent a printed circular letter to all the Brethren of the Order, outlining the situation and warning all Brethren to avoid any connection with the spurious Chapter or any other irregular body - ironic, considering that our Order itself was considered by others to be irregular.

At the Emergency Meeting, the Grand Master reiterated that despite every kindness and the exceptional consideration shown to the Brethren concerned, their attitude and the tone

Seton Challen of Lodge Stability No.5, who with her mother Elizabeth Boswell-Reid went on to found the Honourable Fraternity of Ancient Freemasons.

of their correspondence was an impossible one. The Brethren had put themselves out of court.

The question was put to Elizabeth Boswell-Reid, Howard Challen, Seton Challen and Annie Symonds as to whether, in view of the Obligations that they had taken, they still refused to conform to the edict of Grand Lodge of October, that they should cease working and disband their irregular Chapter. Each considered that they had not broken any vows and refused to conform. The Grand Master, in addressing these Brethren, said that they would understand her reluctance to formally enforce the edict of Grand Lodge, as she wished for no unkindly parting, therefore she left it to them and any other Brother connected with the irregular Chapter to contact the Grand Secretary.

Following this, in November, Elizabeth Boswell-Reid, the two Challens and five other members of Lodge Stability No.5 resigned, together with Annie Symonds of Emulation No.2 and a Bro. Browne of Lodge of Unity No.3. These resignations included the Worshipful Master, Immediate Past Master, both Wardens and the Director of Ceremonies of the Lodge. Stability's meetings were in abeyance because the Warrant and books had not been returned by the Worshipful Master. The remaining members of Stability were summoned to appear before the Board of General Purposes and the position was explained to them. All expressed their loyalty to the Order.

A series of increasingly frustrated letters started - the Grand Secretary to Seton Challen, who referred him to F.W. Lacey, who "replied in disrespectful terms" and resigned; the Grand Master to Seton Challen, who did not reply, and then Lacey - and so on. Lacey's response to the Grand Master was "unnecessarily offensive" and included untrue statements about her and her Officers. As such, the Grand Secretary refused to include it in the Minutes of Grand Lodge.

Grand Lodge directed the Grand Secretary to send a registered letter to Seton Challen, requesting the return of the Warrant and books which were being unlawfully withheld. Bro. Florence Jane Hawkins was instructed to meet the offending Brethren unofficially to try to persuade them to do the right thing, and to report back personally to the Grand Master. Registered letters were sent in February and March 1914, but no reply was received to either.

A letter was then sent to the rest of the members of Lodge Stability, warning them not to attend any Lodge meeting held under the Warrant and welcoming Brethren to the meetings of other Lodges. Finally, a further registered letter summoned Seton Challen and F.W. Lacey to appear before the Board on 30th June 1914 "to explain and be dealt with" and to bring with them the Charter, Minute Book, Attendance Book, Accounts and all the correspondence. Needless to say, they did not attend.

The Quarterly Communication of Grand Lodge having taken place on 24th June, a further Emergency Meeting was called for 9th July, when the Board recommended to Grand Lodge that the Warrant of Lodge Stabilty No.5 be "quashed", and that notice thereof should be sent to the Secretary of each Lodge

Emblem of the Grand Lodge of the Honourable Fraternity of Ancient Freemasons, founded in 1913.

of the Order. The motion was duly carried unanimously that "the said Lodge be formally erased from the Roll of Grand Lodge".

Elizabeth Boswell-Reid and the Challens founded another Masonic Order - the Honourable Fraternity of Ancient *Freemasons,* as distinct from our Antient *Masonry*, on 29th September 1913. Their first three Lodges were consecrated together - Stability Lodge No.1, Fidelity No.2 and Strength No.3. The organisation still exists as the second and smaller women's Order.

Wartime

The impact of the first World War does not feature greatly in the Minutes of Grand Lodge. There are references at every meeting to the absence of the Grand Tyler - Bro. (Mr.) W.L. Lancaster - on military service abroad, and he was mentioned in dispatches from Field Marshal Sir Douglas Haig in 1917. Throughout the war there were attempts to limit expenditure, such as seeking a reduction in the rent of 4 Southampton Row, because of a severe loss of income to Grand Lodge through having fewer meetings and reduced membership.

In 1914 the Worshipful Master of Lodge of Unity No.3 spoke to her Lodge about the war and the sacrifice of lives to make a new world and a new Britain. She continued: "Brethren I ask you to stand to order, as a humble mark of our reverence to the noble men and women who are sacrificing all for Patriotism, Duty and Honour. May the G.A.O.T.U. give these brave men of all nations, both on land and sea, strength to bear their terrible trials and the mothers, wives and children courage to face the cruel ordeals that are being thrust upon them." The following year the Lodge Council proposed that the November meeting be abandoned "owing to the Zeppelin raids and darkened streets and in consequence the difficulty in attending experienced by so many members living at a distance."

Some of the six Lodges cut their meetings to bi-monthly, and this action was regularised by a temporary suspension of the Lodge Warrant and the issue of a provisional Warrant sanctioning fewer meetings. The Lodge of Installed Masters No.6 suspended their meetings in 1916 for the duration of the War and members paid a nominal subscription of 2/6d. In July 1916 Adelaide Litten (then Grand Treasurer) lost her only brother Raymond, the youngest of the family, on active service. In 1918 damage from aircraft was added to the Fire and Burglary insurance policy for Southampton Row.

In October 1914 Marion Lindsay Halsey announced a scheme for "helping women out of work" by setting up a workroom, where they could make and repair clothes and thus earn something. Lodge Golden Rule No.1 (and doubtless the other Lodges) started a scheme to collect and send comforts to wounded soldiers.

The same month also saw Lodge Golden Rule No.1 reduce their meetings from ten per year to one a quarter for the duration of the War and, until further notice, the loss of funds to Grand Lodge resulting from this reduction was to be made good by the Worshipful Master (also Marion Halsey) personally. In March 1918 it was decided to hold meetings on Saturday afternoons each month from April to July, in order to accommodate three candidates waiting for Initiation who could not attend in the evenings when there was a possibility of air raids.

Work and Education

At the Board of General Purposes meeting in March 1913, Grand Master Marion Halsey put to the Board for their consideration a proposition concerning "a sphere of work outside our ordinary Masonic activities." Nothing further is heard until March 1916 when a small Committee was formed to consider suggestions and recommendations for an Outside Work Scheme, which would give members of the Order an opportunity to join in social work as well as providing a possible source of new membership. It was realised that any such scheme could only be on a small scale but there were "good grounds for assuming a fair measure of success." R.W.Bro. Millicent Mackenzie, P.S.G.W., a former Professor of Education at Cardiff University, was a member of this sub-committee and instrumental in the preparation of a scheme to set up a teacher training college which would also train social workers.

The Committee met at the Grand Master's house in London in March, April, May and June 1916. At the opening meeting R.W.Bro. Mackenzie outlined several alternative plans designed to meet the shortage of training for teachers and social workers "on broad and modern lines, fitting them for the modern conditions of social work generally [and equipping them] not only to teach 'subjects', but in the more important work of training and developing character." It was thought that the ordinary Training Colleges were not working in this direction, that ethical considerations and the 'newer' psychology were inadequately represented, that the training was too narrow and that the opportunities for gaining a broad outlook on life were non-existent. A child-centred approach would be adopted, in line with progressive developments in educational theory, many of which were influenced by theosophical principles.

There was also the strong possibility of new educational legislation (subsequently to become Fisher's 1918 Education Act) which would

King's College hostel on Campden Hill, Notting Hill Gate.

introduce compulsory part-time day-release schooling for children aged 14, once they had left full-time elementary school. The proposed college would specifically train teachers for this type of 'continuation' work, and it would be called the Halsey Training College.

One of the plans involved finding premises where lectures on ethical and educational subjects could be given and where students could meet members of the Order, with possible incidental recruitment from both students and teachers. As far as funding was concerned, back in 1913 when the subject was first broached, the Grand Master herself guaranteed to give £100 a year for the first three years.

R.W.Bro. Mackenzie in the meantime told many of her friends and contacts about the possible scheme and received permission from the Committee to circularise a letter - written over her own name and not mentioning the Order - for the notice boards of the principal women's colleges in England, Scotland and Wales. It was thought that a few notices could be sent to America, which would, on the contrary, refer to the Order "as American women were known to be keen about Masonic and kindred organisations, and it was felt that an allusion to the Order might be an added attraction." The Committee were later sharply criticised on this point by the general membership of the Order.

King's College, University of London had a branch and a hostel called Queen Mary's on Campden Hill, very close to Notting Hill Gate. The Warden of this branch saw one of the notices circulated and suggested that they might be able to take students for the scheme if it got underway. Subsequently the Grand Master and R.W.Bro. Mackenzie visited the College and were very satisfied with the situation and accommodation. The students there paid 85 guineas (£89.25) a year - 60 for board, lodging and "their share of the Warden's attention and care" and 25 guineas for the Social and Domestic Science Course provided. The Committee proposed that the Order should charge their students 85 guineas, paying 60 to the College with the other 25 guineas going towards the cost of a special course of lectures and coaching.

An informal meeting of the whole Order was called to discuss the matter and carried an almost unanimous vote to support the scheme, provided it was started up on a sound financial basis. The Board of General Purposes in June passed a Resolution by a majority vote to recommend favourable consideration by Grand Lodge of the Work Scheme. The Halsey Training College would be administered by an outside Educational Committee, aided by two or three Grand Lodge Officers. Grand Lodge duly adopted the proposal.

Guild of Education as National Service

with which is incorporated

HALSEY TRAINING COLLEGE

Recognised by the Board of Education.

Headquarters: 11 TAVISTOCK SQUARE, LONDON, W.C.1.

PROSPECTUS, 1920-21.

President:

Vice-Presidents:

Lord HENRY CAVENDISH-BENTINCK, M.P.
The Right Hon. Sir WILLIAM MATHER, LL.D.
The Hon. Mrs. SPENDER CLAY.

Executive Committee:

Mrs. REGINALD HALSEY (Chair).
PERCY ALDEN, Esq., M.A.
VICTOR BRANFORD, Esq., M.A. (Sociological Society).
Miss M. D. CRESSWELL.
Capt. R. W. ENSOR.
Mrs. R. W. ENSOR.
Miss ESCOTT (Head Mistress, Clapham High School).
Miss MARGARET FRODSHAM, B.Sc.
W. R. HUGHES, Esq., M.A.
Miss A. LITTEN.
Mrs. M. MACKENZIE, M.A.
Miss NICHALLS (Representative of Head Mistresses' Association).
Miss B. RENNIE.
R. H. TAWNEY, Esq., M.A. (London School of Economics).
Mrs. VIR JONES.

Hon. Dean: Mrs. M. MACKENZIE, M.A.

Principal: Miss MARGARET FRODSHAM, B.Sc.

Secretary: THOMAS HARWOOD.

A booklet was printed - *EDUCATION AS NATIONAL SERVICE: New Training Scheme for Teachers and Social Workers, to include a London Hostel.* This gave details of lectures - subjects available to meet individual needs included psychology, ethics, social philosophy, economics and civics *[citizenship]*. Practical training would be given in modern methods of teaching, lecturing and social work, and visits of observation would be made to such special schools and institutions, settlements, clubs, and so on "as are being conducted on the most modern principles." The course was to last three terms and residence would be provided for the first year in the Hostel at Campden Hill. To qualify for admission, students had to be 21 or over and be either graduates or certificated teachers. Interestingly for that time, no one was required to take an examination but students could work for certain teaching certificates if they wished. There were also courses for demobilised ex-servicemen - the College was one of the pioneering organisations to offer these. The scheme would start in October 1916.

Grand Lodge in 1917 received good news of the College's successful first term. Millicent Mackenzie was to keep in touch with the Minister of Education, who had shown considerable interest in the scheme, over the new legislation affecting education. The books showed a modest profit, and progress was being made on all fronts, particularly in forwarding the new educational ideas. Knowledge of our work as Freemasons was also spreading. Apart from voluntary donations, the Order did not formally contribute financially to the scheme, the funding of which was mainly borne by Marion Lindsay Halsey.

The headquarters and main lecture facility for the College - now called the *Guild of Education as National Service* - was at 11 Tavistock Square in Bloomsbury, the premises of the Theosophical Educational Trust. Branches were at Mansfield House, Canning Town, West Ham - home of Mansfield House University Settlement from 1895 - which specialised in inner city work and at Kenton, Harrow where there was a large garden and farm for courses in rural subjects.

Recruiting poster for the Queen Mary's Army Auxiliary Corps - 'The Girl behind the Man behind the Gun'.

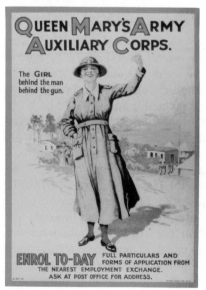

The Petition for recognition of our Order sent to United Grand Lodge in 1920 *(see Chapter Five)* referred to this pioneering educational work. Recognition would help the Halsey Training College, because our sphere of influence would be wider through contact with the men's Order.

Unfortunately there was a great deal of opposition - political, economic and professional - to those parts of the 1918 Education Act relating to day continuation classes, and so although they were law, they were never put into operation. Thus the Halsey Training College lost its entire *raison d'être* and closed, probably in the summer of 1923.

Freemasonry and the Women's Services

At the February 1919 meeting of Lodge Golden Rule No.1, Marion Halsey, speaking as Grand Master, called the attention of the Brethren "to what she felt might be a new and important field of activity for the Order."

Dame Florence Leach, member of Lodge Golden Rule No.1 and Chief Commandant of the Queen Mary's Army Auxiliary Corps.

She had felt for some time that Masonry should especially appeal to the Women's Armies, and more particularly at the time of demobilisation when it might offer a valuable link to cement that sense of comradeship brought about by war service. Bro. Dame Florence Leach, who had been initiated into Lodge Golden Rule in 1909, was Chief Commandant of the Queen Mary's Army Auxiliary Corps. This organisation had been set up as the Women's Army Auxiliary Corps in February 1917 under the control of the War Office, in order to employ women in certain jobs so that men could be released for military service. They worked in very many occupations - as cooks, domestic workers, clerks, waitresses, motor drivers, garage cleaners, storekeepers, checkers, telegraph, telephone and postal operators, grooms, printers, fabric workers, photographers, shoemakers, bakers, technical workers and dispatch riders!

At the same meeting six Q.M.A.A.C. officers were proposed as candidates and initiated at the following meeting. They were variously described as Chief Controller Q.M.A.A.C. (Miss E.H. Horniblow), Assistant Chief Controllers (Miss Blanche Ireland, later to become Camp Commandant of Bostall Heath Camp, Abbey Wood, south east London), Assistant and Deputy Assistant Controllers (Mrs. Dora Esslemont - later to be in charge of Patrols, the equivalent of the Military Police) and a Unit Assistant.

If the movement grew, the Grand Master hoped it might be possible to consecrate a Lodge to be called the United Services Lodge to take officers from all the Women's Corps. In fact, Lodge Harmony No.4, which had been consecrated in 1910, was chosen to be the Lodge primarily for Servicewomen and the six Q.M.A.A.C. officers transferred from Lodge Golden Rule to Lodge Harmony in 1921.

Additional sources

Muriel Mackenzie: 'The Halsey Training College-An Experiment' *Herald of the Star* 8 (1919), 397-400.
Imperial War Museum: *Women's Work Collection database.*

Chapter Five

An Appeal to United Grand Lodge and a New Home for the Order

The Petition

Buried in the Minutes of the Board of General Purposes of 17th January 1919, amongst plans for a banquet to celebrate the signing of peace and a report from the Grand Secretary that he had succeeded in obtaining from the Fuel Controller an adequate supply of coal "to ensure the comfort of the members", is the almost laconic statement "A question arose as to approaching the Grand Lodge of England relative to a possible understanding between their Obedience and our Order." It was proposed and carried that a Special Committee be appointed to consider the matter and to draft a petition. The Committee consisted of Grand Master Halsey, Deputy Grand Master Peter Birchall, Grand Treasurer Adelaide Litten and Grand Secretary Peter Slingsby.

They had met by 18th March when the Grand Secretary reported to the Board that a sympathetic letter had been received by the M.W. The Grand Master in response to an enquiry she had made to United Grand Lodge, but several points of policy meant that the greatest care had to be taken in submitting the petition to ensure its favourable reception. Grand Lodge were to be informed that favourable encouragement had been given to the movement but that negotiations were likely to be lengthy and the matter was to be left in the hands of the Special Committee for at least six months before it was brought forward again.

At Grand Lodge in October 1919 Grand Secretary Slingsby referred to a recent circular from the Board of General Purposes of the Older Obedience, again relating to association with irregular bodies. Grand Master Halsey stated that in conference with her senior Grand Lodge Officers she had agreed that a diplomatic protest on behalf of our Order was necessary and that if left to her, she would take steps to see that it reached the proper quarter. Philip Colville Smith was then

Grand Secretary of the United Grand Lodge of England. She duly had a "satisfactory" interview with him in an official capacity. "When leaving his office she told him he must look to seeing her again later on *[regarding the Petition]*. He received her suggestion in a very kindly manner ...".

The Special Committee had meanwhile finalised the text of the Petition and it had been inscribed on parchment. The wording was thought by Grand Lodge to have strength and dignity and thanks were duly expressed to the Committee. *(The Petition and the full accompanying correspondence is included in Appendix I).* The Petition pointed out that the position of women in society had changed greatly because of the War, when women took part in much of the work and responsibilities of men. It requested a full examination of the working of the Order and to have its existence regularised in the Masonic world by the recognition of United Grand Lodge. Integration was neither sought nor desired, but just a removal of the bans of 1910 and 1919, so that men were free to support their ladies in Masonry "without compromising their honour or allegiance."

Grand Lodge formally carried a Resolution approving the work of the Special Committee and begged the Grand Master to present the Petition without delay, for consideration by the men's Board of General Purposes. The Grand Master asked the assembled Brethren "to stand to order with raised hands and looking towards the Volume of the Sacred Law make me a very solemn promise that no word of this Petition or of our proceedings tonight shall be spoken of outside this meeting."

In addition, Marion Halsey sent a personal letter to the Grand Secretary, adding some words of further explanation which did not have a place in the formal document. It spelled out the fact that the Order's prayer was for examination, with a view to possible recognition; recognition which would enable members of Lodges working under the United Grand Lodge of England to visit the Lodges of our Order. It also outlined the reasons why such a small organisation had taken the (to us) momentous step of petitioning the Board at that time, rather than waiting until numbers had grown and our position consolidated. Prime amongst these was the educational work undertaken by the Order in the form of the Guild of Education as

Philip Colville Smith,
Grand Secretary of U.G.L.E. in 1920.

National Service and the Halsey Training College for Teachers. If recognition was granted, the sphere of influence of the Order would rapidly increase through contact with the men's Order and it was felt that this would guarantee the success of the educational scheme.

She concludes "May I say we are quite aware of the magnitude of what we are asking. May we plead in excuse the sincere love we have for our Masonic work, and our deep sense of what Masonic discipline and Masonic teaching can do for women. Amongst the large armies of women - doctors, nurses, teachers and social workers - there is no one organisation which can establish a close link between them all, while embracing every shade of religious opinion. Masonry alone can supply this want, which is every day making itself more felt in our midst."

The reply from Philip Colville Smith, Grand Secretary of United Grand Lodge, did not come until February 1921. The answer was terse:
    "The Board, after giving full consideration to this petition, ... directs me to state that it cannot recommend the prayer of the petition for acceptance by Grand Lodge ... [The admission of women] affects a principle on which the United Grand Lodge of England has always stood firm, and concerning which it admits no compromise. No woman can be a Freemason according to the original Plan of Freemasonry to which English Freemasons have from time immemorial adhered ... Every Brother is pledged ... to discountenance all dissenters from that original Plan, and to admit that it is not in the power of any man or body of men to make innovation in the Body of Masonry ... [The Board] will continue to exercise its disciplinary powers towards any member working under the English Jurisdiction who violates his obligation by being present at or assisting in assemblies professing to be Masonic, which are attended by women."

Peter Slingsby sent a remarkably restrained reply:

"M.W.Bro. Marion L. Halsey ... desires me to acknowledge your letter ... and to express her gratitude for the very kind and courteous way in which you received her on the two occasions on which she came to your office.

She and her Officers regret the answer of your Honourable Board to the Petition handed to you in November of last year, an answer containing a refusal basing the exclusion of women solely upon adherence to the 'original Plan of Freemasonry', but feeling, as she and her Officers do, that the recognition of women's place in Freemasonry is nevertheless only a question of time and patience, they will continue to devote their best energies to developing their part of the Movement in the true spirit of Masonry, so that, when recognition is finally granted, the Honourable Fraternity of Antient Masonry will be seen to be securely founded upon the three grand principles of Brotherly Love, Relief and Truth."

M.W. Bro. Halsey read the response of the Older Obedience to Grand Lodge in March 1921. She also told them that subsequent to the reply, two male Brethren, Bro. Fox-Warner and Bro. Perkins (both of whom had wives in our Order and were friendly towards us) proposed to United Grand Lodge that the decision should be referred back to their Board of General Purposes for reconsideration.

Bro. Fox-Warner then made a bad mistake. In explaining his proposal he said that "this little organisation *[our Order]* could not be as black as it was painted (solely because they admitted women) as the Grand Master of the Order was the daughter-in-law of their own beloved Deputy Grand Master, and further, these ladies had no doubt got the genuine Masonic secrets." This reference to the relationship between Marion Lindsay Halsey and her father-in-law Sir Thomas Halsey was, in the circumstances, unwise and not unnaturally led to some protest by the men. Grand Master Halsey said that she was satisfied with the response, although its arguments were weak. It was obvious that United Grand Lodge would continue with their disciplinary measures against any of their members who continued to associate with us.

It would be necessary for us to determine our attitude in future towards 'English' Masons who still wished to visit us. The Grand Master then read Peter Slingsby's acknowledgement to United Grand Lodge, which

Sir Thomas Halsey, Deputy Grand Master of U.G.L.E. 1903-1926.

had been approved by the Special Committee and confirmed by our Board of General Purposes. She finished by saying "That, Brethren, concludes our first effort towards recognition and I do not regret anything that has been done." Following an enquiry from the Grand Secretary, a resolution was passed by Grand Lodge absolving all Brethren from the vow of secrecy they had taken concerning the Petition. It was stressed, however, that there should no indiscriminate talk.

It appears from the membership records of the early Lodges that men were admitted as candidates up to 1916, although the numbers are few because of war service and the penalties imposed by United Grand Lodge of England. The policy with regard to receiving visitors from the Older Obedience was considered at two meetings of the Board of General Purposes in 1921. The Grand Master felt that, so long as we did not send actual Summonses to the 'English' Masons, if and when they wanted to attend the Initiation of wives, relatives or friends (knowing, as they would, the penalty to be imposed by their own Obedience) we could permit them to attend. Others considered that we should bar all 'English' Masons from visiting our Lodges, and that we should not initiate any men.

The Board recommended to Grand Lodge that whilst we should be careful not to send a summons or invitation to any male Mason, we should continue not to discriminate against them and to welcome them without comment if they visited us. All visitors were to be proved - either by the Worshipful Master of the Lodge or by an experienced Brother - after which the Secretary was to see that their name and Lodge Number were entered in the Lodge Attendance Book. This was duly approved by Grand Lodge and the Secretaries of the four Private Lodges were informed accordingly. This remained the situation until the next decade.

A new home for the Order

In early 1921 the Baptist Union, as landlords, raised the rent of the Order's premises in Southampton Row by the enormous amount of 60%. This meant that expenditure would then exceed income. It was left to Peter Slingsby to negotiate with the Baptist Union, whilst at the same time trying to improve recruitment to the Order to increase income. He was also charged with looking for alternative accommodation.

In March he secured a reduction to a minimum of £125 per year for the Library (where meetings were held) and £85/10/- (£85.50) for Room 2, used as an office. In June the four private Lodges each agreed to pay a quota as a contribution to the increased rent of Southampton Row. Over the next two years it became increasingly obvious that the Order needed a home of its own.

In June 1923 a meeting of the whole Order was called at Dorset House in order to discuss a possible future home. A sub-committee was formed to investigate finding permanent premises. At this meeting £1,827 was collected in donations with a further £175 per year promised in five-year covenants.

A large freehold house was needed with either a room suitable for a Temple at least the size of that at Southampton Row, or sufficient adjoining land upon which to build a Temple. A Brother "much esteemed by all" offered to purchase a suitable building if found - this was Bro. Florence Emma Turner, a member of Lodge of Unity No.3.

Bro. Florence Emma Turner

At Grand Lodge in June 1923 the Deputy Grand Master Peter Birchall proposed that "a most hearty Vote of Thanks be passed to Bro. F.E. Turner for her most kind and generous donation. This was supported by R.W.Bro. the Grand Treasurer and R.W.Bro. the Grand Secretary and carried by acclamation."

27 Pembridge Gardens

At a meeting of Lodge of Unity No.3 on 10th March 1924 the Grand Master, M.W.Bro. Marion Lindsay Halsey, announced that a deposit had been paid on a house, No.27 in Pembridge Gardens, Notting Hill Gate, London and that the Premises Committee was busily engaged in considering plans for the new Temple to be built in the garden, alterations to the house and re-decoration. It was hoped that Lodges would be able to use the building by October of that year. The minutes of the Quarterly Communication of Grand Lodge of March 1924 also refer to the honour which the Grand Master proposed to confer on Bro. Turner.

27 Pembridge Gardens, as it was in the early part of the twentieth century.

The houses in Pembridge Gardens, Pembridge Square and Pembridge Road had been built as a speculative project between 1849 and 1854. All the houses were built to a standard design of three storeys and a basement. Spacious and elegant detached dwellings, they were later to become Grade II listed buildings in the Pembridge Conservation Area.

Bro. Turner (not even a Warden) was summoned to attend Grand Lodge on 26th March at Southampton Row. After the Grand Secretary's Quarterly Report, all those below the rank of Installed Master retired. Deputy Grand Master Birchall suspended the work of Grand Lodge and formed a special Lodge, then Bro. Turner was called in. She was required to assent to the Ancient Charges read by the Grand Secretary, took the Obligation and was passed through the Master's chair "in regular form". The special Lodge was closed, the Brethren who had retired were recalled and the work of Grand Lodge was resumed.

A Resolution was passed, thanking both W.Bro. Turner for her generosity in purchasing the house and garden at 27 Pembridge

Gardens as a permanent headquarters and M.W.Bro. Marion Halsey for giving the money to build a Temple on the site. As the Deputy Grand Master said "... it is due entirely to your generosity that our horizons have thus far brightened: that your kind action has made possible what we have so long wanted and which has ever been the aim of those who have worked in the Order from its commencement. For myself and the Brethren I sincerely thank you." It was either at this meeting or privately afterwards that Marion Lindsay Halsey presented Florence Emma Turner with an antique Masonic jewel decorated with the two pillars, level, compasses and other Masonic emblems, bearing the inscription 'In affectionate gratitude from M.L.H., March 1924'. The design on this jewel was later reproduced on the banner of Lodge Verity No.7 in 1927.

In what must have been a nerve-racking and emotional ceremony for one who had only belonged to the Order for three years, the newly elevated W.Bro. Turner replied:
"It is quite impossible for me to adequately thank you all for the high honour you have done me. I will always endeavour never to disgrace the trust you have placed in me, and I thank you all very, very sincerely for being so extremely generous to me. I do not think I alone merit all the kind things said to me, for I would like to say my late father, who was a Mason, set aside certain money for my brother and myself, but the purpose of its use could not be carried out, therefore as a tribute to my father, I had every pleasure in using this money for the good of our Order, knowing my doing so would have pleased him. I had hoped to place the title deeds of No.27 Pembridge Gardens in your hands tonight but I have not yet received them, although my solicitors write that they have the keys of the premises, thus giving us possession."

Financial problems immediately came to the fore, but the possession of the freehold enabled a mortgage to be raised. A building contract for £4,000 was signed and work on the alterations began. From first to last the cost of building, decorating and furnishing the Temple and offices amounted to £7,600 between 1923 and 1937.

The Grand Master then informed the Brethren that the laying of the foundation stone of the new Temple would take place on Wednesday evening, July 2nd 1924. Grand Lodge would convene, for the first time, in the long room at 27 Pembridge Gardens at 6.15 p.m. A Grand Lodge procession (including the four reigning Masters of the private Lodges, carrying the Consecration vessels) would then be formed and proceed to the new Temple, afterwards returning to the long room for the Closing of Grand Lodge. By her order a Command notice, with a book of the Ceremony, was to be sent to all Members of the Order.

So Grand Lodge was opened in due and ample form on 2nd July. The Worshipful Master of Lodge Golden Rule No.1, W.Bro. Antonia Collet, carried the vessel of corn; W.Bro. A. Gascoigne of Emulation No.2 carried the wine; R.W.Bro. M.E. Cook of Lodge of Unity No.3 the oil and W.Bro. Maud Litten (sister of the next Grand Master Adelaide Litten) carried the salt. Others present whose names resonated in later years were Florence Jane Hawkins, who acted as Grand Junior Warden and lived to be the oldest surviving Founder

Member of the Order (dying in 1949), and W.Bro. Alice Muirhead Hope, mother of Mary Gordon Muirhead Hope, Grand Master from 1948 to 1964. Peter Slingsby carried the silver presentation trowel (now in the Library at Headquarters) which the Grand Master used during the ceremony. Adelaide Litten herself was Grand Treasurer at the time, and carried silver coins to bury with the foundation stone.

The stone was prepared and the Deputy Grand Master read out the inscription: "This Foundation Stone was laid by Marion Lindsay Halsey, Grand Master of the Honourable Fraternity of Antient Masonry on July 2nd 1924. May God preserve the Craft!" The Grand Treasurer deposited the coins and the Grand Secretary put down a copy of the Book of Constitutions, a list of the current Grand Lodge Officers, a copy of the order of the ceremony and copies of *The Times* and *Daily Graphic* for that day. The cement having been laid, the Grand Secretary handed the Deputy

The silver presentation trowel used to lay the foundation stone of the Temple at 27 Pembridge Gardens.

Grand Master the silver trowel and Peter Birchall read out the inscription on it, together with the fact that it was to be subsequently presented to M.W.Bro. Halsey by the members of the Order.

The stone was lowered and proved by the Grand Master with the square, level and plumb rule. Three knocks were then given with the setting maul and the Grand Master said "In the name of T.G.A.O.T.U. I declare this stone well and truly laid." Corn was scattered: "I scatter corn on this stone, the symbol of plenty", followed by wine: "I pour wine on this stone, the symbol of joy and cheerfulness", then oil: "I pour oil on this stone, the symbol of peace and unanimity", and finally salt: "I sprinkle salt on this stone, the symbol of fidelity and friendship."

The Grand Master prayed on behalf of the whole Order: "Almighty and Eternal God, G.A.O.T.U., we ask Thy blessing on this our undertaking that the Temple that we are raising to Thy honour and to the establishment of our Masonic work, may be built on the sure foundation of true Brotherhood, and supported on the three great pillars of Wisdom, Strength and Beauty. Grant us to pursue our work therein in the spirit of self-sacrifice, with courage and with singleness of heart. Prosper Thou our handiwork, Great Architect, and fit our Order in the future to become a strong tool in Thy hand for the furtherance of honest work and high endeavour. So mote it be."

The Grand Master then gave a short address, the procession reformed and returned to the long room. All this over and done within one hour! There were one hundred and nine members present at the ceremony. In the autumn of 1924 notice was given to the solicitors of the Baptist Union that the tenancy of 4 Southampton Row would be relinquished on 29th September.

At Grand Lodge in January 1925, Marion Lindsay Halsey announced "W.Bro. Florence Emma Turner, I have very great pleasure in appointing and investing you Grand Registrar of the Order. No regular duties are yet entailed by this office but the Grand Secretary will probably tell you, you are to take charge of one of the keys of the Grand Seal" (according to the *Book of Constitutions*, this is still the only formal duty of the Grand Registrar). V.W.Bro. F.E. Turner, Grand Registrar, expressed her appreciation of the honour conferred upon her.

The Consecration of the Temple

The Temple was consecrated on January 20th 1925. In a foreword to the printed version of the Consecration Ceremony, M.W.Bro. Lindsay Halsey wrote that although there were elaborate rituals for the consecration of a new Lodge, incorporating the corn, wine, oil and salt used in the first part of the ceremony, nothing was laid down for the consecration of a Temple and therefore the prayers used were specially written for the occasion.

The Brethren having taken their places in the Temple, with Worshipful Masters and Past Masters on the dais, the western door was closed at precisely 6.30 p.m. On a single knock from the Grand Master the Grand Director of Ceremonies opened the door, called the Brethren to order and admitted the Grand Lodge procession ending with the Grand Master, with her Deputy carrying the censer. The Grand Master took the chair of King Solomon and the Deputy Grand Master conducted the Grand Lodge Officers to their places. The Lodge was opened and the Grand Master saluted with nine (note, not eleven). A special opening hymn was sung - *Holy Father, Lord and Giver/Of that life wherein we move.* This was followed by a few moments silence, then the consecrating procession formed up, consisting of the Grand Master, Deputy Grand Master, Grand Treasurer, Grand Registrar and Grand Secretary. Representatives of the four private Lodges carried the Elements of Consecration, which were scattered or poured in turn during four perambulations.

The Deputy Grand Master then censed the Temple. M.W.Bro. Halsey consecrated the central altar saying: "I cense this central altar with the sweet savour of incense, the emblem of prayer and aspiration", followed by a prayer "May the vows which will be taken kneeling before it, ascend unpolluted to the Throne of Grace. May this sacred spot, the point within the circle of our Masonic ceremonial, a symbol of that Divine Spark which dwells within, become in very truth a point from which a Master Mason cannot err. May the great lessons of the Craft be manifested forth in the work of this our Order, for the realisation of our ideals, and the 'perfecting of Humanity'. S.M.I.B."

The same ritual was followed for the seven officers' chairs, with a different prayer said for each:

The Master's Chair - "May those who occupy this Chair become reflectors of the great Light, which dwells in the East to flood our dark world with wisdom…"

The Junior Warden - "May those who occupy this Chair stand for the dignity and joy of work…"

The Senior Warden - "May those who occupy this Chair stand for that peace and sense of achievement which follow upon work accomplished…"

The Senior Deacon - [May they] "remember their high calling as Guides, and bring to their task all sympathy and understanding…"

Junior Deacon - [May they] "realise themselves not only as Guides, but also as Messengers, linking up the pathway of the Light between those of greater power and understanding than their own."

Director of Ceremonies - [May they] "bring reverence and dignity to our working, once more establishing our ancient ceremonies as a fitting vehicle for the symbolic truth which lies behind the form."

Inner Guard - "May only those who are true Seekers of the Light be permitted to enter the Temple Gates, and approach our hidden mysteries."

The Grand Temple as it was during the 1920s and 1930s, with wooden panelling and the banners of the early Lodges around the walls.

The Deputy Grand Master censed the Temple for the second time and the Grand Master recited the Act and Prayer of Dedication:

"Almighty and Eternal God, Great Architect and Ruler of the Universe, we dedicate this Temple to Thy service, and to the service of the world. Dedicate and consecrate us to Thy service and the service of humanity. May this Temple shelter only pure thoughts and unselfish desire. May high ideals ever be taught within its precincts. From the inspiration here gained may there flow forth throughout the future a great stream of consecrated effort on behalf of the poor, the ignorant and the suffering.

Bind us all together, Great Architect, in the strength of the Masonic Tie, so that caring little for differences of class, creed and nationality, we may be content to work in love and harmony with all those who humbly acknowledge a great Creator. Bless mightily all those to whose self-sacrifice we owe the fulfilment of our hopes in the possession of this Temple. Bless too, all those who have worked for us in its construction, whether with the pencil of the architect, the 24 inch gauge of the surveyor, or the lesser tools of those who labour with their hands. Make all worthy to be used for Thine Almighty purposes, and bring us at last to the Grand Lodge above, where Thou, the world's Great Architect, dost live and reign forever. S.M.I.B."

The Grand Master and her Deputy respectively addressed the Brethren, dealing with the history, development and aims of the Order. On behalf of all the members of the Order R.W.Bro. Peter Slingsby, Grand Secretary, presented the Grand Master with a cheque for one hundred and fifty eight guineas *[£165.90p taking inflation into account]* "being the amount received by him from the Brethren as a token of affection...to purchase something pleasing to herself for use or decoration in the Temple."

The Grand Master replied that she was overwhelmed by this delightful surprise "a gift that would afford her the joy of entering upon certain decorative work in the Temple which up to the present she had thought would have to be deferred owing to the many other calls upon our funds." This is probably a reference to the inscription round the eastern wall of the Temple - *Blessed is he who has known the Mysteries before he goes beneath the hollow earth: that man knows the end of life and its source divine.* The words were written in the third century A.D.

by the Roman philosopher Plotinus, one of the ancient mystics. The 1938 History booklet *(Blue Book)* - written partly by Peter Birchall who was involved in the ceremony and could therefore give a first-

The Worshipful Master's Chair in the Grand Temple.

hand account - records that this inscription was arranged by M.W.Bro. Halsey. We know that she was familiar with the writings of Plotinus, as she donated her own copy of his works to the Library at Headquarters. Grand Lodge was closed in peace and harmony at 8.15 p.m. with the customary Closing Hymn and the National Anthem.

The Temple benefited from many gifts, including the carpet, the Master's Chair (which was an antique gilt Venetian piece, possibly a Bishop's throne from an Italian church, and presented by Bro. Annie Harrison of Lodge of Unity No.3), the Master's pedestal of old walnut and gilt presented by Lodge Golden Rule No.1, the carved chairs on the dais and the Wardens' chairs, which were copies made in London of the Bishop's Chair in St. Mark's at Venice. The 1938 *Blue Book* has photographs of the original Temple with dark wooden panelling from floor to ceiling, decorated with gold. The four Ionic pilasters in the room were given by Lodge of Unity No.3. The banners of the early Lodges hung around the walls, and there was a central altar. The decorated arch behind the Master's chair, with its gilded sunray, was presented by Lodge Emulation No.2.

Three New Lodges

The first ceremony, other than Lodge meetings, to be held in the new Headquarters was the consecration of a new Lodge, Verity No.7. This took place on 28th February 1925 - Verity was the first Lodge to be formed since 1912. The Consecrating Officer was M.W.Bro. Marion Lindsay Halsey, with R.W.Bro. Peter Birchall as Director of Ceremonies and V.W.Bro. Florence Turner, Grand Registrar, as Consecrating Inner Guard. She became a Joining Member later the same year and served Lodge Verity as its Preceptor and Director of Ceremonies until 1939. R.W.Bro. Adelaide Litten, Grand Treasurer, was one of the Element Bearers, as was R.W.Bro. Florence Jane Hawkins, one of the Founder Members of the Order in 1908. W.Bro. Mary Gordon Muirhead Hope was the first Senior Warden and became Worshipful Master of Lodge Verity in 1926-7.

Lodge Verity No.7 consecrated in February 1925

In March 1927 Verity's Banner was dedicated by the Deputy Grand Master, R.W.Bro. Peter Birchall. The design was taken from the jewel given by Marion Halsey to Florence Turner. On a purple background are depicted the two great pillars, the all-seeing eye, the square pavement, the three candlesticks, the sun and the moon, the heavy maul, the perfect ashlar, the chisel, the working tools of the Second Degree and the seven stars. Between the pillars and on the square pavement are three steps, on top of which are the Volume of the Sacred Law together with the Square and Compasses. In the centre of the Banner is the letter G. Seven was the number of Lodge Verity, whose motto was 'When truth comes, evil flies away'.

Banner of Lodge Verity No.7.

Lodge Fidelity No.8 was consecrated in November 1926, a daughter Lodge of Harmony No.4. The two Lodges held an annual combined dinner for some years, and a photograph of this dinner at Harrods in 1931, showing M.W.Bro. Adelaide Litten with R.W.Bros. Peter Birchall and Peter Slingsby, is displayed in the top floor changing room at 27 Pembridge

Lodge Fidelity No. 8 in November 1926

Combined dinner of Lodge Harmony No.4 and Lodge Fidelity No.8 held in 1931.

Gardens. The banner of the Lodge is unique in that it bears no Masonic device, but the name of the Lodge and the names and dates in office of every Worshipful Master since its Consecration, together with the motto in Latin 'May it live forever'. (A new banner - an exact copy of the original but with more space for names - was made and presented in 1995 on the occasion of the Lodge's 500th meeting).

Banner of Lodge Fidelity No.8.

Lodge Loyalty No.9 was a daughter of Emulation No.2, from which came twenty four of the twenty seven Founder Members. The Lodge was consecrated in May 1927. One of the Founders, R.W.Bro. Edith Fisher, P.G.W., took the Chair in 1930-31 and at the completion of her year the Lodge

Lodge Loyalty No. 9 in May 1927

presented her with a jewel. In 1987, R.W.Bro. Fisher, then resident at the Doris Jones Home, gave the jewel to Lodge Loyalty to commemorate their Diamond Jubilee.

Banner of Lodge Loyalty No.9

Grand Master Marion Halsey had been ill on and off for much of 1926 and 1927, missing several Grand Lodge meetings. Her husband Reginald died in May 1927. She seemed to be in better health in the latter part of the year but died on 27th December at her home, 18 Mount Street, W1 in London. A funeral service, attended by the family only, was held at Withyham Church in Sussex, with a Memorial Service at the Grosvenor Chapel in South Audley Street in London at 3 p.m. on the same day, Friday December 30th.

The church of St. Michael and All Angels at Withyham housed the Sackville Vault - Marion Halsey's daughter Diana married the 9th Earl de la Warr, whose family name was Sackville, and Diana's mother-in-law was Muriel, Lady de la Warr, who was also a member of Lodge Golden Rule No.1. Marion Halsey was not buried in the vault, but in the churchyard, in the same grave as her husband Reginald. Their tomb stone bears on the top the square and compasses.

Marion Lindsay Halsey's gravestone in the churchyard of St. Michael and All Angels, Withyham, East Sussex.

Chapter Six

Adelaide Litten - Expansion, Charity and Women Only

Following the death of Marion Halsey in December 1927, Grand Lodge met in January. A Memorial Service preceded Grand Lodge. The hymn *Holy Father, Lord and Giver* was followed by prayers and readings from Ecclesiastes - *Remember now thy Creator* - and the Book of Wisdom - *But the souls of the just are in the hand of God.* After the Address, silence was kept and then came the hymn *Now thank we all our God.* The Service concluded with Chopin's *Funeral March.* Masonic mourning was worn for the first time in this Order - three black crepe rosettes were worn on the apron and one on the collar.

Plans had been under way during her lifetime to set up a Lodge in honour of Marion Halsey. This unfortunately did not come to pass until March 1928, when Lodge Marion Halsey No.10 was consecrated. She herself had chosen the motto - *Arise, Shine*. The banner of the Lodge bears these words and has at its centre the seven-pointed star - seven being the perfect number, of great significance in Freemasonry.

Lodge Marion Halsey No. 10 in March 1928

Banner of Lodge Marion Halsey No.10.

Under the guidance of the Deputy Grand Master Peter Birchall, much thought was given to the Nomination and Election of the next Grand Master. It was within the power of Grand Lodge to defer this until the June Communication, with the Installation to follow in the October. "Very considerable thought [was] given to the choosing of a brother who would be *persona grata* with the whole Order and at liberty to give the attention and time necessary to the proper performance of the duties of this high office."

M.W.Bro. Adelaide Daisy Litten,
Grand Master 1928-1938.

There were three possible candidates, but two withdrew, leaving the name before Grand Lodge of Adelaide Litten, Grand Treasurer for the past fifteen years. There were reasons why a deferment until June was advisable - not only out of respect for the late Grand Master, but because Adelaide Litten was very reluctant to undertake the office and if she did so a new Grand Treasurer would have to be found. She herself would need to oversee the end of the financial year and the Deputy Grand Master would continue to act in the interim.

Adelaide Litten

Later in 1935 Adelaide Litten described her feelings at this time:
"I was approached on the matter but, for many reasons, I at first refused to entertain it in any way. Finally, the pressure brought to bear upon me became very acute, I being informed that if I did not give way to the wishes of the Brethren, the future of our Order (for which we had all worked so hard) would be gravely jeopardised, and that the responsibility for this would rest upon my shoulders. It therefore appeared to me, after the most serious consideration, that my obvious duty was to sacrifice my personal inclinations and consent to serve the Order in the way it was deemed I could do so best."

She had not only been Grand Treasurer but also Preceptor of the Central Lodge of Instruction. As the Tribute to her in *The Gavel* after her death said: "In those capacities she was the guide, philosopher and friend to us all, and it was due to her training that many of our elder Brethren rose to the eminence in Masonic ceremonial which afterwards distinguished them." The eldest of four daughters and a son - her father Tobias was a cigar merchant - in the census returns of 1901 her profession is given as 'Secretary'. She was 55 when elected Grand Master. Her sister Maud, who was three years younger, later became R.W.Bro. Litten, Past Grand Warden.

19th June 1928 duly saw the Nomination and Election of Adelaide Litten to the office of Grand Master. She said then: "Brethren I thank you most sincerely for this great confidence you are placing in me and no-one appreciates more than I do myself the difficulty in following our late dear and wonderful Grand Master, but I can promise you my untiring effort to carry out the work of this high office both faithfully and well, helped by the loyal support of you all." W.Bro. Blanche Ireland was elected Grand Treasurer.

Bro. Diana de la Warr - Marion Halsey's daughter - donated an organ for the Grand Temple in memory of her mother. In addition she gave her mother's jewels to the Order and defrayed the cost of wall cases to exhibit these. Copies of an autographed photogravure of the late Grand Master were available for the Brethren to buy at 2/9d (13p) including postage.

Grand Lodge in October 1928 combined the Enthronement of Adelaide Litten with the consecration and dedication of the organ. Brethren who were not Grand Lodge Officers were invited to attend, and normal Grand Lodge business was suspended whilst they were present. Deputy Grand Master Birchall censed the organ: "I cense this organ with the sweet savour of incense, a symbol of prayer and aspiration ... I consecrate and dedicate this organ to the use of the Order. May the harmonies emanating from this instrument ever remind us of that beautiful character and harmonious life in whose memory it stands as a memorial."

In his preamble to the Installation, Birchall, with the loquacity of the period and of the man, referred to the late Grand Master:
"If I strike for a moment a note of grief - it is but a salute to the memory of that wonderful and splendid personality who for fifteen years governed us so successfully by the compelling power of a great love allied to a wide knowledge and profound wisdom. If by the mercy of Divine Providence she is permitted to be present, though invisible, with us this evening - then I am positively certain that none

is striving more than she is at this moment to make this an occasion of joy and happiness and a special opportunity to strengthen in all good ways the hands of the distinguished Brother whom we have chosen to occupy her place."

He then went on to define a Grand Master, not only as a Master of Masters, one fitted to rule by having perfected themselves in the Three Degrees, but a person fit to occupy the throne of Solomon the King and wield the sceptre of royalty:

"Masonry entrusts to its supreme ruler enormous power, extraordinary privilege, wide-reaching prerogatives, and heavy is the responsibility attaching to the office; not lightly are these powers to be grasped ... intelligence, suavity, balance, a strong will, a deep affection, and incorruptible honesty are its primary necessities."

The *verbatim* record of the Installation, transcribed meticulously from Peter Slingsby's shorthand, occupies nine foolscap pages of Grand Lodge Minutes - which not only reflects the length of the proceedings but also shows how the ceremony of Enthronement had been expanded since that of Marion Lindsay Halsey sixteen years earlier.

Having been interrogated as to whether she would govern without fear, bias or favour, without personal gain in any sense and would always guard the secrets of Freemasonry, Adelaide Daisy Litten took her Obligation. Her attention was then directed to the Great Lights, which "even now in the moment of your exaltation ... will remain infallible guides in the sphere of your predominant authority."

All lights were extinguished save the Master's candle in the East. The Deputy Grand Master then conducted the Grand Master Elect, robed as a Candidate in a white pilgrim's gown, around the Lodge, pausing at the cardinal points:

Standing in the North West: "... In the Antient Mysteries from which Masonry claims descent it was customary, when a Brother was about to be invested with a paramount and responsible position, that he was suddenly stripped of all his insignia of honour, clothed as a neophyte, and made to traverse once again the symbolical path which had lead him into the way of purgation, to illumination and wisdom."

While traversing the North side of Grand Lodge he recited: "... This is the path of the neophyte, through pain, through humiliation, through darkness. It is wise to remember this road by which you journeyed out of darkness into light; lest you be tempted to forget that once you were as those who now with unseeing eyes and halting steps traverse the way which leads to Divine Illumination. Be pitiful! Be very pitiful!! Dedicate the power which will be yours to the help of these, your Brethren, in the hour of their supreme need!"

In the East: "Lift your eyes Brother, this is the mystic East, the symbolical place of rising and increasing Light ... Pledge yourself, so far as in you lies, that you will never be less than a willing and eager vehicle of spiritual illumination to those who sincerely seek it."

Continuing the perambulation from East to South: "Facing the South, the symbolical place of the Sun at the Meridian: the region typical of activity, beauty and knowledge, I charge you to prove yourself a helper, protector and benefactor to all who for the good of mankind seek to increase knowledge and wisdom by honest labour and research of any kind ...".

The east end of the Temple, with dark wood panelling, the throne and the legend.

Continuing from South to West: "Facing the portal of the West, the seat of judgment, the place of the setting sun, you should ever remember that for you an assize is set. That you will be called upon to render an account of your stewardship, that your thoughts, motives and actions will be tested and weighed in the infallible balances of the Divine Justice, in order that you may receive the only award possible - your first due - may yours be an abundant and triumphant entrance into the region of supernal light."

Having been conducted to the East, the Grand Master Elect was invested with the badge, collar and jewel of her office. The Deputy Grand Master called her attention to the Compasses, the particular jewel of the Grand Master:

" ... You are now a Supreme Ruler, and in your sphere you will be called upon from time to time to apply this principle of a wise and beneficial limitation. A restraining hand upon your Officers or upon the Brethren; for yourself an inhibition or limitation of your own will and desire for the general or especial good of the Order you govern. Your compasses are superimposed upon a gauge, it is an emblem of the law which affords you liberty within strict limits, and should remind you that only in obedience to His superior and restraining will can your actions be acceptable to Him, and fraught with blessing on those whom you are set to lead and teach."

Adelaide Litten was then placed in the Chair of the Grand Master, the symbolical Throne of the Royal Solomon. "... Take this heavy maul as the symbol of your authority. Traditionally it is the instrument of death. For you it is the symbol of dominant Life." The ceremony continued with prayer and a corporate act of dedication to the service of God and the Order. The Grand Master herself spoke briefly and with great diffidence: "... I can only pray, my dear Brethren, that I may in some small measure justify your trust, and this, with God's help, will always be my earnest endeavour ...".

She invested Peter Birchall as Deputy Grand Master and Peter Slingsby as Grand Secretary, paying them great tribute: "It is impossible for me to exaggerate the splendid work that these two distinguished Brethren have done for the Order during many, many years; always ready to perform the task requested; ever willing to sacrifice themselves to promote the good and welfare of the Fraternity; always putting personal interests aside in order to help others; and flanked as I am by such pillars of light and learning I feel a sense of security and confidence that I am sure you will understand."

It was particularly pleasing that it had been Peter Birchall who as Worshipful Master of Lodge Emulation No.2 had initiated her in July 1909 and now had placed her in the Chair as head of the Order. Future events were to sour this happy relationship.

Adelaide Litten ruled over the Order for ten years - governing truly and faithfully and with great dignity, being concerned to teach as well as to rule. At the Memorial Service for her in June 1951, M.W.Bro. Mary Gordon Muirhead Hope told the following story, related to her by Adelaide Litten herself. She was talking with her boss in business (she was a secretary by profession), himself a senior Mason, soon after the time when our Order had decided that it would be for women only *[1935]*, and he had said " Well, Miss Litten, the women have it now, an Order of their own; I wonder how long it will last!" To which she had replied swiftly, "Why, for all time! It will grow and spread like that of the men." And he had said "I wonder, Miss Litten, I wonder. I do not want to depress you, but I doubt if you will find that women have the discipline to work together in Masonry. They have not the experience of men in corporate working. I fear you may find that all will go well for a time; and then something will crop up, someone will not get their own way, and the reaction will be that they will have no further use for Masonry."

M.W.Bro. Litten was concerned that the Order *should* develop this sense of discipline and respect for the rights and views of others that would be necessary for us to survive as an all-women Order. She had the essential gift of a real leader - of being able to command the loyal service and enthusiasm of others. She also had a special regard to the care, decoration and improvement of the Temple and Headquarters generally.

During her term of office the membership of the Order increased from four hundred and sixty to double that number. The number of Craft Lodges grew from nine to twenty, but it was to Lodge No.11 that the credit for much of this expansion, both then and in the future, was due.

Lodge Mercury No.11

Lodge Mercury No. 11 in June 1928

On 25th June 1928 the words of a Petition resounded through the new Temple at 27 Pembridge Gardens: "… we…are anxious to exert our best endeavours to promote and diffuse the genuine principles of the art; and to this end we desire to found … a special Lodge to be designated Mercury No.XI for the sole, specific and particular purpose of enabling its officers and members to journey to the provinces to make Freemasons, with the final objective of founding provincial Lodges." So was born the 'travelling' Lodge - consecrated by D.G.M. Peter Birchall and with V.W.Bro. Lucy Bertram O'Hea, Grand Registrar, as its first Worshipful Master. It was to meet at Headquarters or where required every month through the year. Its motto was 'Go forth!' and its hymn was Bunyan's *To be a pilgrim*.

The idea for this Lodge came to V.W.Bro. Lucy O'Hea from the men's military travelling Lodges. Such a Lodge travelled with a regiment and served not only the members of the garrison but recruited from and trained the local population wherever they were stationed. In time new permanent Lodges could be formed and so Freemasonry was spread far and wide. Grand Master Adelaide Litten authorised the formation of a travelling Lodge in order to expand Freemasonry for women throughout the country.

It was founded by one hundred and twelve members drawn from the ten Lodges which then comprised the Order. It came to possess a full set of furniture and equipment, most of which was donated by Brethren, and which was transported round the country by train or car. At the second meeting in July, the Lodge banner, worked by a Steward of the Lodge - W.Bro. Antonia Collet - was dedicated by D.G.M Birchall. This shows the *caduceus*, or wand of Mercury the Messenger, on an amethyst background. The rod is entwined with two serpents and two outstretched wings, with which to carry wisdom to the four corners of the earth. Side panels show the celestial and terrestrial globes, decorated as described in the Second Degree Tracing Board. The sun at the meridian is at the top whilst the motto 'Go Forth' runs across the bottom of the banner.

The third meeting - less than a month after the Consecration - saw the Lodge meet outside London, at Sunderland. The usual pattern adopted in a chosen location was for the Worshipful Master or a senior Officer to address an open meeting, freely advertised to attract ladies who might be interested, on 'Freemasonry and Women'. Lodge Mercury would then in due course initiate, pass and raise those ladies who committed themselves. These

Banner of Lodge Mercury No.11.

would become members of Mercury and when a sufficient number were present in any one place, they could petition for the formation of their own local Lodge.

An eye-witness account from a later phase of Mercury's work, leading to the consecration of Lodge Argosy No.27 at Bradford in 1948, gives an idea of how the procedure worked:

"The gilt-edged, script-printed card said nothing about Freemasonry for Women. It invited us only to meet, and take tea with 'Mrs. Lucy O'Hea and other ladies from London' at the Victoria Hotel, Bradford, and address our replies to 'Miss E.A. McArthur'. That it should evoke suspicion, as well as curiosity was hardly surprising. Even in 1946, seemingly 'innocent' invitations could well be merely the prelude to yet another money-raising appeal, or to the launching of a campaign for some fresh Good Cause. Five years of war had encouraged us to be on our guard against many things besides 'Careless Talk'.

"For a handful of the 40 - 50 guests who accepted it, however, that invitation was to prove the first of many Masonic summonses; and Room 30 in which that all-important Open Meeting was held was to acquire a very special, and a very personal significance - not only for those of us who signed on the dotted line that afternoon - but for many others who, in the years that lay ahead, were to take their "first regular step in Freemasonry" in it.

"Memories of that momentous meeting have inevitably been blurred by the smudging hands of Time. But - as in a faded photograph - a few details still remain vivid.

"Few of us will readily forget Mrs. O'Hea, a dignified and impressive figure, even without the Grand Master's regalia with which we were subsequently to associate her; and for some of us, R.W Bro. D.A. Taylor who, as one of the 'ladies from London' was introduced to us that day as Miss Taylor, will always be associated with 'The Hat', which framed her lovely face, and, conjuring up visions of pre-war Royal Ascots, threatened at times to distract both our fashion-starved eyes and our attention!"

" ... [the Worshipful Master of Lodge Mercury, together with other Grand Officers] had to travel the 400 miles from Kings Cross to Bradford frequently over a period of *two years* to initiate and pass Lodge Argosy's seventeen founder candidates; additional help being provided, as and when required, by other Officers from London or Manchester. Two of our candidates had to journey to London to take their Third Degrees, while several others had to be raised in Manchester."

In the first year of its existence, Mercury personnel held seventeen lecture meetings at Sunderland, Newcastle and Manchester, Southend, York, Northampton, Liverpool, Edinburgh and Hastings. Forty four candidates were initiated, twenty three passed and fifteen raised. The furniture and equipment of the Lodge travelled with the Officers. At the time of its Consecration, the Board of General Purposes had recommended to Lodge Mercury that a Special Standing Order should be adopted to allow V.W.Bro. O'Hea to remain in the Chair for three years to give the Lodge the benefit of her experience and hence a measure of stability.

1930 saw the peak of membership of Mercury - two hundred and twenty three - and it was in that year that the first daughter Lodge, Fraternity No.12 (and the first Lodge outside London) was consecrated to work at Southend. The Consecration largely followed the same form as in more recent times, with the inclusion of passages of Scripture - Psalm 133 *Behold how good and how pleasant it is for Brethren to dwell together in unity!* and the description of the building of King Solomon's Temple from II Chronicles - and an Oration on "the nature and principles of the Institution" by R.W.Bro. Peter Birchall, the Consecrating Chaplain.

Lodge Fraternity No.12 in July 1930

Membership of Mercury included twenty nine ladies returning to the fold from the break-away organisation, the Honourable Fraternity of Ancient Freemasons, who took the Obligation at a special ceremony. They formed their own Lodge at Headquarters, Equity No.16, in June 1931. Although V.W.Bro. Florence Turner, P.G.Registrar was the first Worshipful Master, the Senior Warden was W.Bro. Aimee Coccioletti, previously of the other Order, and she spoke for all those ladies in expressing to the Grand Master and Grand Lodge their gratitude "for having restored to them participation in the active work of Freemasonry." A typical Mercury meeting at this time consisted of three Second Degrees and five First Degrees in the same session.

Lodge Sanctuary No.14 in November 1930

Lodge Perseverance No.15 in December 1930

Lodge Equity No.16 in June 1931

Lodge Sincerity No.17 in January 1932

By June 1932 there were Lodges in Sunderland, Newcastle, Southend and Manchester. In the same year V.W.Bro. Florence Turner, who gave the freehold of 27 Pembridge Gardens to the Order, became Worshipful Master of Mercury. The Immediate Past Master, V.W.Bro. Lucy O'Hea, was presented with a beautiful jewel in the form of a brooch in token of the deep appreciation of the Lodge for her pioneering work. It was a replica of the wand of Mercury, crowned with a black pearl and set with fifty one brilliants, eight rose diamonds, twenty

The Mercury jewel presented to V.W. Bro. Lucy O'Hea when she became the Past Master in 1932.

seven sapphires and four rubies. The Lodge also presented thirty four volumes of *Ars Quatuor Coronatorum* - the research journal of the men's order - to the Library at 27 Pembridge Gardens.

Lodge Joyous No.18 in January 1933

Lodge Progress No.19 in October 1933

Lodge Fellowship No.20 in February 1938

From then until the outbreak of war in 1939 Lodges were consecrated at Liverpool (Joyous No.18), Worthing (Progress No.19) and Cardiff (Fellowship No.20). Open meetings were held as far apart as Gillingham, Stratford and Bridlington.

Charity Work

In July 1928 a questionnaire and covering letter were sent out to all members of the ten Lodges that comprised the Honourable Fraternity of Antient Masonry at that time. The aim was to "fulfil the expressed desire of so many to transmute the ideals of Freemasonry into some practical form of service." In reply, members offered their time and individual skills or expertise, ranging from advice on taxation matters to reading to blind people and painting and decorating - and so the Bureau of Service was born.

By 1930 the work of the Bureau had been formalised into six sections. The largest section made clothes for Queen Mary's London Needlework Guild - founded by the Queen whilst Duchess of York, and which made and distributed clothes to troops at the front and the needy at home. Exhibitions of articles were regularly held at 27

Pembridge Gardens before being sent to the London depot. *The Gavel* for February 1930 contains a letter from the Hon. Jean Bruce, Lady-in-Waiting, thanking the Order on behalf of Queen Mary for the parcel of two hundred and eighty one garments sent in. She wrote "I will see to it that Her Majesty realises what splendid work the Honourable Fraternity of Antient Masonry has done on behalf of the Guild, and I shall take pleasure in showing the Queen your contributions." There was a large consignment of garments from Lodges Sanctuary No.14 in Newcastle and Perseverance No.15 in Sunderland.

Brooch of Queen Mary's Needlework Guild.

Another section of the Bureau worked with H.M. Borstal Institution for Girls at Aylesbury. This cause was adopted because the Governor of the Borstal was a member of the Order, Bro. Lilian Barker. Bro. Barker later became an Assistant Police Commissioner for Prisons, specialising in crime amongst young people, and a Dame of the British Empire. An exhibition and sale of handicrafts made by the women and girls from the Borstal was held every year at 27 Pembridge Gardens and visiting them at Aylesbury was encouraged. Acknowledging the financial help, Bro. Barker wrote "The greatest help of all, however, is the feeling of understanding and sympathy which literally radiates from some of my fellow Brethren, and which gives me courage and further impetus to carry on from here."

Other sections included work with deprived children in Stepney and the Deptford Babies' Hospital and the collection and distribution of Hospital or Convalescent Home Letters - these were vouchers for treatment given to those who made a donation to a hospital, which could then be passed on to needy cases. There was also the provision of hospitality for students and foreign visitors to the country, and an employment service.

The Babies' Hospital at Deptford, south-east London, in the early 1930s.

In 1931 a meeting was held at 27 Pembridge Gardens, chaired by the M.W. The Grand Master, to consider the enlargement of the scope of the Bureau of Service, under the three headings of assisting our own members, assisting women generally and helping children. The meeting was also to ascertain views on the setting up of a definite charitable scheme as an integral part of the Order. The meeting voted for a charity confined to members of the Order, for some kind of home for elderly Masons and for aid to a hospital such as the endowment of a bed. A referendum of the whole Order put as top of the poll the establishment of a Samaritan Fund to assist in times of sickness, with a Home for Retired Masons second.

In 1933 the Bureau of Service was wound up. During 1935 the first suggestion was made at Grand Lodge by the Grand Master for the establishment of an Order Charity Fund to help needy members: "Charity is the duty of everyone, but it is the imperative obligation of the true Mason." The opinions of Brethren in their Lodges were canvassed and sent via the Board of General Purposes to Grand Lodge.

It was decided that the Order should aim at a target of £1,000 with which to launch the Fund. A special collection was taken at the Grand Lodge meeting to form the nucleus of the fund and this raised £24.5s. (£24.25). At the next meeting of Lodge Golden Rule No.1 their Council recommended that a special bag be sent round four times a year for the Fund and this example was followed by other Lodges, becoming the predecessor of our regular collections for charity in Lodge. In 1941 the Order Charity Fund became the Adelaide Litten Trust Fund, in memory of this Grand Master.

1929 saw the introduction of Past Grand Honours for outstanding service to the Order, and the first record of subsidence in the south wall of the Temple - a problem which would come back to haunt us many years later. At the time, the architects thought no serious consequences would follow.

That year also witnessed two important developments. *The Gavel* was revived as our official magazine and Royal Arch Masonry was established in the Order. R.W.Bro. Peter Birchall, D.G.M., agreed to become the new Editor of *The Gavel* under the auspices of a magazine committee. In contrast to the pamphlet written by Dr. Cobb during the first few years of the Order, when "… It was a weapon of offence, polemical, trenchant and utterly unafraid", its aim was now to be educational and informative, and polemics had no place. As well as research papers on Masonic and allied subjects, the activities - both ceremonial and social - of each Lodge were reported and a diary included in each issue. Soon Brethren themselves were asked to submit articles for publication and tributes to distinguished Brethren were printed, as well as reports on the work of the Bureau of Service. There were five issues a year. The first advertisement (for a Masonic outfitter) appeared in 1936.

In the revived journal, considerable space was given over to material on the Holy Royal Arch, such as details of the meetings and of the Triangle Study Circle, together with informative articles. Sixteen years had elapsed since members of Lodge Stability No. 5 unilaterally tried to set up a Chapter and a Supreme governing body, an initiative which ended in their being excluded from the Order. During those years the number of Craft Lodges had increased from six to eleven, with the prospect of considerable expansion in the provinces through the work of Lodge Mercury No.11. The time was now deemed right in 1929 to introduce the Holy Royal Arch.

The Holy Royal Arch

The introduction of Royal Arch Masonry necessitated another amendment to Article 1 of the Constitutions. This was passed in June 1929 so that it read: "It is hereby declared and announced that pure Ancient Masonry consists of three Degrees, *viz.* Those of the Entered Apprentice, Fellowcraft and the Master Mason, including the Supreme Order of the Holy Royal Arch." A previous revision of the Book of Constitutions had deleted the clause on the jurisdiction of Grand Lodge over the Royal Arch Degree as at that time there seemed to be no possibility of acquiring the secrets of it in a constitutional and orthodox manner - in 1913 the introduction of the Royal Arch had been blocked because the secrets had not been obtained in a legitimate way.

Adelaide Litten then explained to Grand Lodge in a statement:

"At length, however, a process revealed itself by which without traversing the canons of Masonic secrecy and without any Royal Arch masons violating their obligation, your Grand Lodge, in the person of your Grand Master, became possessed of the necessary knowledge, whereby she was able to challenge R.A. Masons created and working under what are known as Orthodox Obediences and to secure the essential response and acknowledgment. There already existed within the Order [some] Brethren who were in possession of the R.A. secrets, and this knowledge rendered them capable of co-operating with your Grand Master; and a meeting under Provisional Warrant has been held."

Emblem of Logos Chapter No.2

It appears that she was given the secrets of the Holy Royal Arch by Companions of the Older Obedience.

Under this Provisional Warrant, Premier Chapter No.1 was set up with Adelaide Litten as the first Z., Peter Birchall as H. and Peter Slingsby as J. In due course meetings would be held to exalt other members "invited with due safeguards to receive the Degree" until there were enough Companions to enable a Petition to be presented to the Grand Master for the creation of a duly warranted Chapter under our own jurisdiction.

She continued: "A properly documented description of the whole proceedings and a narrative carefully attested will be executed and placed in our Archives so that posterity may know, without a shadow of doubt, the road by which we have travelled and arrived." Unfortunately, if this account ever existed, it has subsequently been destroyed or lost.

Such was the interest shown by members of the Order in the Chapter Degree that in January 1930 a Charter of Constitution was granted for the consecration of a second Chapter - Logos No.2 - followed quickly by Zodiac No.3. In March 1931 a Supreme Grand Chapter was formed to administer these and future Convocations. Later, Premier Chapter No.1 became a 'travelling' Chapter, on the lines of Lodge Mercury No.11, working particularly in the North and taking around with them by train three large wooden crates of equipment.

Emblem of Zodiac Chapter No.3

In 1930 an application was received from several ladies of the Honourable Fraternity of Ancient Freemasons (the group that had left us in 1913) to be received back into the order. The Grand Secretary said that first they had to sever their connection with H.F.A.F., obtain clearances and

sign a declaration to that effect, and undertake to prove themselves to be Masons to our satisfaction - only then would the question of their admission be put to the Board and Grand Lodge. Irrespective of the office they had held in the other Order, they would have to start their Masonic careers again with us and only progress from the date of their joining.

The declaration was signed by fifty three ladies. When approved by Grand Lodge, they were sent details of the meetings of all the Lodges in the Order so that they could choose which to join. They were to be balloted for in open Lodge and take the Obligations in all Three Degrees.

Various clauses in the Book of Constitutions were being revised at this time. In the course of this, galley proofs of the new Book were sent to all members of Grand Lodge. Most significantly, a new clause was included: "Visitors shall not be received from jurisdictions with which the Honourable Fraternity of Antient Masonry is not in fraternal relations." The resolution to adopt this new rule was carried in Grand Lodge and it formed a further step towards becoming a single-sex organisation.

In the course of Grand Lodge proceedings, the Grand Master gave some pertinent advice to Worshipful Masters about their responsibilities:
"You are expected to be leaders, but you cannot expect your Lodge to be successful and your members to be happy if you simply preside at its meetings. You must keep up the spirit of Masonry in the Lodges; you must not use your authority arbitrarily but you should endeavour so to attach yourselves to your members that they will not follow you as a matter of duty alone, but that it will also be their great pleasure to stand shoulder to shoulder with you in the work of the Lodge."

The early 1930s were a difficult and dispiriting time in this country, following the stock market crash and the Depression, with the rise of the Nazi party already throwing a shadow across Europe. At Grand Lodge in October 1931, the Grand Master invited all members to spend a few minutes reflection each noon and pray for the state of the country -

" ... that the whole nation may be constrained to think and act in such a manner as to ensure that their activities may resound to the glory of God and to the welfare of His realm. And further, that under the compelling force of such an admirable example the nations of the earth may join to expedite the advent of the Golden Age of peace and prosperity.

To this end we invite you to join with us in concentrating for a few moments each day at the hour of high noon, as did our Master Hiram Abif, for the purpose of invoking the blessing of the Most High upon our people and upon our land and that the blessings of righteousness, order and peace may speedily prevail, not only with us but over the whole earth.

Every Mason is a patriot in the highest sense of the term, and at this crisis in the affairs of our beloved country it is incumbent upon every serious and responsible member of the community to exert whatever powers they may possess in the direction of stabilising the affairs of the realm to the immediate, prospective and continued welfare of all its people. As individuals we do our part in the manner dictated by the instructed and enlightened conscience of the good Mason; but the Order might act as a corporate entity, and by the power of its concentrated thought energise to this end."

Miss Bothwell-Gosse and the Order of Ancient, Free and Accepted Masonry

Aimee Bothwell-Gosse was initiated into the Co-Masonic order in 1904 in London, where she became acquainted with Peter Birchall and others of our founder members. She worked with Birchall for some years in that Order. A member of the Supreme Council of the Co-Masons in France, she was admitted to the Worshipful Society of Freemasons (the Operatives) in 1909 and having received the VIIth Degree she became a Grand Master and so qualified to found a Masonic Order. She was also the editor of the journal *The Co-Mason*.

In 1925 she led another group of men and women who seceded from the Co-Masons, as we had done in 1908. Four complete Lodges plus one complete 18th Degree Chapter (Rose Croix) of the Ancient and Accepted Rite, together with other members of Craft, Mark and

Chapter left the Co-Masons because they thought the French Supreme Council had departed from the Landmarks and they wanted to set up a sovereign jurisdiction in England. A Supreme Council was formed by three members of the 33rd Degree of Co-Masonry. The new Order was called *The Order of Ancient, Free and Accepted Masonry*.

In March and June 1925 Marion Lindsay Halsey corresponded with and met Miss Bothwell-Gosse. Discussion centred on the effect the admission of this body of men and women would have on the standing of our Order and whether it would militate against our eventual recognition by U.G.L.E. The issue as to whether closer relations should be pursued went to the Board of General Purposes, which decided by a majority vote to recommend to Grand Lodge that the application should be refused. At Grand Lodge, after long discussion, D.G.M. Peter Birchall proposed that the Board's refusal be endorsed.

At the January 1928 meeting of the Board, presided over by Peter Birchall after the death of Marion Halsey, two further letters from Miss Bothwell-Gosse were discussed, in which she referred to meetings and talks with Mrs. Halsey about entering into fraternal relations. The Board in general felt that this was an exaggeration of the progress of these negotiations. Peter Birchall as chairman proposed that the recommendation to Grand Lodge should be the same as before - not accepted. This was duly agreed at Grand Lodge.

Nothing more was heard for a few years, until in January 1934 R.W.Bro. Antonia Collet, Past Grand Warden, sent Grand Secretary Peter Slingsby a proposal for the Board of General Purposes saying that it was desired by some that a state of fraternal relations should be inaugurated between our Order and the Order presided over by Miss Bothwell-Gosse. A resolution was passed, adjourning further discussion until the meeting of March 1935 and in the meantime R.W.Bro. Lloyd, P.G.W., was to contact Miss Bothwell-Gosse to get the answers to specific questions such as the composition of their Order, the number of men involved, whether men were accepted as Initiates or only as Joining Members, did they receive visitors from U.G.L.E. or any other Masonic body, and which Ritual did they use? A further resolution banned discussion of the matter either at Grand Lodge or anywhere else until the Board had considered the answers to these questions.

In March, in view of the decision of Grand Lodge in 1928, the Grand Master stated that any revival of the subject contravened Clause 10 of the Ancient Charges and Regulations "… and strictly to conform to every edict of the Grand Lodge." The edict would need to be rescinded before further consideration of the subject could be entertained.

However, because of the great interest aroused in Grand Lodge and the fact that many members were unaware of the past history, she read a statement outlining the facts of the matter. Apparently a letter in favour of the proposal had been sent to every Worshipful Master and Past Master of the Order, without the knowledge of herself or Grand Lodge. The letter was signed by no less than R.W.Bro. Lucy O'Hea, G.Reg., R.W.Bro. Antonia Collet, G.S.W., R.W.Bro. Florence Turner, P.G.W. and R.W.Bro. G.I. Lloyd, P.G.W.

Many years before, it had been decided that any point of procedure which was not covered in our own Book of Constitutions should be resolved by reference to that of United Grand Lodge. One such ruling was "… it is most undesirable that any appeal should be made by letter, circular or advertisement from private Lodges or individual members of the Craft in general, to support particular objects, causes or movements, without the sanction of the Most Worshipful The Grand Master." The circular letter that had been sent out went directly against this ruling.

So, it had been made abundantly clear that there would be no discussions about closer links between the two organisations. It was therefore very surprising when the Grand Master referred to the recent Annual Celebration dinner when the Deputy Grand Master brought up this subject in his address. In this, she said:

"… notwithstanding the resolution passed by the Board of General
Purposes … [he proceeded] to enlarge upon the advantages he
conceived would accrue to us if such a suggestion came into effect.
This, in spite of the fact that for the last twenty years the D.G.M. had
never failed to inform me how impossible it would be to work with
Miss Bothwell-Gosse." Nobody could understand what had caused
Peter Birchall to make such a *volte face* - he had previously been
very much against the idea of closer relations.

Adelaide Litten felt strongly that the decision to bar men, both as members and as visitors, was very important for the sake of our future relationship with U.G.L.E. It would be wrong to destroy the fragile links that had been built up and to prejudice our position by going back on that decision and to enter into relations with a body which accepted male members.

As far as she could see, the only reason for wanting links with Miss Bothwell-Gosse's Order was so that we could obtain the secrets of the 18th to the 33rd Degrees of the Ancient and Accepted Rite - but when we were ready for the Higher Degrees, we would get them, and without plunging our Order into discord and dissension. Adelaide Litten said she endorsed a united Women's Order in due course, but not in a rush and not until everyone wanted it.

The four Brethren who had signed the circular letter each spoke to Grand Lodge, explaining their reasons. They felt that nothing but good could come of unity - not union - with another order, enabling us jointly to spread Freemasonry for women and extend our influence. "We could not find a more suitable body of women with whom to take a first step towards mutual understanding than these people, who left Co-Masonry for exactly the same reasons as our own Order did, to practise pure Masonry according to the true ideals of the Institution."

After a short discussion, the Grand Master repeated that if it was desired to call for a rescindment of the Grand Lodge decision on 'fraternal relations', a notice of motion should be sent to the Grand Secretary, who would bring it to the Board for consideration, and report to Grand Lodge. This was the end of the matter for the time being, but not for good.

Grand Master Adelaide Litten summed up her own devotion to the Order during an address to a dinner held by Lodge Emulation No.2 in 1935. She told the guests:
"I am exceedingly proud that I can lay claim to the honour of having been initiated into this Lodge nearly twenty six years ago, and I can recall to this day the thrill that I experienced when I realised that a long-cherished dream had come true, and that I was henceforth and for ever privileged to describe myself as a Freemason.

I have no doubt that there are among our visitors this evening some who do not yet enjoy that distinction, and if so, I most earnestly advise them to repair the omission so soon as they conveniently can; for until they do so they cannot understand what a wonderful thing Freemasonry is, and that if we give it of our best what a difference it makes in our lives.

It is not only an Order which recognises human Brotherhood, but an Order which reposes faith in man. It does much for those who come into it in the right spirit and with an open mind. Freemasonry may be described as a great University where people meet together on a common ground of mutual esteem, respect and Brotherhood; where differences in creed and politics are forgotten, and where each one of us is vividly conscious of the goodwill and encouragement of the other."

1935: Women Only!

One of the most significant events in the reign of M.W.Bro. Adelaide Litten was the move in 1935 to restrict the membership of the Order to women alone. Back in the 1920s, after the rejection of the Petition for recognition by United Grand Lodge, it was decided not to admit any more men as Initiates or Joining Members and that an Order consisting of women only would be the best way forward. In 1930 Grand Lodge resolved "that visitors shall not be received from Jurisdictions with which we are not in fraternal relations" - this of course would include all male visitors. To develop a strong and well-run female Order which did not impinge in any way on the activities of the men would give us the best chance of recognition in the future. This at the time did not affect the position of men then in Grand Lodge office, such as Deputy Grand Master Peter Birchall and Grand Secretary Peter Slingsby. These two men had, since the beginning, contributed much to the development and organisation of the Order.

Peter Walter Slingsby was initiated into Lodge Emulation No.2 in 1909 and his business abilities very soon found him in the office of Secretary of that Lodge. It was characteristic that from the very start of his Masonic career he proceeded deliberately to master by-laws, Constitutions, usages and customs in order that he might be properly equipped to assist the Worshipful Master and be of help to the Lodge. He recorded every detail of procedure for the sake of future generations.

So painstaking, forceful and well-marked a personality could not fail to attract the attention of our Grand Lodge, and by a special ruling of the then Grand Master, the Rev. Dr. Cobb, he became Assistant Grand Secretary. When R.W. Bro. Marion Halsey became Grand Master in

Peter Walter Slingsby, Grand Secretary 1912 to 1935.

1912, she appointed him her Grand Secretary, and he continued in that office until his death in 1935. He was given the secrets of an Installed Master at Grand Lodge in October 1912. Slingsby took a shorthand record of Grand Lodge transactions and wrote them up in great detail - useful for historians - in a small, extremely neat and rather cramped hand.

He would often speak of himself as a builder of foundations and liked to say that however magnificent the superstructure with its appeal to the eye and the imagination, so desirable a splendour could have no stability or future unless the foundations were well and truly laid, and it was to this work that he dedicated his life. His economies, his demands for adequate charges and fees, were all part of a deliberate plan, admirably conceived, and at times ruthlessly administered, in order to make the Order 'safe'. "He nursed it, watched it and protected it with unremitting diligence and affection." After the opening of the Grand Temple in 1928, he took responsibility for its maintenance and upkeep. He was what we now call a workaholic, and it was rarely, apart from his official duties in Grand Lodge, that he allowed himself to enjoy a Lodge meeting 'off-duty'.

A land surveyor by profession and a Yorkshireman, he is said in his Obituary, which appeared in *The Gavel*, to have been very conservative and extremely adverse to rapid changes, a characteristic which permeated all his activities, conduct, clothes, food and the practice of his religion. It continues: "He had a keen shrewd mind, a fine memory, incredible industry and an acute moral sense based on a profound religious belief." He never married, sacrificing his own happiness for the sake of looking after his widowed mother and his sisters and brother. In spite of his efficiency, he was never a rich man and his professional work was very much reduced by the first World War. He devoted all the time he could spare to the welfare of the Order and more perhaps than he should have legitimately given, seeing that as a professional man he had to battle hard to keep his family comfortably. In 1923 he was voted an honorarium by Grand Lodge of fifty guineas "in recognition of the services he had so long rendered."

He died in 1935, aged 69, from coronary artery disease and the tribute paid to him in Grand Lodge in October of that year spoke of the lifelong and devoted service he gave to the Order. That he worthily maintained the dignity of his important office and the prestige of our Order by his conscientious devotion to duty; his strong sense of justice, his wise counsel, his unfailing kindness and courtesy, and the example of his life. To his zeal and enthusiasm much of the success achieved then - and indeed now - was due.

Peter Birchall was one of the Co-Masonic founders of our Order in 1908, when he took office as the first Senior Warden of Lodge Emulation No.2 and became the first Grand Secretary of the Order for four years. The earliest Minutes of Grand Lodge are recorded in his bold and flowing handwriting. When R.W.Bro. Marion Halsey

Peter Birchall, Deputy Grand Master from 1912 to 1935.

became Grand Master in 1912, she chose Peter Birchall as Deputy Grand Master - an office he held until 1935. During those twenty three years he loyally and effectively supported the rulers of our Craft. There was at that time a Central Lodge of Instruction and for twenty years he was Preceptor of this. To him we owe, to a very large extent, the establishment and preservation of our ceremonial workings. He was a tall, distinguished-looking man who must have had a wonderful presence as a Director of Ceremonies.

He was Worshipful Master four times of Lodge Emulation No.2, twice Master of Lodge Harmony No.4 and six times Master of the Lodge of Installed Masters No.6. When the publication of *The Gavel* was resumed in 1929, R.W. Bro. Birchall was the new Editor.

In August 1935 Peter Slingsby, the Grand Secretary, died. This left Peter Birchall, as Deputy Grand Master, the only man remaining in high office. At October Grand Lodge in that year, before appointing the Deputy Grand Master, Adelaide Litten said that in view of the Resolution passed some time before, it was felt to be inconsistent that a man should hold an important office when men were no longer admitted into the Order. "It was deemed by a great many that the appropriate moment had arrived when the executive offices of this Order should be occupied by women only."

The Grand Master told R.W.Bro. Peter Birchall in an interview that she felt it her duty not to reappoint him as Deputy Grand Master, at the same time expressing to him the profound gratitude which would always be felt for the splendid services he had rendered to the Order "in endeavouring to raise a superstructure perfect in its parts and honourable to the builder." R.W.Bro. Birchall assured the Grand Master that he recognised that in taking this step she was actuated solely by what she believed to be for the good of the Order, and that it would be his pleasure in the future to endeavour to assist the Order in every way within his power.

It is difficult to avoid the conclusion that there was a degree of personal antagonism between these two, and that the decision to dispense with his services was not completely altruistic, whatever was said publicly. The bad feeling shown towards Birchall by the Grand Master over the Bothwell-Gosse affair must, at the very least, have contributed to her attitude and what was in effect his sacking rather than his resignation.

On his retirement as Deputy Grand Master, R.W.Bro. Birchall was sent (by post) a gift of £120 from the Brethren of the London Lodges in recognition of his outstanding services to the Order, together with an embroidered Grand Lodge collar and a Past Deputy Grand Master's jewel, presented by an anonymous Brother. His apron "altered to meet the exigencies of the case" (converted to a Past rank) was also sent. M.W.Bro. Litten wrote "May I reiterate how deeply I deplore the circumstances which necessitate your retirement from the office of D.G.M. and how earnestly I hope that the future may hold nothing but happiness and good health for you." His reply was brief: "Will you be good enough to convey to those interested my very sincere thanks for this most munificent expression of their kindness and appreciation."

The wording of the report given by his Mother Lodge, Emulation No.2, under 'Lodge Activities' in *The Gavel* is interesting: "... the oldest member of the Lodge, R.W.Bro. Peter Birchall, P.D.G.M. *had been retired from* the office of Deputy Grand Master." *[Author's italics]*.

A few months later, Peter Birchall wrote to the new Grand Secretary, R.Bro. Florence Leveridge, P.G.W., with reference to the editorship of *The Gavel*, asking for a decision as to whether the Brethren were satisfied that a man should be editing the organ of the Order, and offering to vacate the post. He was assured by the Board of General Purposes that it was earnestly hoped that he would continue. However, two Assistant Editors were appointed. This provoked a letter of resignation:

R.W.Bro. Florence Leveridge, Grand Secretary from 1935-1950.

"Grand Lodge having so emphatically declined to permit me to co-operate in the official work of the Order, I am convinced my position as Editor of *The Gavel* must, logically, be equally objectionable. I felt that from the moment it was suggested, that the appointment of two capable assistant editors (thus ridiculously overweighing so small a magazine) was a quiet hint that if I were sensible I should adjust the balance. I do so by resigning my editorship."

As it was nearly time for the December issue to be printed, he offered - if permitted - to do whatever possible to ensure that it was published on time.

It seems that he withdrew his resignation and continued as the editor until the issue of February 1944 when W.Bro. Louise Gordon-Stables took over. He died in September 1946 from prostate cancer, aged 81.

When Grand Lodge stood to order in his memory in October 1946 M.W.Bro. Lucy O'Hea said of him: "R.W.Bro. Peter Birchall was the last of that splendid and courageous band of pilgrims who with wonderful foresight saw what Freemasonry could mean to women. For thirty years and more his interest and advice was always at our disposal. He was indeed a pillar of strength and wisdom at all times. For twenty years he was the Preceptor of the Central Lodge of Instruction - he was intolerant of bad work as some of us will remember - only the very best was good enough for him."

In order to make the existence of the Order more widely known, in 1936 the Board of General Purposes decided to put an advertisement in *The Times, Morning Post, Sunday Times* and *Time and Tide*:

"The Honourable Fraternity of Antient Masonry (the Pioneer Order of Women Freemasons) whose Headquarters are at No.27 Pembridge Gardens, London W2 had a very representative gathering on Saturday, January 18th at the annual Celebration to commemorate the Consecration of their Temple at the above address."

In October 1937 Peter Birchall wrote to Grand Lodge to suggest that photographs of the Grand Temple should be published in *The Gavel* of January 1938. The Board recommended that a 30th Anniversary Souvenir Supplement should be published with the February *The Gavel,* including photographs of the Temple at Headquarters, the Temples at Liverpool and Newcastle and some of the Lodge banners. This was the first of the history 'Blue Books', others being published in 1951, 1953 and 1963. The 1938 edition was written by Peter Birchall and Mary Mostyn Bird, who had been Worshipful Master of Lodge Mercury No.11 during the war years, and frequently wrote for *The Gavel,* of which she had been Assistant Editor for a while.

As a footnote to the Masonic history of this period, in 1930 R.W.Bro. Anne Charlotte Harrison, P.G.W., was buried in her full Masonic regalia, and on behalf of both Grand Lodge and the Lodge of Unity

No.3 (her Mother Lodge) a sprig of acacia was placed at the head of the grave. R.W.Bro. Harrison's son led the perambulation round the grave, followed by over thirty relatives and friends.

Another noted Brother who passed to the Grand Lodge above in 1933 was Dorothea Frances Forster Irving. She was the daughter-in-law of Sir Henry Irving, the famous actor-manager, and was an actress herself. "Her natural and technical qualifications carried her rapidly upwards in the Craft; the beauty of her voice, the restrained but powerful and intensive diction, the carriage and gesture all combined to make her rendering of our wonderful ritual a delight." She was well-known for creating the role of Trilby, the subject of the hypnotist Svengali in the play by George du Maurier.

W.Bro. Dorothea Irving, in her role as Trilby
in the play by George du Maurier.

Chapter Seven

Lucy O'Hea, Wartime and the Mark Degree

At the Quarterly Communication of Grand Lodge in March 1938, M.W.Bro. Adelaide Litten made an announcement. Coming to Item 7 on the Agenda - To Nominate the Grand Master for the ensuing year - she said: "From the moment, Brethren, that I accepted the high office ... I resolved for my own sake and the sake of the great Order to which I am proud to belong, that the moment I felt that I had given the best of what I had to give, I would ask to be relieved of the burden of office, and to my deep sorrow I have come to the conclusion that the time has now arrived for me to retire."

During her period of office the membership of the Order had doubled and the ten Lodges of 1928 had grown to twenty Craft Lodges and three Chapters. Over the last few years she had suffered from increasingly bad health. Although she believed her judgement to be still sound, "I am conscious that my vitality is to a certain extent sapped; that I get more tired and need more rest; and with the fear that I may gradually become much more tired, and consequently really impair the work of the Order, I deem it better to retire ... ".

She was supremely confident in the successor she had chosen :
    "The office of Grand Master ... will be filled by one who has earned the respect and affection of you all; who possesses more than her share of character and intellect; who has rendered yeoman service to the Order ... [and] will maintain in its fullest integrity all the traditions and greatness of the high office of Grand Master. I may tell you that I have had unspeakable difficulty in persuading her to take upon her shoulders the burden of this great Trust; but because of her overwhelming love for the Order, her high sense of duty and her heartfelt desire to help the Order in every way in her power, I am rejoiced to tell you that my reiterated pleadings have at last prevailed." She then formally nominated R.W.Bro. Lucy Bertram O'Hea, C.B.E., P.S.G.W., P.G.Registrar to succeed her as Grand Master.

At the Enthronement in the following October, for the first time admission was restricted by ticket. In addition to the members of Grand Lodge, twelve tickets were issued to each of the Private Lodges for any of their members. Refreshments were served after the meeting at a cost of 1/6d (7.5p) per head. There were three hundred and fifty present.

After emphasising the great work that Lucy O'Hea had already achieved, Grand Master Adelaide Litten went on to say "From the depths of my heart, Brethren, I commend her to your sympathetic and affectionate consideration, and I beg you to support and co-operate with her to the utmost limits of your power. Remember the magnitude of her task, and realise that with your help her pathway can be made brighter and her service more grand and glorious."

After the business of the meeting, the Grand Master vacated the Chair in favour of her Deputy and left the Temple. The Visiting Brethren entered and were seated. The Lodge having been opened in all Three Degrees, the Grand Master Elect was escorted in by a procession of the Masters and Past Masters of the provincial Lodges - in recognition of her work with Lodge Mercury No.11 in spreading Freemasonry for women throughout the country. The Grand Master was then escorted into the Temple. After the hymn *O God, our help in ages past ...* and a reading from the *Book of Wisdom*, Chapter Six, *Wisdom is glorious and never fadeth away,* Lucy O'Hea was presented, obligated, invested, enthroned and saluted according to ancient custom.

Following the Proclamation by the Grand Director of Ceremonies, the Lodge was resumed in the First Degree and the Past Grand Master was presented with a jewel and a cheque from the Order. She said "This beautiful jewel I shall always prize as a memento of the most interesting years of my life; and this most generous cheque will enable me to do much that I could not otherwise have done; and one of the first things I shall do is to buy a portable typewriter, which I have coveted for years." She was appointed President of the Board of General Purposes.

Lucy Bertram O'Hea also had the title of Lady Markham. Her first husband was Sir Arthur Markham, Baronet, who died in 1916. Her second husband was Lt.Col. James O'Hea, and after his death she reverted to the Markham family title, becoming the Dowager Lucy, Lady Markham. She was initiated into Lodge Harmony No.4 on the 1st June 1923 by Adelaide Litten. This Lodge was set up primarily for Servicewomen, and it was through their work for the Women's Auxiliary Army Corps in the First World War that Lucy O'Hea's great friend, Dame Florence Simpson, introduced her into the Lodge. In what may have been second sight, or just a happy remark, M.W.Bro. Marion Halsey told the Brethren at the Initiation of

Lucy Bertram O'Hea,
Grand Master from 1938 to 1948.

Lucy O'Hea: "We have today initiated our future leader." W. Bro. O'Hea was Worshipful Master of Lodge Harmony No.4 in 1928-1929.

She had of course been the inspiration behind Lodge Mercury No.11 and taking Freemasonry for women to the provinces. Her pioneering spirit was further well illustrated in 1937, when, together with her son Sir Charles Markham, she undertook an extended trip through Africa. They travelled for six months in a motor lorry which R.W.Bro. O'Hea had fitted up as a bedroom for herself and drove from Algiers across the Sahara, through the Congo, Uganda, Kenya, Tanganyika, Northern and Southern Rhodesia and Transvaal to the Cape. On the way, they broke their journey to visit Bro. Dame Florence Simpson who was staying with her step-daughter - also in the Craft - in the Orange Free State. For Christmas 1937 she sent the Brethren of Lodge Joyous No.18 in Liverpool a painted plate showing her route, with the scenes and animals likely to be encountered. "These mementos will be treasured as another expression of R.W.Bro. L.B. O'Hea's abiding love and thoughtfulness for the Brethren."

108

Banner of Lodge Joyous No.18, Liverpool, named after the daughter of Grand Master Lucy Bertram O'Hea.

The Gavel of April 1937 carried a further report:

"The travellers had a very trying journey in crossing the Sahara, experiencing extreme cold and drifting sand storms, the latter being so severe that, just before reaching In Salah, they completely lost the motor tracks, and Sir Charles Markham, her son, had to go off and explore for help. Two days later they broke down at a place two hundred miles from water, where they had to remain for six days. This of course made them late in reaching Kano, in Northern Nigeria, which they left somewhere about 1st February.

Letters report that on reaching the French Cameroons, road conditions improved and by 19th February they had arrived in Stanleyville, in the middle of the Congo, where of course being so near the Equator it was exceedingly hot but daily rain afforded some relief. R.W.Bro. O'Hea found the heat very exhausting, but all the Brethren will be glad to know that otherwise she is well, and looking forward to moving on to higher ground, where the climatic conditions will greatly improve."

Lucy O'Hea was not an intellectual, but a woman possessed of great practical energy, vision and determination, with an almost childlike zest for everything. Direct in speech and a practical woman, she had a noble presence which did not, in conversation, mask her lively interest in people and events. However, her speech after her Enthronement was characteristic in its reference to humility "I am filled with anxiety as to my worthiness to occupy this Throne ... May the G.A.O.T.U. give me wisdom and understanding in all my dealings, so that I fail you not." She also looked forward - "We cannot live in the past, great as that past has been; we cannot stand still, we must progress … Let us go forward with a renewed enthusiasm and determination to make our masonry a real live force in the world."

She was awarded the C.B.E. for her work with the Red Cross during the First World War. Her only daughter, Joyous Raczynska, was a member of Lodge Harmony No.4. Joyous married a young diplomat, Edward Raczynski, who was related to the House of Hapsburg, and lived in Warsaw. After two miscarriages, she died in childbirth in 1931. Lucy O'Hea chartered a light plane and flew through severe storms via Berlin to be with her daughter before she died. Lodge Joyous No.18, named in her memory, was one of the first to have and maintain their own Temple at 19 Devonshire Road, Liverpool. Joyous' husband represented the Polish Government in exile in London during the second World War, eventually becoming the President of Poland in exile in 1979.

Wartime

The years of the second World War brought many difficulties for the Order, for Lodges and for their members. In 1939 the Board of General Purposes at a special meeting made recommendations to Grand Lodge about wartime measures. Private Lodges should be allowed to meet (by Dispensation) every two months if they so desired, but it was suggested that meetings be held on Saturday or Sunday at any hour during daylight.

If any Lodge felt that it was impossible for them to meet, a Dispensation must be applied for, to temporarily suspend their meetings. The Central Lodge of Instruction would be suspended for the time being, as would practices for Private Lodges held at Headquarters. The Annual Dinner was cancelled.

In October 1939 "the Masters present were informed of the procedure it was proposed should be adopted should an Air Raid warning be given while a Lodge meeting was in progress, *viz*. The Worshipful Master should gavel and say: "Brethren I call this Lodge from Labour to refreshment." If gun fire were heard, the members could go down to the basement if they so desired; if a gas alarm were given, members should proceed to the second floor dressing rooms."

As in the First War, Lodges had to make up the deficit in rent due to Grand Lodge through the reduction of meetings. Many members were absent on war work, for example W.Bro. J.M. Lloyd-Edwards. A nursing sister who had served in the previous war, she was called up with the reserves at the outbreak of war and joined a hospital ship: "…by all accounts [she] is not enjoying a life on the ocean wave, being a particularly poor sailor." She was Matron on the *S.S. Brighton* which was bombed in Dieppe Harbour and she was later posted to the East.

In 1940 the size of *The Gavel* was reduced from twenty eight pages to twenty, thus "saving 8/6 to 10/- per page." The frequency was subsequently reduced to three issues only per year, in October, January and April. Also in 1940 the retirement was reported from active work in the Order of R.W.Bro. Florence Turner, P.G.W., who had given the freehold of 27 Pembridge Gardens to us in 1924. In the previous August she had had a serious motoring accident in France, resulting in concussion and severe eye problems. The report of her retirement was written by Peter Birchall, who was still editor of *The Gavel*, and he seems to have upset people yet again, whether deliberately or not. He wrote: "[The disabilities caused by the accident] worked upon a mind suffering the reaction natural to a very severe physical shock, and for a moment the picture of life, with all its circumstances and interests, inevitably became perhaps a little blurred. Genuine grievances and remembered slights, kept at bay by the physically sound, tend to deepen into tragedies. It is sympathetically understood, but difficult to explain."

Maybe the "genuine grievances and remembered slights" which had assumed such importance referred to some previous altercation between the volatile character of Peter Birchall and Florence Turner, but whatever it was, it was enough to prompt a letter from Mrs. Turner's solicitors. Peter Birchall printed an apology in the next issue of *The Gavel:* "… certain paragraphs of my comments … have been construed by you in such a way as to cause you annoyance and pain. I express to you my sincere regrets and apologies that the paragraphs in question should have been construed or be capable of construction by you or certain of your family and friends in the way which your Solicitors indicated."

Brethren met regularly at the Grand Master's house in London to make clothes for the Polish refugees and knit items for the Middlesex Regiment serving in France. From her country home at Sandhurst in Kent Lucy O'Hea ran two mobile canteens for the West Kent Home Guard, and appealed for clothing such as gloves, socks and scarves for those men who often had to report for duty direct from their work on the farm.

The Gavel ran a section called 'Lodge News' where Brethren could request details of friendly contacts wherever they were billeted and where information about war work was given. The Deputy Grand Master (R.W.Bro. Lilac Parker-Jervis) was driving a mobile canteen day and night around the dark and foggy Surrey commons to take hot meals to the lonely A.R.P. *[air raid precautions]* personnel scattered around the district. They also drove into central London and to Plymouth and Gosport. Through blitzes, blackouts and under great difficulties they supplied food and drink to exhausted firemen and bombed-out people. The Deputy Grand Master summed up the attitude of her ladies, mostly middle-aged: "If there is any bombing going on we just ignore it." This war work made it impossible for the Deputy Grand Master to come to London to attend Grand Lodge.

Lilac Parker-Jervis, the Deputy Grand Master, who organised and drove mobile canteens during the War.

Brethren drove ambulances, manned first aid posts, one worked for the Secret Service Department at the War Office, many did nursing, and they knitted, knitted, knitted…

The Consecration of Lodge Inspiration at Liverpool was postponed due to the evacuation from coastal towns, troop movements, enemy action and the difficulties of travel. It was not until 1943 that a new Lodge was consecrated - Lodge Hope and Integrity No.21 (Kent) in May of that year.

The main Temple at Headquarters was closed for the duration of the War, and meetings were held in the Lecture Room. The services of the handyman and Housekeeper's husband, John Prebble, were dispensed with, and Mrs. Prebble took over the work of the house for £75 a year. The Committee Room was rented to the Grand Master for an office at £25 annually.

In *The Gavel* of April 1943 there was trouble over an article entitled *Symbolism of the Masonic numbers 3,5,7* which was considered too explicit in disclosing Masonic secrets. It was ordered to be withdrawn and the article was cut out of every single copy, even those retained in the Library, so it is not possible find out exactly what the offence was. Peter Birchall thereupon resigned as Editor (for good this time), together with his Assistant Editors Mary Mostyn Bird and C.M. Upright. Louise Gordon-Stables became the new Editor.

The following year the Board recommended that Worshipful Masters suggest to their Lodges that meetings be restricted to a maximum of five per year for the duration of the war, to save on light and fuel. The men in United Grand Lodge dispensed with white gloves at meetings because of their unavailability, but with feminine practicality the Grand Master showed her Grand Lodge a pair of white knitted gloves which would be an economic solution and were washable.

1944 saw two events of note. The first was the appointment of Mary Gordon Muirhead Hope as Deputy Grand Master, despite still being a 'light blue' - she had twice refused to accept Grand Rank. This followed the precedent created when Marion Halsey was appointed Deputy Grand Master in 1911.

The second occasion was the Grand Master's 70th birthday on 2nd August 1944, when the Brethren of the Order presented her with a cheque for £165 "… which is but a slight token of our overwhelming gratitude to you for your unfailing efforts on our behalf, and for the high sense of duty and sacrifice of personal inclination that has always actuated you in your Masonic career." It was accompanied by an illuminated address bearing the signatures of the Worshipful Masters of each of the private Lodges of the Order. In the following January the twenty third Craft Lodge of the Order was consecrated and named after the Past Grand Master, M.W.Bro. Adelaide Litten.

Lodge Adelaide Litten No.23 in January 1945

The postponed Consecration of Lodge Inspiration No.24 at Liverpool took place in March 1945, and in the same month Lodge Faith and Friendship No.25 was consecrated. For some time it met at 'The House of the Red Cross' in Cranley Gardens, Kensington and listened to research papers such as *The significance of the Pentagram and the Pentagon in the Third Degree.* In later years, particularly in the time of M.W.Bro. Frances Hall, it became the custom for the Grand Master to occupy the Chair, as permanent Worshipful Master.

Lodge Inspiration No.24 in March 1945

Lodge Faith and Friendship No.25 in March 1945

Following the end of the War in 1945 Lodge Fellowship No.20 wrote to Grand Master Lucy O'Hea:

"The Worshipful Master and Brethren of Lodge of Fellowship No.20 Cardiff offer you a message of love and congratulation on your courage, strength and sacrifice for the cause of Freemasonry during the strain and burden of the War years. Your fortitude in difficulties and danger were an inspiration to the Brethren, who are very mindful of all that you and the London Brethren have endured. So on the successful termination of War in Europe, please accept the loving greetings and congratulations of the Worshipful Master and Brethren."

The banner of Lodge Fellowship No.20

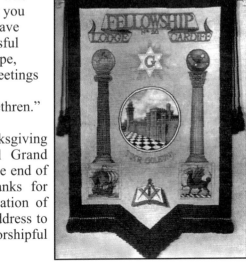

On 29th September a Thanksgiving Celebration and Especial Grand Lodge was held to mark the end of the War and to give thanks for peace and for the preservation of the Temple. During her address to the Brethren the Most Worshipful The Grand Master said:

"... we would wish to express to our Brethren who have lost dear ones owing to the War, or their homes destroyed, or their business ruined, our very deepest and loving sympathy. And last, but not least, we come to our own thanksgiving. I know that we, one and all, most earnestly desire to express our profound and heartfelt gratitude to the G.A.O.T.U. for the preservation of our Temple. Our spiritual home has been spared, and to show our gratitude may it be more than ever the centre of inspiration for us all. May it ever shelter pure thought and unselfish desire; may high ideals continue to be taught within its precincts, so that we may go forth with renewed strength and resolution to take up our share of those very heavy responsibilities which undoubtedly lie ahead, for the building of a new, and we hope and pray a better and happier world.

So Brethren, let us re-dedicate this our beloved Temple, and more especially let us re-dedicate ourselves to the service of God and the Brotherhood of Man ... ".

The Mark Degree

The following year the Grand Master announced that she was able to give the secrets of the Mark Masons Degree to the Order. She had received them "in a perfectly legitimate manner", presumably from a member of the Older Obedience. Grand Lodge thanked her for her work and research in enabling the Order to progress. Several Brethren had been advanced in the Mark Degree to form the nucleus of the first Mark Lodge, Keystone, which was consecrated on 22nd March 1946. The officers of the first Lodge were appointed in strict order of seniority of Mastership in the Craft. The Grand Master also informed Grand Lodge that a cheque presented to her two years previously for her 70th birthday would now be used to buy the necessary regalia and equip the Mark Lodge.

The Grand Master was the first Worshipful Master of Keystone Mark Lodge No.1, past Most Worshipful Bro. Adelaide Litten was Immediate Past Master and Mary Gordon Muirhead Hope, Deputy Grand Master, was Senior Warden. Six meetings, both Regular and Emergency, were held within three months to advance Candidates. In the Book of Constitutions Clause 1 was amended to read "... pure

Antient Masonry consists of the three Degrees and no more, *viz.*:-those of the Entered Apprentice, Fellow Craft (and the completion thereof, the Degree of Mark Mason)…"

The end of 1946 was overshadowed by the news of the serious illness of the Grand Master. She was away from her duties for some time and in early 1947 left to spend an extended period in the South of France. The Past Grand Master was also ill. The beginning of the system of Grand Inspectors to oversee Areas came in 1947 when a resolution was passed in Grand Lodge that "eminent Brethren" should be selected by the Grand Master to visit provincial Lodges to guide and advise.

In the same year the Grand Master presented a collection of books to the Library at Headquarters, which she wanted to be called the 'Besant-Scott collection'. Mabel Emily Besant, married name Besant-Scott, was the daughter of Annie Besant, who played an important part in the early days of Freemasonry for women in this country. Mabel had been initiated into Lodge Human Duty No.6 of the Co-Masons in 1911 and had become a senior figure in that movement, culminating in her appointment as Head of the British Federation of Co-Masonry after the death of her mother in 1934. However, in another split, she and seventy two members resigned from the Federation in 1935. It is not clear whether the books in this collection were originally owned by Mabel Besant-Scott, or what the reason was on the part of Lucy O'Hea for so naming them.

The Grand Master returned to this country in the summer of 1947 but was advised by her doctor to spend the following winter abroad to avoid a recurrence of her illness. She spent the winter in Santa Barbara, California.

Lodge Concord No.26 in July 1947

Post-war shortages are illustrated by a few lines from the report of the Board of General Purposes in 1948: "The Masters of the Private Lodges agreed with the suggestion that each should supply two cakes of toilet soap during the year, for use in the dressing rooms, until such time as toilet soap is off the ration."

At the same meeting permission was given to W.Bro. Auriel Gotch to proceed with the production of an Annual Diary or Calendar, giving

Lucy, Lady Markham.

the dates of regular meetings. This was to be sold to members of the Order and the proceeds given to Lodge Mercury No.11 towards the Lodge's Expenses Fund. W.Bro. Gotch offered to finance the total cost of production.

At Grand Lodge in March 1948, the following was read on behalf of the Grand Master:

"... I have after long and serious consideration, come to the following decision. I am sure you will agree with me that owing to my bad health and age, the time has come when it is right that I should give place to a younger Brother. I find the office and duties of Grand Master are now too arduous for me.

Without stressing the point, you will all understand what this means to me - for twenty four years my thoughts, time and energy have nearly all been given to Masonry. It has been a great happiness to serve the Order which I dearly love. You have one and all helped in times of sorrow and taught me lessons of inestimable value. You have always given me such affection and loyal co-operation that I find it hard to express adequately my deep appreciation. I can only add that the honour of being your leader had been a real privilege and joy - a very wonderful experience in my life.

I name as my successor R.W.Bro. Mary Gordon Muirhead Hope, Deputy Grand Master. Her great knowledge, her enthusiasm and her selfless devotion to our Order has already won our affection and admiration. I have every confidence that she will carry on the good work she has already done, and that the Order will progress under her guidance."

A letter from M.W. The Past Grand Master, Adelaide Litten, seconded the Nomination:

"Grand Lodge Officers and Brethren. As the Past Grand Master of our Order it is my great privilege and high honour to second the nomination as Grand Master for the ensuing year of R. W. Bro. Mary Gordon Muirhead Hope, Deputy Grand Master, whom I have known intimately for over thirty years and for whom I have the greatest admiration and regard. As the health of our beloved Grand Master unhappily necessitates her relinquishing the office she has adorned for the last ten years, I am convinced we could find no more suitable Brother than the Deputy Grand Master to succeed her. Endowed as she is with such outstanding qualities of leadership, deep Masonic knowledge, erudition and modest charm of manner, she is peculiarly fitted in every way to follow in the footsteps of our beloved Grand Master whose retirement we so deeply deplore."

The Deputy Grand Master and Grand Master Elect replied by saying: "… this is not the time to express what we all feel on the sad message in the letter from the Most Worshipful The Grand Master. We are at present suffering from a stunned sense of loss. Few fraternities can have been so blessed in their head, for her regal ardour of spirit was matched by perfect vehicles of expression. The work she has done for us is beyond calculation and has passed beyond our praise into our Order's history. What the Order has meant to her we all know; what she has meant to it is something which we cannot even yet appreciate to the full.

As regards her nomination and that of our dear Past Grand Master I will say little. No one in our Order would accept such an office gladly for it must always be a hard and lonely path, and especially to take the mantle of such an Elijah. I am very conscious of the many qualifications of a Grand Master which I do not possess, yet my deep sense of my own weakness must not frighten me from obeying the call of our two Leaders to carry on their work. One thing however, I know to be essential - the Grand Master of this Order must continue to enjoy the confidence of its members. Mistrust, hesitation and doubt would break our unity and blunt our purpose; 'where harmony is not in the heart it is not in the Lodge, where it is not in the Lodge it is not in the City'. This is an issue which must be decided with the head and with the heart so that at our next meeting you can give your answer caring for nothing save the prosperity and welfare of our Order, and then let your Yea be Yea, or your Nay, Nay, and may God guide us all aright."

At the June Quarterly Communication, a ballot was taken to elect the Grand Master and R.W.Bro. Mary Gordon Muirhead Hope was duly elected. In thanking Grand Lodge for their confidence she said:

"You have offered me the greatest honour the Order has in its power to confer on any of its members; it is difficult to find the right words in which to try to express my feelings in response.

At our initiation we are taught we have become 'Accepted Masons' and this word 'accepted' runs like a thread through both the Craft and the Higher Degrees. Whatever maybe the historical derivation of 'the Acceptance' I take it the inner meaning of the word in our Symbolic rite today is that as Masons we must learn to live by the great law of Acceptance. To accept life as we find it, to accept people as they are and above all to accept the path of life to which the Great Weaver spins our thread - not to refuse it because we would have desired another, nor to rebel because we have not the ten talents granted to others and which seems to be so necessary for the work.

'To do our duty in that state of life in which it shall please God to call us.' In that spirit I shall try most humbly to take up the heavy responsibility you offer me, and I ask for the tolerance, the kindliness and the prayers of my Brethren and mutual Faith and Hope in the great work of Spiritual brotherhood to which we are called."

At the same meeting, V.W.Bro. Mildred Rhoda Low was elected Grand Treasurer.

The next chapter will tell of the great expansion of the Order, both at home and overseas, and the introduction of several Degrees beyond the Craft under the guidance of Mary Gordon Muirhead Hope.

Chapter Eight

Mary Gordon Muirhead Hope and the Expansion of the Order

October 1948 duly saw the Enthronement of the new Grand Master. Having been presented, Mary Gordon Muirhead Hope was interrogated by the Installing Officer, M.W.Bro. Lucy O'Hea:

"Will you exercise the prerogatives attaching to that high office without reference to your personal aggrandisement, advancement or profit …? Will you in the spirit, as well as in the letter, interpret and exercise the powers, both potential and active, which though unrecorded and undefined, are traditionally among the prerogatives and privileges wielded by the Grand Master, your sole regard being the honour, reputation and usefulness of the Order or whatsoever may tend to the advancement of the Masonic Art? Will you with peculiar care and with unremitting vigilance guard the traditional secrets of Masonry, so that under your governance no deviation be made from, or aught added to, the accepted Landmarks or Ancient Form or Mysteries? … ".

The Grand Master Elect then took her Obligation at a central altar, after which her attention was directed to the Three Great Lights:

"No office in Masonry is so exalted that its occupant can afford for a moment to forget those Great Lights in Freemasonry to which the greatest as well as the most humble in the Craft is indebted for guidance, direction and discipline, so that once more I direct your attention to the Volume of the Sacred Law, the Square and the Compasses … The Volume of the

Sacred Law inculcates the paramount claims of God and Duty ...
The Square will continue to be the guide to all your actions ..."

Lucy O'Hea then raised the Grand Master Elect and led her to the East, where she was anointed by the Grand Chaplain to the words "And he set all the people from the right side of the Temple to the left side of the Temple, along by the altar and the temple, by the King round about. Then they brought out the King's son, and put upon him the crown, and gave him the testimony, and made him king. And Jehoida the Priest anointed him and said, 'God save the King'. And behold the King stood at his pillar at the entering in." These words come from the second Book of Chronicles, Chapter 23, where Jehoida the High Priest anoints Joash, King of Judah and covenants to serve the true God rather than idolatrous idols.

The Investiture and Enthronement followed:
  "To the Glory of the Most High and to the perfecting of humanity, in the name and under the auspices of the Grand Lodge of Antient Masonry, and by virtue of the power in me vested, I place you in the Chair of the Grand Master of the Honourable Fraternity of Antient Masonry, a symbolical throne of the Royal Solomon. Take this heavy maul as the symbol of your authority. Traditionally it is the instrument of death. For you it is the symbol of Dominant Life...".

As the Grand Director of Ceremonies censed from north to south in front of the pedestal, she recited "As smoke of this incense ascends upwards to the Heavens, so may the daily supplications of this Fraternity ascend to the Throne of Grace on your behalf, that you may in abundant measure become a channel for the Eternal Wisdom, an exponent of the Everlasting Strength and a reflector of the Divine Beauty." There followed as an anthem the prayer of St. Patrick *I bind unto myself today, the power of God to hold and lead ...*

R.W.Bro. Dorothy Alice Taylor was appointed, obligated and invested as Deputy Grand Master, a position she held for twenty five years. She died the year after the Grand Master she served for so long, in 1975.

The Address given by the new Grand Master presaged the outstanding characteristics of her reign - spirituality, expansion and an interest in the Higher Degrees. Speaking on the spiritual and symbolic meaning of the setting square and the three sides of the Pythagorean triangle on the Past Master's Jewel, she then went on to emphasise the hard work to be done as an Order to secure:

"an ever increasing expansion of numbers, a deepening understanding of the Masonic philosophy and the adorning of our main Craft structure with the beauty of the further Degrees about which you have heard this evening, the cultivation of a new friendliness not only among ourselves but the holding out of our hands to all true masons in the faith and earnest hope that in the not too far distant

R.W.Bro. Dorothy Alice Taylor,
Deputy Grand Master from 1948-72.

future we may see all women's masonry united on terms of fraternal affection thus preparing ourselves for the great day (though it may not come in our lifetime) when all masons, men and women, can join in the work of the building of the great Temple not made with hands."

The ceremony concluded with a presentation by the Grand Master to M.W.Bro. Lucy Bertram O'Hea, on behalf of the Order, of a breast jewel and a cheque for two hundred guineas. In making the presentation, the Grand Master said:

"Most Worshipful Grand Master, (for so you will ever be addressed in our hearts) it is my first privilege to act as the spokesman of the whole Order and ask you to accept two things, our love to you, and our gratitude for all you have given us. The first, I think, is appropriately not Masonic, for we wish first and foremost to express our feelings towards you as a person, as our dearly loved leader and Mother-Superior-in-the-Craft. So we ask you to accept this cheque for the purchase of a gramophone and what records appeal to you for your new home in Africa, whither our love and our thoughts will follow you.

Secondly, I have here a small antique Masonic jewel, which according to the ancient traditions of the Craft, I offer you as a *tessera*. As the fruits of your long work for our Order, both before and after your Grand Mastership, you have left us not only with Craft Lodges spread over all England and reaching out to Scotland, with Arch Chapters in London and in the provincial centres, and the Mark Lodges also both in our two London Temples and in the provinces, you have also on the eve of your departure given us as a trust the further adorning of our Masonic Temple with the Degrees of the Cryptic Rite and the nucleus of the high Chivalric Degrees.

This small jewel bears the St. Andrew's Cross of the Cryptics, the Cross Pâté of the Templars, and the Passion Cross and Crown of the Rose Croix, in rubies and diamonds. On the back it bears the Mark, and surmounting all, it carries the helmet and vizor which by Masonic traditions belongs to the arms of a Grand Master. Therefore, we pledge this to you, as a Mark and a *tessera*, that we will not only be grateful for all you have given us, but we will, God helping us, worthily carry on your work, so that you may look at this jewel when you are far from us and see in it a pledge of our faith, and wear it when you return and see (we trust) the fruit of your labour, and be satisfied."

M. W. Bro. O'Hea, Immediate Past Grand Master, in returning thanks for the presentation, said:
"The years I have spent in working for the Order have been the happiest of my life. I am going to miss you all very much. As you know it is my intention to buy a gramophone as a gift from you all, with special records to ensure that I shall have the music I desire. And there is nothing I would like better than a record of the voices I know in the Order."

The Past Grand Master had been advised to winter abroad every year and had bought a house in Nairobi to be near her son, Sir Charles Markham. She left for Africa early in 1949, and a collection was taken at Grand Lodge for flowers to be sent to the boat before she left.

Grand Lodge resolved that the Mark Degree would be governed by its own Mark Council, under the supreme authority of the Grand Master.

London Grand Rank apron and collar jewel.

The dignity of London Grand Rank was introduced for "long and meritorious service to the Craft in London." The Grand Secretary reported to Grand Lodge that the House Committee at 27 Pembridge Gardens had discussed the safe custody of members' valuable coats, and in future expensive coats or furs were to be given to the Tyler to keep in her cupboard in the Crush Hall.

New Degrees

At the Grand Lodge meeting held in June 1948, the M.W.The Grand Master was petitioned to "establish as time and circumstances permitted Chapters and Lodges to work further Masonic Degrees recognised by the Grand Lodge of England as being 'in amity' with Craft Masonry and as such open to Master Masons." In general, there are two main systems of Masonry practiced by different Constitutions - the so-called York Rite of the three Craft Degrees plus Mark, Ark Mariner and Chapter, and the thirty three Degrees of the Ancient and Accepted Rite, which includes some of the Higher Degrees.

Lodge Courageous No.30 in January 1930

During the following summer, M.W.Bro. Lucy O'Hea and R.W.Bro. Muirhead Hope had many discussions on how such Degrees should be worked in our Order without altering our Constitutions. They decided that it would be logical and proper for us in our Order to work further deistic Degrees by bodies attached either to our existing Mark lodges or Chapters. Councils of the Cryptic Rite series would be established by Supreme Grand Chapter and Ark Mariner would be 'moored' to Mark Lodges as in the male Order in England.

The Chivalric Degrees - Knights Templar and of Malta, the Red Cross of Constantine and Knight of St. John - could not, however, be dealt with in the same way because they are chivalry and as such not part of the 'pure and antient masonry' of the York Rite. As the Grand Master said "In them their members meet not as builders but as warriors; their emblems are not the working tools of the masons but the sword, shield and spurs of medieval chivalry." Formerly, the men had worked Knights Templar and Rose Croix as linked together until a Supreme Grand Council was set up in 1845 to administer all the Degrees connected to the Ancient and Accepted Rite. It was decided in 1949 not to establish a Supreme Grand Council in our own Order, because this would necessitate working not only the 18th Degree (Rose Croix) but the 30th Degree (Kadosh) and up to the 33rd Degree.

Lodge Sirius No.31 in April 1949

Lodge Herakles No.32 in May 1949

Having studied the various rituals, a small group had been practising the Knights Templar Degree for three years. The time had come to consecrate a Knights Templar Encampment with the right to also work the Rose Croix. Membership was open to all Royal Arch Companions professing the Christian faith, and Avalon Encampment No.1 was consecrated in March 1949. A Rose Croix Chapter followed in March 1950. The Grand Master put on record the Order's gratitude to the Past Grand Master who "with her characteristic energy and imagination" arranged for the making and embroidery of the clothing for the officers, and presented more than half the equipment necessary for the working of the Rose Croix Degree, [of] "which it was her dearest wish, as well as [that] of our Most Wor.Bro. Marion Lindsay Halsey, to see established here."

The first Cryptic Council was held in London in October 1948, with M.W.Bro. Lucy O'Hea as Thrice Illustrious Master. Further meetings took place to form the nucleus of Private Councils attached to individual Chapters, for it was felt at the time that the linking of the Cryptic Degrees to the Holy Royal Arch, as organised in Scottish Masonry, was the correct procedure. The four 'Cryptic' Degrees - named after their connection with a secret vault, which was also their link with the Holy Royal Arch - had originated on the Continent to further elaborate the legend of King Solomon's Temple. From there they had transferred to America and came to England in the 1870s.

The original members were granted a Charter forming them into the Aleph Cryptic Council, made up of members of Supreme Grand Chapter, with the three Grand Principals as its chief Officers. The Council was to meet as and when called, primarily to carry Cryptic Masonry to the provinces. Light Invisible Cryptic Council No.2, attached to Logos Chapter No.2, was consecrated on 31st May 1949. Hidden Mysteries No.3, sponsored by Zodiac Chapter No.3 and Aries Council No.4, sponsored by Zerah Chapter No.4 were consecrated in the following September. Clearly much of the preparatory work on the introduction of these 'Degrees beyond the Craft' had taken place under M.W.Bro. Lucy O'Hea, although Mary Gordon Muirhead Hope was an enthusiastic supporter.

R.W.Bro. Florence Jane Hawkins, P.G.W. was the last living Founder Member of our Order - one of the group which, with the Rev.Dr. Cobb at their head, formed the Honourable Fraternity of Antient Masonry in 1908. She was a member of the Lodge of Unity No.3, and when the Grand Temple was built and being furnished, she donated the original blue carpet. She passed to the Grand Lodge above on 14th February 1949.

Lodge Constancy and Faith No.33 in September 1949

Lodge Dueguarde No.34 in July 1949

At Grand Lodge in October 1949 the ceremonial sword of the Order was carried in procession for the first time. Lodge Constancy and Faith No.33 had been consecrated the previous month in Sheffield, city of steel. At the Consecration the sword, made in Sheffield, was presented to the Grand Master for the use of the Order. With a silver blade and a hilt of gold and enamel, its name was also 'Constancy and Faith'. It was therefore necessary to introduce into Grand Lodge the office of Grand Sword Bearer, and the first holder was W.Bro. Kate Coast, Immediate Past Master of Lodge Constancy and Faith No.33.

Lodge Endeavour No.35 in October 1949

Lodge Felicity No.36 in November 1949

The sword 'Constancy and Faith', presented to Grand Lodge by Lodge No.33, Sheffield.

More Fraternal Relations

At the same Quarterly Communications, the Grand Master made a statement on the question of fraternal relations of this Order with other women's orders.

"We want, I am sure" she said "our Order to be strong, and to spread over Great Britain and Ireland, and perhaps the English-speaking world. It is evident that unity is strength ... our aim should be that all Masons should be united. This Order is the strongest one, and with the most Degrees, therefore, we should take the first step. If and when the Union or Fraternal Relations come, it would come ... from the main body of the two Orders. It would come from the hearts and goodwill from the members of this Order, and the members of the other Order would know that we have stretched out our hands in sincerity and brotherhood, and may the G.A.O.T.U. put His blessing upon it."

Lodge Fortitude No.37 in January 1950

Lodge Herewe No.38 in February 1950

Lodge Adherence No.39 in July 1950

The other Order referred to was the one which had broken away from ours in 1913 - the Honourable Fraternity of Ancient Freemasons - following a dispute over the introduction of the Holy Royal Arch Degree.

With the unanimous consent of her Advisory Council (the most senior members of Grand Lodge) the Grand Master had written to the Grand Master of the other Order, Mrs. Seton Challen, suggesting the setting up of a reconciliation committee to make recommendations towards the establishment of fraternal relations or a complete union. This move follows the pattern in the Older Obedience, when a Lodge of Reconciliation was set up to pave the way to union between the Antients and the Moderns in 1813. Mrs. Seton Challen was said to be considering the suggestion, although over the following two years she was unable to agree any dates to meet and eventually the matter lapsed.

January 1951 brought the news that, although the offer of closer relations with the Honourable Fraternity of Ancient Freemasons under Seton Challen had not materialised, some of their members who had come over to us had petitioned for the revival of Lodge Stability No.5 - the Lodge which was suspended following the defection of many of its members to form the new Order in 1913. They wanted Stability to

Banner of Lodge Stability and Peace, consecrated in 1951 with the number of the old Lodge Stability, No.5.

become the Mother Lodge of all those who came to us from other Orders. This Petition was granted and Lodge Stability and Peace No.5 was re-consecrated in April 1951. For some years, Joining Members were accepted from Lodges such as Elizabeth Boswell Reid No.7, City of Birmingham No.18 and Countess of Warwick No.24, all of the Honourable Fraternity of Ancient Freemasons.

Lodge Stability and Peace No.5 in April 1951

Over the next year, still in the spirit of extending fraternal relations, an approach was made to another Order that included women Masons, the Order of Ancient, Free and Accepted Masonry, with which discussions had taken place back in 1935. The difference in 1951 was that this other Order had now changed their structure so that women practised Masonry separately in their own Lodges, not in mixed Lodges. At Grand Lodge in October 1951, Mary Gordon Muirhead Hope recalled that M.W.Bro. Marion Halsey had wanted three things for the Order - recognition by the Grand Lodge of England; a full Masonic life for women (which could in fact now be offered in terms of the different Degrees practised); and fraternal relations between the women's orders.

"In pursuance of this aim we tried three years ago to heal the breach with our own breakaway order the H.F.A.F. This effort failed. There was a third order, one that had broken away from the Universal Order of Co-Masonry, as our Order had done. It worked the Masonic series of the Ancient and Accepted Rite, having sufficient numbers of Brethren upon [whom] the 33rd Degree had been conferred. When they were first established ... they had applied to our Order for fraternal relations, but had been refused as their numbers consisted of both men and women. Since then many of their numbers had adopted the view that women should work Masonry completely separated from men, and local autonomy had been granted to all their Lodges to restrict their membership to

Emblem of the Ancient, Free and Accepted Masonry.

women only should they so decide. About two thirds of the Lodges were so restricted."

The Heads of the two Orders had already been on friendly terms, and the Grand Master said that with the consent of her Advisory Committee and of the Board of General Purposes, she had approached the current Lt. Grand Commander of the Ancient, Free and Accepted Masonry, Very Puissant Brother [Marjorie] C. Debenham, to see if we could not agree on terms of amity between our Orders. The proposals were that such terms would include consultations between the heads on matters of mutual Masonic interest, interchanges of formal visits by Senior Members of both Orders (on our side limited to visits of Lodges restricted to women only), such visits to be arranged between the heads of each Order.

Lodge Granta No.41 in October 1950

Lodge St. Mary's No.42 in November 1950

The Grand Master submitted a letter which she proposed should be sent to the Supreme Council 33rd Degree of the Honourable Fraternity of Ancient, Free and Accepted Masonry, and asked all members of Grand Lodge to express their views. She would not move without their consent. The proposal was carried without opposition and so the letter went out:

"To the Supreme Council of the 33°, Ancient and Accepted Rite, of the Honourable Fraternity of Ancient, Free and Accepted Masonry.

Greeting,
    We, the Grand Lodge of the Honourable Fraternity of Antient Masonry, having the interest of the Craft at heart which we are convinced is best served by brotherly love between all true Masons, desire to salute you and express our hope that friendly relations may be inaugurated between us.
    …We know that you share with us a belief in the spiritual basis of Masonry, and we understand that you allow local autonomy to your private lodges to decide whether they should admit men, but that several lodges have elected to follow the path we have steadfastly chosen, of limiting membership to women only.
    …We would welcome the establishment of formal relations of amity between us; in meeting for discussion from time to time on Masonic

matters of joint interest; in welcoming formal visits from your Principal Officers as may be arranged between us, and in delegating our Grand Lodge Representatives to visit, when invited, any of your lodges that are limited in membership to women only. In this way we hope to work for and reach a better understanding between women masons generally."

A few months later it was proposed that consultations should take place twice yearly between the Heads and Senior Officers of each Order to discuss matters of Masonic interest and importance to both sides. The M.W. The Grand Master said that since the last Quarterly Communication of Grand Lodge she had been in touch with V.Puiss.Bro. Debenham and had discussed with her the spread of Freemasonry for women in Australia. We had neither the time nor the money to go there at present, but there were five Lodges there for women only belonging to the Ancient, Free and Accepted Masonry who would accept our members as visitors, and later as affiliated members should they desire it.

There was also a very enthusiastic Past Master of the same Order who was willing to take open meetings in other areas in Australia, with a view to starting up other centres. Miss Debenham had suggested that our members might help in interesting their friends in such a proposed development. She would also be happy that any new Lodges overseas which would be shared between us should be authorised under the name of *The Alliance of Womens Masonic Obediences*. This however would be discussed at the meetings to be arranged.

Lodge Voyagers

Lodge Voyagers breast jewel.

In tune with the emphasis on expansion, it was decided in late 1950 to consecrate a Lodge to initiate applicants from overseas. The Lodge was called Voyagers No.40 and the first Worshipful Master was Lucy Bertram O'Hea - most appropriately, as she had done so much to spread Freemasonry for Women within this country. There were over three hundred Founders. The first

Lodge Voyagers No.40 in December 1950

Banner of Lodge Voyagers No.40.

member of the Lodge was Bro. M.R. Brock, who was initiated at an Especial Lodge convened by the Grand Master. Bro. Brock worked in Abadan, a centre of oilfield activity in southern Persia (Iran), and she was on leave in this country. In the following year Grand Lodge stood to order to send their thoughts to Bro. Brock, now back in Persia, where serious disputes were endangering the oilfield region.

Applications for Lodge Voyagers had also been received from potential members in the Channel Islands. Later Lodge Voyagers visited there and initiated twenty seven candidates before forming Lodge Isle of Sarnia No.50 in 1952.

Lodge Phoenix No.43 in March 1951

Lodge Isle of Sarnia No.50 in November 1952

In the same year R.W.Bro. Florence Leveridge, P.G.W., Grand Secretary, retired - having had the unenviable task of succeeding Peter Slingsby as Grand Secretary.

Grand Master Mary Gordon Muirhead Hope (second from right) with Grand Lodge Officers on the way to Guernsey in 1952 to consecrate Lodge Isle of Sarnia No.50.

Continuing the expansion of the Degrees available to members of the Order, in 1950 the Grand Master told Grand Lodge that she was now in possession of the secrets of the Ark Mariner Degree, and would communicate them with the approval of Grand Lodge. Ark Mariner Lodges would be attached to Mark Lodges.

In June 1951 Adelaide Litten died and a Memorial Service for her was held prior to Grand Lodge at Headquarters that month.

The Grand Master's Standard

Mary Gordon Muirhead Hope is the only Grand Master to have had her own personal standard. It was the gift of an anonymous Brother in 1951 in recognition of the tremendous expansion which had taken place in the Order in the three years since her Enthronement. On her retirement the Grand Master gave the standard in perpetuity to the Brethren of Liverpool, with whom she had a close relationship.

The background is garter blue and on each side rise the pillars of the House of Masonry. The top of the arch is hidden, as the keystone is only inserted in the next life. On the square ashlars along the wall at the base of the banner are the

Lodge Tranquillity No.44 in May 1951

Lodge Valiant No.45 in June 1951

The personal standard of Mary Gordon Muirhead Hope.

numbers of the Lodges already consecrated up to that time. The central panel is the almond shape of the *vesica piscis*, which is both a pagan symbol of the feminine and a sign of the Christian religion. On this are the emblems of the Degrees worked by the Order at that time - the top section has Knight Templar, Knight of Malta, Rose Croix and the Kadosh; to the right, the Royal Arch and the Cryptic rite; to the left, the Mark and Ark Mariner; and at the bottom, the Scots Masonic emblem of the square and compasses enclosing a G, with above it the breast jewel of the Royal Order of Scotland. In the two bottom corners are the Grand Master's personal mark and her family crest.

In April 1952 the Degree of Knight of the Red Cross of Constantine was introduced. At that time it was divided into three 'grades', Conclave, the Order of St. John and that of the Holy Sepulchre.

February 1952 saw the introduction of the Charity Sash. A sash of dark crimson and silver was to be awarded to each Immediate Past Master and to the Lodge on the Installation of her successor, if the minimum quota amount of money had been forwarded to Headquarters. The first Lodge to receive this sash was Harmony No.4.

The Home at Worthing

Lodge Good Report No.46 in March 1952

Lodge Mystic Tie No.47 in February 1952

For some years the Order had been looking for a suitable house to convert to a residential and retirement home for elderly members, which would be owned and maintained by the Adelaide Litten Trust Fund. In early 1952 a house, built in 1906, was finally found at West Worthing in Sussex and purchased by the A.L.T.F. Members of the Order were invited to vote for a name for the house, and it duly became known by a majority vote as *Porchway House*. It had spacious rooms for permanent residents and a music room which would be let as a Temple.

Lodge Bond of Friendship No.48 in June 1952

The official opening took place on 7th June 1952. As the Grand Master said "May this house always radiate happiness, friendship, hospitality and right feelings." Over one hundred Brethren spent time looking over the house, then assembled for tea on the lawn. The main aspect of the house is south and west: the climate of Worthing is suitably mild and temperate, and the sea and sheltered Marine Gardens were a few minutes away from the house.

At that time there was accommodation for twelve people and when the house was opened there were five permanent residents. On each landing there was an innovation - a table with gas ring and grill (with a penny-in-the-slot meter) for preparing drinks or snacks. "We have deliberately left many gaps in the furnishing" said the Grand Master "these are gaps for the members to fill" - a policy still practiced today and which helps to make *Porchway House* feel like home for the residents.

Porchway House at Worthing, as it was in 1952. The building on the right with tall windows is the music room, dedicated as a Masonic Temple. It was later extended into the garden when the nursing home wing was built.

The following day, the house was consecrated as a Residential and Rest Home by R.W.Bro. Maud Litten, P.G.W. on the first anniversary of the death of her sister, M.W.Bro. Adelaide Litten, Past Grand Master. A procession moved through the house to the strains of *Bless this House, Praise my soul, the King of Heaven* and *How lovely are Thy dwellings*. The same day the music room was dedicated as a Masonic Temple. Initially it was let to Lodge Progress No.19 which met at Worthing. After the dedication, Progress opened a Lodge in the new Temple. A remark by a male Mason at the Opening of the house made the point that we had achieved something that U.G.L.E. had never done so far - opened a home with a Temple attached, so that the residents could continue to enjoy their Freemasonry.

M.W.Bro. Muirhead Hope was again installed as Grand Master in the October of 1952, but this Quarterly Communication was unique in that present were V.Puiss.Bro. Debenham and some of her senior Officers of the Ancient, Free and Accepted Masonry. Before the close of Grand Lodge the Deputy Grand Master rose to say that the members would like to show their great appreciation to the Grand Master for all the work she had done for the Order. The Worshipful Master of Lodge Golden Rule No.1 and her Wardens then presented a cheque for £625

Lodge Gordon No.49 in October 1952

"to be used for whatever purpose you wish." The M.W. The Grand Master said that she considered it a great compliment that something like two thousand women could keep a secret and that it was only within the last few days she had known something was happening! She intended her gift to go towards "the expansion and adorning of our Masonic Edifice." This included increasing our membership, offering a full Masonic life to women in terms of the Degrees offered, and in having friendship with other Orders who also followed the Masonic path. She expressed her pleasure in seeing V.P.Bro. Debenham and her Brethren on this occasion. Miss Debenham thanked the Grand Master on being allowed to share in the ceremony and congratulated the Order on their Grand Master.

M.W.Bro. Mary G. M. Hope - a portrait painted in 1954.

Lodge Faith and Zeal No.53 in April 1953

Lodge Radiant No.54 in May 1953

Lodge Corinthian No.55 in September 1953

Lodge Orion No.56 in September 1953

Lodge Doric No.57 in October 1953

Mary Muirhead Hope continued to keep in contact with Miss Debenham, even after she retired from the position of Grand Master, and to look for ways of affiliation rather than amalgamation. In 1968 Miss Debenham wrote to her "The Supreme Council wish to confer the 33rd Degree upon you & invite you to become an honorary Member in recognition of your magnificent work for Women's Freemasonry and as an expression of their personal affection, friendship and admiration."

Canada

1953 and in particular 1954 saw very important developments on the expansion front. The 50th anniversary of the Order in 1958 was approaching. At the time there were fifty nine Lodges, and the hope was that in the next five years we would reach one hundred Lodges. This meant the staggering total of forty one new Lodges to be consecrated in that period, an average of over eight per year. In September and December 1953 two special Lodges were consecrated

- Lodge Peace and Harmony No.58 was the late City of Birmingham Lodge of the other Order (the H.F.A.F.) and Lodge Arbitrium No.60 had formerly been the City of Warwick Lodge of the same Order. December 1953 saw the first Lodge in Northern Ireland - Lodge Loyal Ulster No.61.

Lodge Peace and Harmony No.58 in September 1953

Lodge Contemplation No.59 in October 1953

The Grand Master and Deputy Grand Master flew to Canada in the autumn of 1954 on the first intercontinental venture. This was the culmination of nearly three years work. A Brother in Lodge Meridian No.28 had a cousin in Toronto, Mrs. Dorothy Garde (who later became Grand Inspector for Canada). She met up with a member of Lodge Marion Halsey No.10 who lived in Toronto, and the two held a series of meetings for friends and acquaintances. Eventually they asked Headquarters for a Lodge in Toronto.

Lodge Arbitrium No.60 in November 1953

Lodge Loyal Ulster No.61 in December 1953

On their arrival the Grand Master and Deputy started to interview intending candidates. Over forty Canadian women had signed declaration forms and already paid one third of their ceremonial fees (at their own request). They were from Toronto, London in Ontario and Niagara. Five other senior Grand Lodge Officers from England arrived in Canada on 13th October and for sixteen days they worked two ceremonies a day, with evening meetings every other day.

Lodge Ashlar No.62 in January 1954

Lodge Steadfast No.63 in March 1954

In the two weeks, fifty four Master Masons were made, a Lodge was consecrated, a Worshipful Master installed and officers invested. The Lodge was Lodge Pioneer Hope of Toronto No.72 (No.1 Canada). Bro. Garde was given the secrets of an Installed Master and installed as the first Worshipful Master of the Lodge. One of the visitors from England, W.Bro. Sarah Hallam J.G.D., stayed in Toronto for nearly a year to oversee progress and to advise. The consecrating party managed to fit in a visit to Niagara, where they saw the rainbow over the Falls by day and the illuminations by night.

R.W.Bro. Dorothy Garde, P.J.G.W., G.M's.G.S., care of Canada.

Lodge Ionic No.64 in April 1954

Lodge Justice No.65 in April 1954

Lodge Tuscan No.66 in May 1954

Lodge Western Light No.67 in June 1954

W.Bro. Garde later wrote to *The Gavel*:

"We in Ontario can never be thankful enough to all of you who made it possible by your many gifts, thoughts and prayers for all of us to receive the Degrees of Freemasonry. For us it was a dream come true, and the realisation far exceeded the imagination. We know how fortunate we were, in having those Degrees conferred by M.W. The Grand Master and other Grand Officers, and we do appreciate the sacrifices they made in undertaking the trip ... They have set us a very high standard which we shall certainly strive to maintain. By their presence they turned a somewhat dingy room into a place of beauty and inspiration. They captured the hearts of everyone, the building superintendent, janitor and elevator woman, to say nothing of the clerks in the stores, the taxi men and waitresses. As for their hosts and hostesses, they say unanimously 'Come back as often as you can, as soon as you can, and stay as long as you can'."

Lodge Albanus No.68 in June 1954

Lodge Vigilance No.69 in June 1954

Lodge St. Barbara-in-Teesdale No.70 in September 1954

Lodge Patience and Industry No.71 in October 1954

Lodge Pioneer Hope of Toronto No.72 in October 1954

Lodge Pillar of Strength No.73 in October 1954

In 1956 and 1957 further visits to Canada were made. The Grand Master took a joint banner for Lodge Pioneer Hope No.72 and Lodge Trillium of York No.79, which had been paid for by Brethren in this country. She also presented on her own behalf a banner for London Lodge of Accord No.78. Another Lodge was consecrated - Lodge Heritage of Oshawa No.84.

The banner of Lodge Victoria No.124, Vancouver Island.

The fifth visit to Canada was in October 1959, when the Deputy Grand Master left England on the *Empress of Britain* and the Grand Master followed shortly afterwards by air. The existing Craft Lodges were visited, and at the Installation meeting of Keystone Mark Lodge No.6 Brethren were elevated into the Degree of Royal Ark Mariner, so that this Degree could be worked in Canada. In addition, meetings were held for interested ladies in Vancouver in the west and other centres back east. They were to return in the spring in order to consecrate two new Lodges in Vancouver - Lodge Victoria No.124 on Vancouver Island and Lodge

Vanguard No.125 in Vancouver City. In April the following year the 'advance party' initiated, passed and raised twenty nine candidates in three sessions a day. Similarly, seventeen candidates awaited their three Degree ceremonies before the consecration of Lodge Vanguard.

The support to the Canadian Lodges continued, with another visit by the Grand Master and her team in May 1961. They met as many members as possible of the three Toronto Lodges, held 'open' meetings, attended Installations and generally gave encouragement. After flying to Calgary, the party went by train through the Rockies and visited the Brethren in Vancouver.

The honour of Provincial Grand Rank was introduced in 1955 for Past Masters of Provincial Lodges who have "rendered long and meritorious service to the Craft." There was to be no more than one award for every three Provincial Lodges.

A Banner for the Order

A Masonic Service was held at the Seymour Hall in London on 12th April 1955, attended by over eight hundred Brethren. The occasion was the presentation by the Grand Master of a banner to the Order. First to enter the hall was a procession of reigning Worshipful Masters and their Lodge banners. The Volume of the Sacred Law was carried by an Entered Apprentice and the Square and Compasses by a Fellow Craft. The Assistant Grand Master, R.W.Bro. Rhoda Low, then gave an Oration, which was followed by a procession of the Rulers of the Further Degrees.

The Order's new Banner was processed in and dedicated by the Deputy Grand Master, R.W.Bro. Dorothy Taylor. Before the service drew to a close, the Grand Chaplain, V.W.Bro. Kate Coast, dedicated a plaque, naming a bed on behalf of the Order, to be placed in the Florence Nightingale Hospital. This was a small hospital for women in London and a charitable cause which we supported at that time.

Lodge De Laci No.74 in February 1955

Lodge Kedron No.75 in April 1955

Lodge St. David No.76 in April 1955

Portsmouth Lodge of Duty No.77 in May 1955

The Banner of the Order of Women Freemasons, showing the <u>partly</u> Open Door of Masonry, with our insignia of the Three Pillars above and the emblems of the countries where we work. The three stars on the triangle at the bottom represent the first three Lodges consecrated in 1908.

The banner was described at the time:

"It shows the great door of Masonry half open (for the entrance is not yet fully open to women), and leading into the Holy House of Wisdom. The door is reached up worn steps, steps worn by the feet of the many who have passed this way before us, into the House of Wisdom, which is symbolised by the seven white pillars through which the light streams: the Degree of the Seven Pillars is the final of the York Rite.

The Badge of the Order is centred above the portico, and is in brilliant colour against the grey stone of the arched entrance. And, as Masonry is a sanctuary, the great knocker on the door is copied from the sanctuary knocker of Durham Cathedral.

The heraldic emblems to be seen below and on either side of the main design, are those of the countries in which our Order works; first, the Rose of England - and the triangle, with its three stars which can be seen beneath it stands for the three lodges, Golden Rule, Emulation and Unity, with which the Order began, the three lodges being consecrated together in June 1908 - then the Dragon of Wales to the right of the Rose and the date 1938 which was the year when our first lodge was opened in Wales.

On the left is the Thistle of Scotland, where our first lodge was opened in 1948. The emblems on the left hand side-piece are of the Channel Islands (1952) and the Red Hand of Ulster (1953). On the right, there is the Maple of Canada, with the year of our first lodge in that country, 1954. May the blank spaces be filled soon with the emblems of the other countries of the Commonwealth!."

Later were added the emblem of Australia, the wattle (1957), the flame flower of Zimbabwe (Southern Rhodesia) (1957), the dogwood flower of British Columbia (1960), the George Cross of Malta (1961), the three legs of the Isle of Man (1962), the harp of the Republic of Ireland (1966), the palm tree of Nigeria (1971), the *protea* of South Africa (1982) and the *bougainvillea* of Spain (2005).

Also in 1955 extensions were made to the Headquarters at 27 Pembridge Gardens - a refreshment room, a small Temple and further cloakroom accommodation. At this time the use of a central altar in the Temple was discontinued, and replaced by an altar in the East. The use of incense in ceremonies in general was stopped because of difficulties in hotels and halls used for other purposes.

The Name of the Order

During 1956 there was considerable discussion over changing or adding to the Order's name, which was at that time still the Honourable Fraternity of Antient Masonry. When the Order was founded, it included both men and women so that 'women' was not incorporated in the title. The words 'Antient Masonry' were to suggest that we looked back for our spiritual inspiration to the Ancient Mysteries in which women had participated rather than to the operative craft where women were forbidden. Although 'Fraternity' was perhaps not the most suitable description of an all-women order, many Brethren were reluctant to change the name we had held for nearly fifty years.

Lodge Staffordshire Knot No.81 in January 1956

Lodge Serenity No.82 in January 1956

The Grand Master felt that in view of the difficulties in explaining to outside bodies that we were a women-only organisation, it would serve the purpose to leave the title as it was but to add a sub-title incorporating the word 'Women'. The matter was adjourned to give time for feedback from the Lodges. One objection was that the inclusion of the word 'Women' or 'for Women' might prejudice our chances with the men if and when we were reconsidered for recognition by United Grand Lodge of England.

Lodge Acacia No.83 in April 1956

Lodge Heritage No.84 in May 1956

When canvassed, seventy votes were in favour of a sub-title and ten against, indicating that there was a general wish that there should be no alteration to the original title. In choosing a sub-title, it needed to illustrate the fact that we were an order of women only and that, according to United Grand Lodge, the correct description of a Speculative Mason was Freemason rather than Mason. It was decided to take a written ballot. The Grand Master hoped that Grand Lodge would have confidence in the general principles she had laid down, and that they should think on the words of Adelaide Litten at another occasion: "I do strongly beg you to remember that the Grand Master has, in deciding any matter, sources of information and fields of thought which cannot possibly be known to others, of the general principles of the Order or even of Grand Lodge and therefore it is only under serious consideration that you should reject her advice."

Lodge Amethyst No.85 in November 1956

Lodge York No.86 in September 1956

The question of a possible name change for the Order was shelved for the time being, when there was the possibility of a merger with Miss

Dagenham smaller Order. However, two years later, with the merger rejected, it was thought that the word 'women' should be in our new title. It was finally decided in October 1958 that our name should be the Honourable Fraternity of Antient Masonry with the subtitle 'The Order of Women Freemasons' - and this is still the case, with both titles appearing on our emblem.

The honour of Grand Master's Grand Star was instituted in 1956 - a personal award from the Grand Master in recognition of outstanding work for the Order.

The Grand Master's Grand Star

Lodge King Solomon No.13 in April 1958

In 1958 Lodge King Solomon No.13 was consecrated by the Grand Master. The number '13' had been left vacant since 1930. The purpose of this Lodge was to train and initiate Candidates prior to new Consecrations, somewhat similar to the function of Lodge Mercury No.11.

Further Expansion Overseas

Banner of the Lodge of King Solomon No.13.

The Deputy Grand Master, R.W.Bro. Dorothy Taylor, visited Australia in July 1957 to prepare for the consecration of a Lodge in Adelaide in the autumn - Lodge Pathana No.96.

There was further interest elsewhere overseas in Freemasonry for women. In Rhodesia a group of women found a suitable hall and met fortnightly to prepare themselves by reading and research and to canvass suitable candidates. This was in advance of a visit from the Grand Master in October 1957, when twenty six candidates were

Banner of Lodge Zimbabwe No.98.

Bury Lodge of Goodwill No.88 in March 1957

Lodge St. Wilfred No.89 in May 1957

Lodge Sussex Downs No.90 in June 1957

Lodge of St. Anne No.91 in June 1957

initiated, passed and raised in groups of up to six. Lodge Zimbabwe No.98 was consecrated on 6th November 1957. In the little spare time available, the Grand Master and her party visited Victoria Falls and took a trip by motor launch up the Zambezi.

Further expansion took place when the Grand Master consecrated Lodge St. Michael and St. George No.132 at Sliema, Malta in March 1961. Many of the seventeen candidates belonged to service families stationed on the Island. The first Worshipful Master Elect, Bro. L.E. Williams, a member of Lodge Voyagers, had formerly belonged to the other women's Order and had enquired at Headquarters to see if there was a Lodge of ours on Malta. She was assured that if she could gather together a nucleus, this might be possible. So in March the Grand Master and Officers arrived for the Consecration, including Grand Secretary R.W.Bro. M.V. Ellis, P.G.W., who was the reigning Master of Lodge Voyagers.

Later in the year, R.W. Bro. Marjorie Ellis also visited Salisbury (Harare), Southern Rhodesia, in August to meet and encourage the members of Lodge Zimbabwe. Lodge Voyagers promoted Lodges both near and far, and in April 1962 the Grand Master, Assistant Grand Master and their team flew to the Isle of Man to consecrate Lodge Barrule No.151. Barrule is the Manx name for the mountains that rise in the centre of the island. R.W.Bro. Clara Cooper, S.G.W., Master of Voyagers, visited Malta for a week and the Grand Master went to Rhodesia in August to initiate, pass and raise (on consecutive days) the first candidates from Bulawayo, with the hope of interesting other ladies there and forming a Lodge. The Grand Master also visited Canada again to give her support to the two Lodges in Vancouver, who were experiencing difficulties in recruitment in an area where the American adoptive orders such as the Eastern Star were strong. Other senior Brethren went to Adelaide and Sydney.

In October 1963 the Grand Master, accompanied by a party which included W.Bro. Doris Hoadley, A.G.D.C., arrived in Salisbury, Southern Rhodesia via Khartoum and Nairobi. Thousands of jacaranda trees were smothered in blue blossom, and these together with scarlet, pink and orange hibiscus, golden acacia and crimson amaryllis made a sharp contrast with the rain-sodden leaves of autumn at home. Having flown to Bulawayo, the party were soon at work - initiating, passing and raising candidates who had been prepared over the previous few months. Ten were raised "in what was virtually a continuous performance of the Third Degree ceremony." A few days later Lodge Pambili No.166 was consecrated, with W.Bro. Hoadley giving the Oration. The name Pambili is an African word meaning upward and onward. One hundred and seventeen Lodges from around the world sent telegrams of congratulation and goodwill.

Lodge Assheton No.94 in October 1957

Lodge Thorpe No.95 in November 1957

In the following summer of 1964 the Grand Master and Grand Secretary again flew to Salisbury. They went to see the new Temple at Hatfield and visited Lodge Zimbabwe before flying to Bulawayo, where they visited Cecil Rhodes' grave in the Mtopo Hills and attended a meeting of Lodge Pambili. Back in Salisbury Paternoster Conclave No.9 was consecrated and eighteen candidates were taken in. In spite of almost losing her voice through 'flu, the Grand Master took Craft Degrees for Lodge Voyagers and consecrated Lodge St. Kilda No.180.

Mary Gordon Muirhead Hope at the Consecration of Lodge St. Michael and St. George No.132 in Malta.

Lodge pathans No.96 in October 1957

Lodge Courtesy No.97 in November 1957

Lodge Zimbabwe No.98 in November 1957

Golden Jubilee of the Order

Having described how the Order expanded overseas, we return to 1958. The fiftieth anniversary of the Order was celebrated at the Albert Hall in London on the 7th September that year. Present were representatives of nearly one hundred and ten Lodges, from England, Scotland, Wales, Northern Ireland, the Channel Islands, Canada, Southern Rhodesia and Australia. The first part of the meeting

The Grand Master, Deputy Grand Master (R.W. Bro. Taylor) and Assistant Grand Master (R.W. Bro. Low) in 1958.

included a pageant illustrating the development of the Order and the events of the half century, preceded by a prologue given by W.Bro. E.V. Smith.

During the proceedings Grand Master Mary Gordon Muirhead Hope looked back on her forty years in the Order:

" ... what eager masons we were in 1918! In every walk of life doors were opening to admit women for the first time, and we thought, surely after the Great War the door of Masonic toleration might be opened? Our hopes in this respect were not unfounded, for soon after, in 1920, a circular letter was issued by the Grand Orient of the Netherlands *[a body in fraternal relations with the United Grand Lodge of England]* to all lodges within its jurisdiction concerning the admission of Women into their Order, which, after considering all the arguments for and against, summarised what they advised as the best solution as follows:

'The Order should provide opportunity for women to assemble in a suitable organisation, but without men ... Should it appear that such bodies develop in the proper direction, then, in our opinion, full initiation into the Mysteries of our Order must essentially follow'.

But the door of Masonic toleration, as some other doors, remained locked and barred, and we realised that a long period of probation lay before us."

The pageant at the meeting, according to the account in *The Gavel*, "demonstrated the birth and growth of the Order by the consecration dates of the Lodges over the last fifty years. Inevitably history touched the scene; there was the occasional burst of success, followed by severe checks which were often caused by factors well outside our control, such as the infant Order having to survive the first social strains of the Great War, a short prosperity and the world-wide Slump, partial recovery, and again the long ominous threat over Europe, culminating in the second World War of 1939-45, with England under siege and London itself a wide mark for bombs and rockets. Miraculously, the Order not only survived the anticipated normal displeasure and opposition to its existence, but also these almost major setbacks, until as we could hear with our ears and see with our own eyes, the trickle of new Lodges over the last ten years became a flood.

… Perhaps for the first time, many members caught the magic of a living continuity of tradition. Among the Elder Brethren watching, who had been known in the past to many as among the Rulers of the Craft, it was heart-warming to see [M.W.] Bro. Lucy O'Hea, Past Grand Master and, no doubt, it was heart-warming for her to look down on the crowded ranks of the younger Brethren … A living tradition is one which continually adapts itself to the needs of its time and yet loses nothing of its central idea … and the tradition of this Order of Freemasons founded in 1908 is, we hope, *to work well*."

Lodge Elizabethan No.100 in February 1958

Lodge of the Three Lights No.101 in March 1958

An outstanding tribute to the Grand Master was paid by the Deputy Grand Master:

Lodge Cornerstone No.102 in January 1958

"It is unusual to publish an appreciation of any living member of our Order, but in our history, this year of 1958 is unique, and it justifies a needed tribute to the architect of the great post-War increase in our numbers - our present Grand Master.

Golden Jubilee jewel.

Lodge Pentagram No.103 in February 1958

It is easy for all of us to take things and people for granted, and in the rush and bustle of the present rate of expansion in the Order we may be in danger of losing sight of the immense and dynamic contribution towards that expansion which has been made by M.W. The Grand Master. In a small organisation (for our Order is still small) there is no place for a non-working figurehead, and the Grand Master is the very last one to be thought of as such. In all weathers, and at all times she travels the length and breadth of England, Scotland and Wales: journeying also to Northern Ireland and the Channel Islands: flying as often as she can to Canada, and Rhodesia. Later, she will go to Australia."

"Since her enthronement the great increase in the number of our Craft Lodges and of the Associated Degrees witness to her untiring effort and her knowledge of Masonic history and her study of symbolism, together with her lucid powers of exposition, all make her an outstanding Freemason.

The time spent in guiding our Order and in visiting remote lodges means that a long stay in her own home is not often possible, but whenever she is able to enjoy her charming house one finds her absorbed in her lovely garden, her dogs, and, perhaps surprisingly, her budgerigars, which she breeds most successfully. A number of them have been presented by her to hospitals dealing with mental cases where the staff report that these birds have been of great interest to the patients.

Our Grand Master, is of course, a dedicated person; dedicated to the Order which, at times, and in the natural order of every day, takes her for granted without meaning to do so. In 1948, our newly enthroned Master said clearly - 'In the obligation I took today, in the presence of you all, I undertook for all time to subordinate my own position to the enlargement, honour and magnification of the Craft'. How wonderfully that promise has been fulfilled."

Following the Golden Jubilee pageant, the Grand Master and her Deputy and Assistant Grand Masters were obligated, clothed, proclaimed and saluted. All the other Degrees saluted the Grand Master - the Mark, Ark Mariner, Chapter, Cryptic, Red Cross of Babylon, Royal Order of Scotland, Red Cross of Constantine, Knights Templar, Rose Croix, the Kadosh and Knights Templar Priest.

R.W.Bro. Florence Emma Turner, P.G.W., was invited to the Golden Jubilee and a box was put at her disposal. The Brethren had cause to be grateful to her for donating the freehold of 27 Pembridge Gardens to the Order as a Headquarters, and also for her enormous energy and enthusiasm in promoting the work of Lodge Mercury No.11 in the provinces. It was uncertain whether she would be able to attend because of the state of her health, but, as D.G.M. Dorothy Taylor wrote later in *The Gavel* " ... to our great pleasure she came and was delighted to see for herself the vast increase in the Order which she had served so well."

Looking forward rather than back, 1958 also saw a proposal for a Building Fund. The time would come when we would have to acquire new premises or extend the present ones as they were inadequate. At

The banners of the Order ranged behind the Grand Master, the Deputy and Assistant Grand Masters at the Golden Jubilee celebrations at the Royal Albert Hall in 1958.

Lodge Crusader No.108 in February 1959

Lodge Tradition of Wigan No.109 in December 1958

Lodge Edinburgh Castle No.110 in January 1959

Lodge Mercury North No.111 in November 1959

Lodge St. Thomas of Canterbury No.112 in January 1959

Lodge Meditation (Installed Masters) No.113 in March 1959

Lodge Southern Light No.114 in September 1959

Lodge Ewenny No.115 in October 1959

Lodge Hampton Court No.116 in October 1959

Lodge The Cedar and the Olive No.117 in November 1959

27 Pembridge Gardens the refreshment room, office and staircases were unsuitable; it was an old property and maintenance would become expensive. We also needed a smaller Temple to accommodate smaller Lodges. The Grand Master said it might be cheaper to pull down the house and rebuild it rather than add to the present structure. It was suggested that Lodges might like to give a thank-offering for the fifty years of the Order, that the resulting Fund might be further boosted by legacies and that any surplus from the celebrations at the Royal Albert Hall could be used to start it.

In 1959 Lodge Mercury North was founded to fulfil the same role in the northern counties as Lodge Mercury No.11 had done in the rest of the country for so many years - to introduce Freemasonry for women. It took the number of Lodge No.111, as the daughter Lodge of No.11.

On February 5th 1960 Lucy O'Hea, Lady Markham, Past Grand Master died. "Her own enthusiasm for spreading the cause of Freemasonry among Women inspired all who worked with her … Her quiet handling of difficult situations and her marked quality of leadership, aided by her fine presence, won for her the affection and respect of all who had the privilege of knowing her."

Grand Lodge was held outside London for the first time in June 1962 when it was convened, by Dispensation, at York, a historic centre of Masonic activity. In the following June the Quarterly Communication meeting was held at the Midland Hotel, Manchester, to give the northern Brethren an opportunity to see the Grand Master enthroned. In May of the same year the Euphrates Council No.2 of the Allied Masonic Degrees started to work the Degree of David and Jonathan (now resumed after a long absence and known as the Order of the Secret Monitor).

Retirement

At the Nomination meeting of Grand Lodge in March 1964 M.W.Bro. Mary Gordon Muirhead Hope announced her retirement after nearly sixteen years in office, opting to leave centre-stage whilst still at the height of her powers. When nominated as Grand Master by M.W.Bro. Lucy O'Hea back in 1948, the latter said "Her great knowledge, her enthusiasm and her selfless devotion to our Order have already won our affection and our admiration. I have every confidence that she will carry on the good work she had already done and that the Order will progress, expand and enlarge under her guidance."

The Gavel writer continues: "Never were words more prophetic! In October 1948 we had twenty six Craft lodges in our Order; five Chapters of The Holy Royal Arch and six Mark Lodges. Not quite sixteen years later and reckoning only up to this April 27th we have one hundred and seventy three Craft lodges, twenty one Mark lodges - fourteen of which also work the Royal Ark Mariner - twenty Royal Arch Chapters, two Cryptic Councils, and one lodge working two of the Allied Masonic Degrees. Of the Chivalric Degrees we have eight Conclaves of the Red Cross of Constantine, one which works the appendant Orders of the Holy Sepulchre and of St. John the Evangelist, one Chapter of the Royal Order of Scotland, two Encampments of Knights Templar and Knights of Malta, two Chapters of the Rose Croix of H.R.D.M., and in addition the Degree of Knight Kadosh and that of Knight Templar Priest are worked at Headquarters.

…We owe to our present Grand Master, M.W. Bro. Mary Gordon Muirhead Hope, not only the explosion of expansion which is still taking place, but the fact that her foresight, courage and imagination, tireless energy (as well as the beautiful example of her ritual work), has lifted us, almost willy-nilly, out of the shadows of disapproval in which the Order existed for so many years. It is odd to remember now, but between the World Wars the climate of opinion was such that few women risked people knowing they were a Mason. Then it was possible for a woman be asked to leave a boarding house, or to lose her job if it unfortunately became known to the unsympathetic that she was a Mason. Living through those years one was indeed 'taught to be cautious'.

Lodge Farley No.118 in February 1960

Lodge Integrity No.119 in February 1960

Lodge Three Pillars No.120 in February 1960

Lodge of Honour No.121 in March 1960

Lodge St. Seiriol No.122 in May 1960

Lodge Reading Abbey No.123 in May 1960

Lodge Victoria No.124 in April 1960

Lodge Vanguard No.125 in May 1960

Lodge Achievement No.126 in June 1960

Lodge Northern Light No.127 in September 1960

Lodge Milestone No.128 in September 1960

Lodge St. Andrew No.129 in February 1961

Lodge Stronghold No.130 in March 1961

Lodge Alnwick No.131 in April 1961

Lodge St. Michael and St. George No.132 in March 1961

Lodge Courage and Hope No.133 in April 1961

Lodge Tudor Manor No.134 in June 1961

Lodge City of Rochester No.135 in May 1961

Lodge Calder Vale No.136 in June 1961

Lodge Sir Fon No.137 in October 1961

Lodge Danum No.138 in October 1961

Lodge Tolerance No.139 in October 1961

Lodge Cartref No.140 in October 1961

Proper caution is still with us but the greater liberality of thought since then aided the vision of the Grand Master. She knew that our Order would remain unregarded unless our membership increased. And without respite, she has led the members of those few lodges almost ruthlessly into the Modern World. ... We have toiled after Mary Hope, thinking sometimes that she must prove to be mistaken but in the end it seems that she was justified! With her, to conceive a way was also to see vividly how it could be accomplished. New in terms of years most of our Lodges are, but there was true endeavour and great purpose in their consecration. A great pioneer has

Mary Gordon Muirhead Hope at the House of Commons in 1964.

pulled us out of the shadows and it is up to each and every member to prove that what has been done with almost prodigal vitality and high seriousness has been well and truly done so that the result will mean strength and continuity throughout our lodges 'from generation to generation'."

The Grand Master herself summed up the changing attitudes both inside and outside the Order:

"To nominate her successor is surely one of the most anxious and difficult decisions to be faced by a reigning Grand Master, for on the plans of the Chief Architect depend the building of the Temple. Looking back over forty-six years of membership of the Order, I can see it, like many of our great Cathedrals, embodying three different styles of architecture. Masculine masonry was evolved from the Craft Guilds; masonry for women was evolved from philosophical circles. The deep roots of the English Craft gave masculine masonry a priceless heritage; but our later start spared us the difficulties of transition that had to be faced in the 18th Century.

Our first two Grand Masters saw our work as essentially a quest for Truth; our Order a small, select body devoted to the study of ancient symbolism. Under our next two Grand Masters we strove to adapt ourselves more exactly to the model of present English Craft Masonry. The adaptation to a small Order of the caste, rank and dignities of an old established and mighty one presented many difficulties; while the storm of opposition from all sides that assailed us in the mid-twenties gave us, I think, a slightly defensive complex, that unwillingness to say one was a Mason that is still sometimes found.

But by the end of the 1940s we had become more realistic and more practical. We saw ourselves rather as one of those little lodges of Guild masons that used to be sent forth in the Middle Ages to erect a more modest building according to the plans and ways they had learned in the erection of some great Cathedral or Abbey …
It is to this change of attitude that I attribute the great expansion of our Order in the last fifteen years. We have been a dedicated band of builders under a Grand Master who was no all-wise Sovereign, but merely one 'first among her equals'."

In thanking those who had helped her along the way, the Grand Master added:

"I also thank humbly and gratefully in my heart four true friends not of our ranks or sex, 'leaders of the people', honoured by the outside world, who believed in our mission and integrity, and who have helped us more than anyone knew - except perhaps myself - by proclaiming their respect and belief aloud to a rather cynical and supercilious world. It would not be proper to give their names; all but one have passed to the Grand Lodge above. May the Great Architect raise up for the Order more valiant friends like these!"
[These four men, probably members of the Older Obedience, surely included the Grand Master's father, the Rev. Walter Muirhead Hope, who had been a regular visitor to our Lodges when so permitted].

"Now, after five years as Deputy Grand Master and fifteen and a half as Grand Master, I feel the time has come when I have probably given the best I have to give to the Order, and it would be better to have a fresh mind in charge and new vigorous leadership. I do not part with my charge lightly; for twenty-one years my life has been filled by the Order and I know I am going to feel very lonely without it; but the Obligation I took as Grand Master was to place the good of the Order at all times above my own wishes; so that is my duty

Priory Lodge of Christchurch No.141 in November 1961

Lodge Curtana No.142 in November 1961

Lodge Le Bolyn No.143 in December 1961

Lodge of Freedom No.144 in December 1961

Lodge North Cestrian No.145 in January 1962

Lodge St. Crispin No.146 in March 1962

Lodge Dyffryn No.147 in May 1962

Lodge Venturer No.148 in May 1962

Lodge Remembrance No.149 in June 1962

Lodge Landmark No.150 in May 1962

and that I will do. I wish I had attained nearer to all the goals that I set out to reach. We have increased our Craft Lodges nearly sevenfold, and spread them throughout the world. We have added the Further Degrees of English Masonry, which I felt was a development of great importance, for while Craft is the trunk and therefore of paramount importance, the Further Degrees are the branches and their life enriches the life of the whole tree.

We have opened our first Masonic Home and are half way to another. We have broadbased our Charities, both for ourselves and for others. Our help has been gladly accepted in beautifying many of the great Cathedrals built by our forebears.

But the uniting of the smaller Orders offering initiation to women into our larger Order; and the building of a more suitable Headquarters, both objects very dear to my heart, were not given to me, and; like King David, I bequeath them to my successor. Like King David, I leave her some material gathered on the way towards union, three strong lodges and many valiant brethren who have crossed the bridges to join us; and for the building, considerably more wealth in our common purse that will help to set the foundations of the larger Headquarters which our increased numbers now demand.

You will have noticed that amidst the names of the Officers who have so greatly helped me during my term of office, I omitted one most important name - that of our Assistant Grand Master, RW.Bro. Mildred Rhoda Low. I did not include her name, not because her contribution has been less important or that I have appreciated it less, but because I feel her greatest work for Freemasonry lies in the future rather than in the past. After May of this year she will be free to devote her time to the Order, and I know that she can and will bring to it great powers of administration, a great belief in Freemasonry, great love of its spiritual and symbolic side, beautiful ritual working and an always welcome presence at our family gatherings.

I have now much pleasure in nominating Right Worshipful Brother Mildred Rhoda Low, Assistant Grand Master, as Grand Master of The Order of Women Freemasons for the year 1964-65. And I would like to offer it to her, both as a promise from every Brother, both present and absent, and as the vocation to which she is called in the words that our late Grand Chaplain used to me in this Temple, on a similar occasion: 'And we will cut wood out of Lebanon as much as thou shalt need, and bring it to thee ... and *thou* shalt carry it up to Jerusalem' ."

R.W.Bro. Low had been Assistant Grand Master since 1951 but was not known to as many Brethren as one might expect from the years of her service in the Order. Her public avocation as Financial Director of the large commercial and manufacturing firm of Gestetner, with its own factory and world-wide agents and connections, meant that she had not been able to visit as many Lodges as she would have liked to do. "In case it may be thought that Mildred Low is to be recognised as a 'business tycoon', we must emphasise that anyone who has ever walked even half the miles of her firm's factory must be alive with admiration for the obvious welfare of the workers shewn there and her personal concern for their happiness."

Her managers at Gestetner said of her: "[she] had the general care of our thousands of women. There are few people with her strength of character, her administrative ability and her simple humanity. She has always found time for the individual's smallest problem and her colleagues speak for countless friends in wishing her health and happiness in retirement."

R.W.Bro. Mildred Rhoda Low, as Assistant Grand Master.

The nomination was seconded by the Deputy Grand Master. R.W.Bro. Low replied "briefly and feelingly." Having said how honoured she was by the Nomination, she concluded with the words "There is, however, one important thing we should remember, and that is *Except the Lord build the House, their labour is lost that build it.* May He who can make all things out of nothing, guide us in what we do. Show us the right

Lodge Mariners No.161 in May 1963

Lodge Perpendicular No.162 in June 1963

Lodge Blythe Harbour No.163 in June 1963

Lodge Exonian No.164 in September 1963

Lodge Bryn Golau No.165 in September 1963

Lodge Pambili No.166 in October 1963

Lodge Haven No.167 in November 1963

Lodge Masonic Pioneers No.168 in February 1964

Lodge Friendship No.169 in April 1964

Lodge Shalom No.170 in April 1964

154

*Lodge Gothic No.171
in April 1964*

*Lodge Keele Gate
No.172 in May 1964*

*Lodge Fealty No.173
in April 1964*

*Lodge Hospitality
No.174 in May 1964*

*Lodge Clemency
No.175 in May 1964*

*Lodge Composite of
Shrewsbury No.176 in
May 1964*

*Lodge of Truth No.177
in June 1964*

*Lodge St. Cuthbert
No.178 in June 1964*

*Lodge Diligence
No.179 in June 1964*

*Lodge St. Kilda
No.180 in July 1964*

choice to make. And bless and prosper this Order of ours, this work to which we have set our hands and hearts."

At the same meeting, W.Bro. Doris Jones was nominated Grand Treasurer.

June saw the Election meeting, when, R.W.Bro. Low having retired from the Temple, a ballot was taken for her which proved unanimous in her favour. On her return she addressed the Brethren:

"I am most appreciative of the honour which has been conferred on me but I am also deeply conscious of the obligations and responsibilities which are annexed to this supreme office. I am not unaccustomed to shouldering the burdens of a position which involves a considerable amount of trust and responsibility for the well being and contentment of a number of people. Therefore I come to this high office well aware of the magnitude of the task which I am undertaking and the impossibility of being of myself to discharge these duties worthily and with the perfection to which my vision will aspire.

*Each age is a dream that is dying
And one that is coming to birth.*

With the retirement of our Grand Master an epoch in the history of the Order is coming to an end. I believe that in time it will indeed show that it was a golden epoch. A new phase comes to birth in the Albert Hall this October. ... I do ask, my Brethren, that when we come together on that solemn occasion you will be with me silently in the obligation which I shall take, because you as well will be embarking with me on a high and noble venture..."

Chapter Nine

Mildred Rhoda Low and the Diamond Jubilee

Mildred Rhoda Low was initiated into Lodge Equity No.16 on April 5th 1932 and was the Master of that Lodge in 1937/38. She had also been the Master of Lodge Faith and Friendship No.25 in 1948-49 and 1959-61, and the first Master of Lodge Kedron No.75 in 1955-56. She held the office of Grand Treasurer from 1940 to 1948, and had been Assistant Grand Master for thirteen years.

So many overseas Brethren were coming to London to be present at the Enthronement in 1964, that R.W.Bro. Low, who was also the Worshipful Master of Lodge Voyagers No.40, decided to hold a reception where they could all meet. More than a hundred Brethren met in the Peers' Reception Room at the House of Lords to be received by the Grand Master Elect, take refreshment and tour the Lords and the Commons.

An Especial Grand Lodge was convened on 13th September 1964 for the Enthronement of the new Grand Master. Significantly, the event was reported in *The Times*, albeit briefly -

Mildred Rhoda Low receiving guests at the House of Lords reception in 1964.

The Order of Women Freemasons, established in 1908, celebrated the Enthronement of their new Grand Master at the Albert Hall yesterday. Nearly 3,000 members were in attendance and this number included members from all over England, the Channel Islands, Northern Ireland and the Isle of Man, Scotland, Wales, Malta, Ontario and British Columbia, Canada and Rhodesia.

The Enthronement saw two innovations. The first was the presence of a delegation of Women Masons from Finland. Following a procession of all the Craft banners of the Order, grouped by area, the delegation was welcomed by the M.W. The Grand Master, Mary Gordon Muirhead Hope.

After the hymn *Immortal, Invisible, God only wise ...* a presentation was made to the Grand Master. In doing so, her faithful Deputy and friend, R.W.Bro. Dorothy Taylor addressed her with these words:

"M.W. The Grand Master, the day has arrived which you and I have envisaged for some time and now that it is here it hardly seems possible that you are really about to hand over the reins of your high office to your chosen successor.

Sixteen years of high endeavour have passed like a flash and now that the day has come, we perhaps meet it with a sense of shock. I am not going to give a catalogue of the work which has been done in those sixteen years - the new Lodges, the further Chapters, the Allied Degrees, fascinating and wonderful days of endeavour, for here in this great Hall today is the living evidence. But *this*, I must say, for numbers count. When you became our Grand Master in 1948, our membership was well under nine hundred; it is now over six thousand! Towns in England, Scotland, Wales, Northern Ireland, Malta, or the Islands round our coast, and in the far-flung Commonwealth - all have reason to be proud of your pioneering spirit, your driving power and your forward vision.

Swiss Masonic gold watch presented to Mary Gordon Muirhead Hope in 1964 to mark her retirement.

M.W. The Grand Master, I promised to be brief and indeed I must be, for we have much to do. But first I want to hand you this envelope which contains a cheque, which the Brethren ask you to accept as some small token of the deep affection and esteem in which you are held. They ask me to say that it is their urgent desire that you should use this money in any way you think fit. Secondly, Grand Master, your reigning Grand Lodge Officers wish me to present you with this Masonic Gold Watch in the form of a triangle and with many Masonic emblems on it, which we hope will remind you of happy hours spent with them. We hope too that you will accept the small cheque that goes with it and buy something - perhaps some special bulbs for your garden. Thirdly, Grand Master, this Scrap Book, which we hope will please and divert you. Fourthly, the Order asks you to hand over this cheque of £2,500 to the Chairman of the Florence Nightingale Hospital, as a Thank-offering for your reign of sixteen years. And we ask the Hospital to put this money to the Pathological Clinic to be named *The Mary Gordon Muirhead Hope Pathological Clinic*. We wish you all happiness and would remind you that your work for Freemasonry with us is not by any means finished. Blessings on you, now and forever!

The Grand Master replied "R.W. Deputy Grand Master, my Brethren. If I may borrow the words of a great Queen, 'though I am proud to have been called to preside over this Order for sixteen years, yet this I account my chief joy, if I have reigned with your love.' You all know how much I love Freemasonry and will therefore understand what it has meant to me to see our Order expand in numbers and in knowledge during these years.

Now what can I say but 'Thank you', and again thank you, for all the support, help, courage and enthusiasm you have given for the work. This most imaginative book prepared by our Deputy Grand Master with so much labour, will keep green many memories and be a cause of pride, of thankfulness, of laughter and, perhaps, a few tears. The lovely gift from the Grand Lodge Officers will always be my favourite jewel and is most appropriate for one whose life has been ruled by clocks (mainly alarm clocks) for many years! The further gift you have entrusted to me I will try to use as I have used the other generous presentations you made to me on former occasions - for good, to help the distressed, and in both to reflect honour and glory on the Craft."

M.W.Bro. Mary Gordon Muirhead Hope then turned to the Chairman of The Florence Nightingale Hospital, Mr. P.M. Studd, who was accompanied by other representatives of his Board and the Hospital Committee. Since 1955 the Order had donated money to this private hospital in North London - set up "to provide medical and surgical treatment for educated women of limited means" - both for equipment

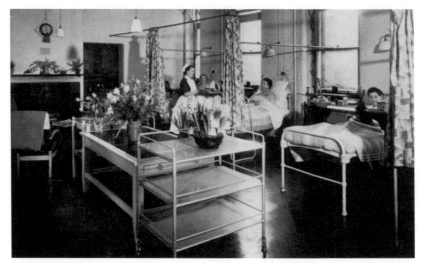

A ward in the Florence Nightingale Hospital for women, supported for many years by the Order of Women Freemasons in sponsoring beds and donating equipment.

Lodge Humility No.181 in October 1964

Lodge Grand Design (I.M.) No.182 in October 1964

Lodge Caredig No.183 in October 1964

Lodge Avenham No.184 in September 1964

Lodge Harbour No.185 in November 1964

and to sponsor a two-bedded ward, named after us. The Grand Master handed the cheque for £2,500 to the Chairman with these words:

"Mr. Chairman, from our inception, we have seen our efforts to open the great door of Freemasonry for women as a Crusade. It seems fitting therefore that it should be the wish of my members to commemorate our work by forging another link between this Order and the hospital which stands for ever in memory of a greater Crusade, one to bring to women an equal share in helping the needs of the world, led by a woman whose name will never be forgotten, Miss Florence Nightingale."

The Chairman of The Florence Nightingale Hospital accepted the cheque towards *The Mary Gordon Muirhead Hope Pathological Clinic* with much pleasure on behalf of the Hospital and thanked the Order for its continuing interest in the Hospital. He and the other representatives of the Hospital then retired, together with all non-Masons. The Grand Master then opened the Especial Grand Lodge.

In the course of the Enthronement ceremony representatives of the Further Degrees advanced and saluted the Most Worshipful The Grand Master as their Supreme Head. The Past Grand Master, M.W.Bro.

Muirhead Hope, said: "Brethren, Companions and Knights of the Orders of Masonic Chivalry, whereas our Most Eminent and Illustrious Brother Mildred Rhoda Low has this day been proclaimed Head of the Further Degrees worked under the auspices of the Order of Women Freemasons, I beseech you therefore as many as are here present to join together in hearty prayer to Almighty God that He will vouchsafe to this our Brother grace to perform aright the duties that appertain to so sacred and grave a trust: for which purpose silence shall be kept for a space."

The new Grand Master pledged herself "to continue unabated the expansion of our Order" and also to maintain our charitable efforts: "This way we can bring honour and credit to our Order, for it is something the outside world can understand and admire..."

Two days after this meeting, the twelve ladies from Finland attended a ceremony at the Grand Temple, after which they presented the Grand Master with a Rough Ashlar - a piece of quartz from the Finnish mountains. In return, M.W.Bro. Mildred Low gave them an antique Grand Master's jewel to take back to the Grand Master of their own Order. Founded in the want and suffering following the War, the Finnish Order had about one hundred and eighty members. The fraternal links with Britain helped them to feel less isolated, and they were avid readers of *The Gavel*.

Ever since *The Gavel* re-started publication in 1929, details of the principal officers of every Lodge and the

Lodge Runnymede No.186 in November 1964

Lodge Invicta No.187 in February 1965

Lodge Carmel No.188 in February 1965

Lodge Gateway No.189 in March 1965

Lodge Cheviot No.190 in April 1965

M.W.Bro. Mildred Rhoda Low.

Lodge Burnley No.191 in May 1965

Lodge of Peace No.192 in May 1965

Lodge Mercia No.193 in May 1965

Lodge Rectitude No. 194 in June 1965

Lodge Coeur de Lion No.195 in June 1965

ceremonies held were included in it. With two hundred Craft Lodges and an increasing number of further Degrees, this clearly had become unwieldy and impracticable. In 1965 it was decided to publish a separate Yearbook, starting the following year, which would give the details of the three principal officers, Secretary and Treasurer of all the Lodges and the other Degrees. The remainder of *The Gavel* would stay as it was.

The Penalties

For some time the Older Obedience had been debating alternative wordings for the penalties in the Obligations of the Craft Degrees. The draconian measures which had been there from time immemorial clearly had little actual meaning in the present day, and had been known to put off potential candidates. Our Board of General Purposes, following the example of the men's Board, had ruled that "it was not a matter which it was competent to judge but it was a matter for Grand Lodge itself to decide." The Grand Master at the Quarterly Communication in May 1965 said that the penalties were ancient and traditional parts of the ceremonies, and a study of the Ritual showed that any alterations to them would cause difficulties in later parts of the Degrees, where further alterations would be needed to make sense of the whole.

R.W.Bro. Clara Cooper, M.B.E., Assistant Grand Master 1962-1968.

She suggested that one way of dealing with the problem would be for the 'Office of Preparation' sometimes read to the Candidate outside the Lodge at Initiation to be brought into regular use by the Private Lodges, and for it to be re-written to include an explanation of the Obligations and the symbolic nature of the penalties associated with them. M.W. The Grand Master asked Grand Lodge if they would agree to the matter being referred to the Grand Master's

Advisory Council *[a group of the most senior Grand Lodge Officers]* to consider the question of the desirability of providing an alternative wording for the penalties and the form it should take, if any, and to report their findings back to Grand Lodge. The Council was also to examine the various forms of the Office of Preparation at present in use and consider a revised form which should contain wording to impress upon Candidates the symbolical nature of the penalties and of what they were about to experience. This motion was carried unanimously. The recommendations of the Grand Master's Advisory Council would be put to Grand Lodge in the following January.

Lodge St. John Prescot No.196 in June 1965

The matter was, in fact, dropped for the time being and not raised again until 1986, when the Older Obedience finally made changes to the wording of the Penalties. The Grand Master assured the Brethren that " ... We will also be making changes, but it cannot be done quickly. The changes will be made as easy as possible and the penalties would be retained in a different part of the Ritual. Brethren were urged to be discreet. A meeting of Grand Inspectors will be held at which they will be briefed to ensure that the changes are implemented properly."

Lodge St. Peter No.197 in July 1965

Lodge Airedale No.198 in September 1965

The first year of office of M.W.Bro. Mildred Low was eventful, as she told Grand Lodge in October 1965:

Lodge Wyndleshora No.199 in September 1965

" ... it had been a very strenuous and difficult one in many respects; the loss of the late Grand Treasurer *[Doris Grace Jones, her great friend]* was a grievous blow to her. However, thanks must be given to God for another year of great progress in that eighteen new Craft Lodges had been consecrated, and the total would soon be two hundred and five, with more to come. She hope to devote time and consideration to the administration and expansion of the Higher Degrees, being as anxious as her predecessor that the Order should cover as wide a field as possible, and that its growth should be both upwards and onwards."

Lodge Torbay No.200 in October 1965

The Grand Master had recently appointed several senior members of the Order to act as her Representatives for groups of provincial Lodges. With so many Lodges now, it was clearly impossible for her to supervise them all personally, and we were not able financially or in terms of numbers to support a system of Provincial Grand Lodges.

"The M.W. The Grand Master then outlined the position and duties of the Grand Inspectors whom she had appointed, and who would be her permanent representative in the Lodges in their respective groups. Through them she hoped to be able to keep in personal touch with all the Lodges; their duties would be those of friend, counsellor, adviser and guide. By visiting and being in constant touch with their Lodges they would have the advantage of a first-hand appreciation of local matters and difficulties, which would be of inestimable assistance when decisions had to be taken at headquarters. A letter would shortly be sent to the Lodges within the groups making the position of the Inspectors quite clear. She thought that this new departure would add to the strength the unity of the Order."

Lodge St. Gwynllyw No.201 in September 1965

Lodge Queensway No.202 in November 1965

Lodge Croeso No.203 in November 1965

Headquarters

In the time of Mary Gordon Muirhead Hope the expansion of the Order meant that the limited space at Headquarters was becoming a serious problem, and at one stage the demolition and reconstruction of the building was even considered. How much more desperate then had the problem become with the tremendous expansion taking place under Mildred Low? Rather than demolition or relocating elsewhere, plans were drawn up to extend the present building.

The plans submitted to the Local Authority consisted of a single storey extension behind the platform at the east of the Temple to act as a storeroom for equipment; a room to be built on to one side of the Crush Hall which could be used for council meetings and with sliding doors which could be pushed back to enlarge both the Temple seating area

Lodge St. Clare No.204 in January 1966

Lodge Tudor Rose No.205 in February 1966

Lodge St. Lawrence (I.M.) No.206 in April 1966

*Headquarters at
27 Pembridge Gardens, Notting Hill Gate.*

and the Crush Hall (this room is the present-day Committee Room); on the other side of the Crush Hall a Tyler's and Candidate's Room and three toilets and washbasins. The attic floor would be extended out to the front facade and a lift was to be installed on the outside of the building from basement to attics. The existing coke boilers were to be replaced with gas central heating throughout the building, and finally the Temple was to be redecorated and its heating and ventilation attended to. The works were to be completed in time for the Diamond Jubilee celebrations in 1968.

These additions and improvements would cost at least £25,000 so the problem arose of how to finance it, since it would be wrong to use up all available funds. The Grand Master particularly wanted to make the raising of the money part of the effort to celebrate the Diamond Jubilee in 1968. "The Order was now getting known and must have a dignified face to show the world. When the proposed improvements had been completed, she felt the Order would have a headquarters of which it could be proud."

It had been approved by the Board of General Purposes that a commemorative jewel should be issued for the Diamond Jubilee. At a cost price of one and a half guineas (£1.575) and a sale price of three and a half guineas (£3.725), if only half the members of the Order bought it, this would raise £6,000 towards the building work. Another suggestion was that each Lodge should raise a sum of £200 over the next two and a half years for the Diamond Jubilee Building Fund and if achieved, they would be awarded a ten-pointed star to fix to their Lodge banner for all time.

At the same meeting, members of Grand Lodge were advised that a member of Lodge Pentagram No.103, Bro. Edna Vincent, who was partially-sighted, had written a Ritual in Braille which she had presented to the Order for use by others in her circumstances.

Lodge Carreg Harlech No.207 in May 1966

Lodge Horizon No.208 in June 1966

Lodge Kingdom of Fife No.209 in September 1966

Lodge Cabot Tower No.210 in October 1966

Lodge Emerald No.211 in October 1966

Lodge Sussex Martlets No.212 in December 1966

Lodge Allegiance No.213 in December 1966

The Diamond Jubilee Commemorative jewel.

Provincial Matters

Lodge Bedale No.214 in April 1967

In April 1966 a Masonic Service was conducted for the Northern Brethren at York Minster, with which the Order had many links. The Grand Master read the First Lesson. In his Address the Canon of the Minster summed up perfectly the essence of Freemasonry for women - in speaking of builders and building, he said "Freemasons, with the chisel, the square, the trowel, display the traditional signs of an ancient craft. But apart from the ceremonial, the concept of building - the creation of something that is true and solid and beautiful and enduring - that surely is precisely what your Order is for." He then suggested a text for us from the *Book of Proverbs*, Chapter 14 - "Every wise woman buildeth her house."

Lodge Faversham Abbey No.215 in April 1967

Lodge Cefnllys No.216 in July 1967

In the same month M.W.Bro. Low made her first visit to Canada in her capacity of Grand Master. She and the Grand Officers accompanying her attended the Installation meeting of Lodge Victoria No.124, and, on the other side of the continent, exalted fifteen Companions prior to the consecration of Golden Triangle Chapter No.24 in Toronto.

Lodge Aspiration No.217 in August 1967

A development during 1966 was the dedication of four Temples for our Lodges in Sunderland, Leigh-on-Sea in Essex, Aberdeen and Doncaster. That in Essex was the first Temple to be designed and built for this actual purpose by provincial members; the other buildings had been adapted to our needs. *(See Appendix IV)*.

Lodge Endurance No.218 in August 1967

Lodge Connaught No.219 in November 1967

In October 1966 the first Lodge in the Irish Republic was consecrated - Lodge Emerald No.211 in Dublin. The design of their banner incorporated part of the Old House of Parliament in Dublin, with the flax flower representing Irish linen and the candlestick *Nir Tamid* denoting everlasting light. The two tablets with Hebrew letters represent the Ten Commandments. Unfortunately this Lodge did not survive the troubles which blighted Ireland over the following decades.

Lodge Sarum No.220 in December 1967

The Banner of Lodge Emerald No.211 in Dublin.

Grand Lodge in October 1967 was divided into two sessions - the Enthronement on 7th and the business part of the meeting on 14th. This was to give as many Brethren as possible the opportunity to see the newly decorated Grand Temple in London.

Lodge Whytchurche No.221 in December 1967

Diamond Jubilee Year

In the week before the Albert Hall celebrations in 1968, the Temple at Headquarters was re-dedicated by the Grand Master, according to ancient custom. As *The Gavel* described it "In the months of stripping down the old decor and some re-building the undoubtedly numinous atmosphere which had accrued over the last nearly forty years quite naturally disappeared and some of the elder Brethren, in particular, although ready to adjust to the new lightness of colour, felt that the atmosphere to which they had grown accustomed had vanished altogether."

Lodge Hala No.222 in December 1967

Lodge Cashio No.223 in January 1968

Some of our brethren from Canada and Australia were among those present. The Order Banner was carried into the Temple, followed by Reigning Masters who carried the Working Tools and the Consecration Elements. After the entry of The M.W. The Grand Master and the

Lodge of Grace No.224 in February 1968

The Grand Temple, with the dark wooden panelling of 1925 removed.

Lodge Diamond Jubilee No.225 in April 1968

Lodge Algum Tree No.226 in March 1968

Lodge St. Mildred No.227 in March 1968

Grand Lodge Officers and her assumption of the Chair, all joined in the opening hymn, *Eternal Wisdom whose decree / Made light dawn and darkness flee.*

Lodge Quantocks No.228 in April 1968

There followed an Address by The M.W. The Grand Master, an Anthem, the Dedication Prayer and the Invocation. The contents of the glass vessel were stated by the Grand Secretary and lowered into the cavity. The Memorial Stone was then tried by the Junior Grand Warden, proved by the Senior Grand Warden and tested by M.W. The Grand Master. The Stone was then lowered into the Cavity by the Wardens during the reading:

Lodge Pen Dinas No.229 in May 1968

"Except the Lord build the house; their labour is but lost that build it. Except the Lord keep the City; the watchman waketh but in vain." "Let the beauty of the Lord our God be upon us; and establish Thou now the work of our hands: Yea, the work of our hands establish Thou it".

Lodge Brawdgarwch (I.M.) No.230 in June 1968

Lodge St. Dorothea No.231 in June 1968

Then Corn - the Sacred Emblem of Plenty - was presented to the M.W. The Grand Master who strewed it upon the Stone, followed by the presentation of Wine - the Sacred Emblem of Truth - and this was poured on the Stone. Then Oil - the Sacred Emblem of Charity - was presented and sprinkled on the Stone, and then Charcoal - the sacred emblem of Fervency and Zeal. The Cover was then placed upon the stone. Corn, Wine, Oil and Charcoal are ancient symbols not to be thought of as pagan, but as representing four of the ancient blessings for Man. The Grand Master was presented with Salt, which was scattered on the Lodge floor.

Lodge Alliance (I.M.) No.232 in July 1968

Lodge Dormer Light No.233 in August 1968

The Grand Director of Ceremonies censed the Lodge Room three times in silence. This was followed by a solemn dedication, the hymn *Now thank we all our God*, and a Blessing.

The Royal Albert Hall Meeting

Lodge St. Barnabas No.234 in August 1968

Tickets for the Diamond Jubilee celebration at the Royal Albert Hall were set at £2. It was hoped to hold Thanksgiving Services around the country as close as possible to 20th June, the date of our founding in

1908. These services would be open to non-Masons, and possibly have a standard format. That in London was at St. Paul's Cathedral on 15th June 1968. There were Thanksgiving Services held in eleven cathedrals and eight churches throughout the world.

The great celebration meeting at the Albert Hall on 5th October 1968 was in two parts: the Enthronement of the Grand Master, then a break for tea, followed by a pageant illustrating our history. There were 3,600 Brethren present including ninety five reigning Grand Lodge Officers, the stock of programmes ran out and they had to be reprinted later.

Lodge Hestenga No.235 in September 1968

The ceremony started with a procession of all Past Grand Officers across the arena from east to west. Then came the reigning Grand Lodge, followed by the Volume of the Sacred Law carried by an Entered Apprentice and the Square and Compasses carried by a Fellowcraft. After the hymn *Praise my soul, the King of Heaven* the Deputy Grand Master opened Grand Lodge in due form. Two Senior Deacons escorted the Proposer and Seconder of the Nomination, and those of the Election, followed by the M.W. The Grand Master. The procession halted for the anthem *I bind unto myself today*, and the Grand Master was presented to the Deputy Grand Master and installed.

Lodge Glaslyn No.236 in September 1968

Lodge Jasper No.237 in October 1968

Lodge Vinovium No.238 in November 1968

The Diamond Jubilee meeting at the Royal Albert Hall.

Lodge Revelation (I.M.) No.239 in December 1968

Lodge Oxford Temple No.240 in December 1968

After the appointment and investiture of Grand Lodge Officers and the conferment of Honours, the Grand Master presented R.W.Bro. Dorothy Taylor with the breast jewel of her office - wrought in gold with a diamond to acknowledge the Jubilee - to commemorate her twenty years of service as Deputy to two Grand Masters. As the Grand Master said:

"Throughout this time you have worked closely with - and loyally supported - two Grand Masters possessing widely different ideas and temperaments. Only your great love of and whole-hearted devotion to Freemasonry could have made this possible for you ... It is a rare combination of qualities that has enabled you to fill your high office for so many years without feeling any resentment at being so near to and yet remaining beside the Throne. Therefore your great contribution to the welfare and prosperity of the Order has been unspoilt by the jealousy and envy which would have troubled a more petty and conceited nature...".

In the course of her address, the Grand Master reflected on what had been achieved in the past and the hopes for the future: "We have been united in our determination to leave behind us tangible evidence of our love of Freemasonry and of our pride and joy that our Order has reached its Diamond Jubilee; also with a humble desire that we may leave to those who come after us inspiration, hope and encouragement, thus emulating the example of our early Brethren." She echoed the writer of the early *Blue Book* in 1938: " ... the work will go on and on, in wider circles and in a larger measure of influence. We trust that we shall not have lived and laboured in vain".

She also spoke of what had been achieved as a result of our charitable donations, both within and without the Order, and what could still be done. Although we had a retirement home at Worthing, and would shortly have another in the north, neither of these were suitable or able to give nursing care. To obtain and equip such a haven would need a lot of money and the cost of upkeep would be considerable. In the Adelaide Litten Trust Fund there was a sum of £500 which had been given in memory of Doris Grace Jones, a close friend of the Grand Master and the late Grand Treasurer, who had long wanted the establishment of such a nursing home. This cause was to be the next charity of the Order.

Lodge Prescelli No.241 in February 1969

Lodge True Light No.242 in March 1969

Lodge Semper Fidelis No.243 in April 1969

Lodge Ribble Valley No.244 in May 1969

Lodge Perfect Ashlar (I.M.) No.245 in July 1969

The Brethren sang the hymn *Immortal, invisible, God only wise* and the Especial Grand Lodge was closed in ample form. At this point, all the Brethren were asked to turn towards the west so that a series of photographs could be taken. The Grand Master and Grand Lodge Officers then retired in procession.

A welcome interval of forty five minutes gave the opportunity for a cup of tea and a 'comfort break'. Part Two of the proceedings opened with the hymn *Praise to the Lord, the Almighty, the King of Creation*. The Grand Master then presented to the Chairman and Representatives of the Florence Nightingale Hospital a plaque to be placed in the Nurses' Dining Room, the modernisation of which was the Order's gift to the Hospital to commemorate the Diamond Jubilee. After a further hymn, *All creatures of our God and King,* the Welsh Choir sang three pieces.

The Pageant of the Banners followed. Each Lodge was represented in numerical order from No.1 to No.236 by its reigning Master (presented where possible by the first Worshipful Master), preceding her Lodge banner. The Welsh Choir then sang some music composed by Masons - two extracts from *The Little Masonic Cantata* by Mozart and two from *Masonic Ritual Music* by Sibelius.

The Pageant of the Banners at the Diamond Jubilee celebration in 1968.

The next item was an historical pageant *Sixty Glorious Years*. This was illustrated by slides projected onto a huge screen and enhanced by a floorshow of changing fashions and appropriate regalias. The commentary was written by (the then) V.W.Bro. Doris Smyth and read by her, R.W.Bro. E.V. Smith and W.Bro. Marjorie Howard, the Deputy Grand Master's sister. The pageant traced our history from the beginnings in 1908 through the vicissitudes of sixty years and placed it in the context of events in this country and social change, particularly with respect to the position of women.

Lodge Simplicity No.246 in July 1969

The afternoon closed with the hymn *Now thank we all our God*, followed by the National Anthem. A book was published, which included the commentary to the pageant and the text of the various addresses made at the Thanksgiving Services round the country, with pictures of some of the gifts presented to cathedrals and churches by the Order.

Lodge Resolution No.247 in August 1969

There were many instances of donations by both the Order as a whole and by individual Lodges to churches and cathedrals. One of the most notable examples of this is York Minster. English Freemasonry has always been linked with the Operative Masons of York and our Order felt a particular affinity with the building as it housed a special memorial to the Women's Services of the Great War of 1914-18. A new set of Eucharistic vestments was presented in 1956 as a thank-offering by York Lodge No.86, followed by funds to make up vestments from rare Chinese silk.

Lodge Montpellier No.248 in September 1969

Lodge Minerva No.249 in September 1969

In the year of the Golden Jubilee 1958, the Chivalric Degrees of the Order paid for the cost of gilding most of the York Choir stalls which had been replaced in the 19th century. The most striking monument is, however, the tiny Paternoster Chapel. Set in the main body of the Minster near the west entrance doors, this Guild Chapel was put there originally so that medieval workmen on their way to work could look in and say a quick *Our Father ...* , hence the name.

Lodge Brig O'Doon No.250 in September 1969

The chapel was in a serious state of disrepair in the 1950s, having been dismantled during major renovation work in the Minster. With the Order's funding, an architect was asked to design wrought-iron railings to enclose the north and south sides of the chapel and to form a canopy over the altar. The iron work, painted blue and gold, incorporated medallions bearing the Three Pillars of the Order, the Square and Compasses and the Six Pointed Star with the All-Seeing Eye. The side rails also had the maple leaf of Canada and the flame flower of Rhodesia in acknowledgement of contributions from the Lodges in Toronto and Zimbabwe. Members of the Order also gave the six Regency chairs which fill the tiny Chapel.

The Paternoster Chapel in York Minster.

An application had been made by some members of the Honourable Fraternity of Ancient Freemasons to attend the Diamond Jubilee meeting. This was refused by the Grand Master, because it was felt that their presence at the meeting would not alter their allegiance to the other Order. There had most probably been clandestine visits by our own members to Lodges of the H.F.A.F., as at Grand Lodge in 1969 it was clearly stated that such visits were not permitted.

Grand Lodge Matters

Since 1935, during the tenure of Grand Master Adelaide Litten, it had been the tradition in the Order for the Grand Master, if living, to nominate her successor, and for the transfer of power to be uncontested. This was the accepted practice but was not explicitly stated in the Book of Constitutions. However, as occasionally happens in all organisations, sometimes dissenting voices are heard.

One such instance occurred at the beginning of the 1970s, when a Past Senior Grand Warden became involved in a dispute with the Board of General Purposes, concerning the funeral and memorial fund of a late friend of hers. The R.W.Brother concerned - a Freemason for some

172

Lodge Durnovaria No. 251 in October 1969

Lodge St. Martin (I.M.) No.252 in October 1969

Lodge St. Mary's Priory No.253 in November 1969

Lodge Ner Tamid No. 254 in November 1969

Lodge White Cliff No.255 in December 1969

Lodge Anwyl No.256 in December 1970

fifty two years, having served under six Grand Masters - contravened the Book of Constitutions and Standing Orders by circulating various accusatory and personal letters both to members of the Board and directly to members of Grand Lodge. These letters included a suggestion that a secret ballot should be taken at Grand Lodge to nominate the Grand Master for the following year, contrary to tradition. The dispute escalated and an Appeal was dismissed. The R.W.Brother's transgression and the fact that she refused to meet the Board of General Purposes to put her case in person led in time to her suspension for three years by vote of Grand Lodge, and, because she broke the terms of the suspension by writing yet more letters to members of Grand Lodge, to her eventual expulsion from the Order.

At the same meeting of Grand Lodge in March 1970 - which was the Nomination Meeting of the Grand Master - M.W.Bro. Mary Gordon Muirhead Hope, Past Grand Master, uncharacteristically also tried to deviate from the traditions of the Order in nominating an alternative candidate and moving that the election in June should be by poll. This move was strange, as she herself had nominated M.W.Bro. Mildred Low as her successor and commended her in glowing terms, promising her support. The proposal was deemed procedurally out of order, as no prior notice had been given, and also because outside agencies had been consulted. The nomination of M.W.Bro. Low as Grand Master for the ensuing year was duly proposed and seconded and a Vote of Confidence in her passed.

R.W.Bro. E.V. Smith, P.G.W., Grand Chaplain

In order that such divisive efforts should not disrupt the harmony of the Order in the future, it was felt that it would be advisable to officially spell out in the Book of Constitutions the procedure for the Nomination and Election of the Grand Master. The Board of General Purposes recommended to Grand Lodge that several additions should be incorporated in the Constitutions to regularise the tradition that the election of the Grand Master was not contested, and that "It is the right and the privilege of the reigning Grand Master to nominate and install her successor".

Some words from the Grand Master's Address to Grand Lodge in October 1969, in the midst of this period of the Order's history, sum up the feelings of any true Mason:
"…there is one great lesson which we have to learn in Freemasonry and should always remember. The spirit of Freemasonry is greater than any one individual and greater than any one set of individuals. It is concerned with the verities, the eternal truths and values…"
Her speeches regularly had a theme of reverting to the basics of Freemasonry, of watching our behaviour and controlling our tongues.

R.W.Bro. E.V. Smith resigned the Editorship of *The Gavel*, as she had been told that the content of the Order's journal was in future to be under the supervision of the Grand Master's Advisory Council. She was not prepared to work under this restriction. The Grand Master announced the appointment of R.W.Bro. A. Johnstone Heath, P.J.G.W., G.M's.G.S. as Editor and V.W.Bro. E. Chaplin, Grand Treasurer G.M's.G.S. as Assistant Editor.

The expansion of the Order accelerated under Grand Master Mildred Low - in the first six years of her reign an average of thirteen new Craft Lodges per year were consecrated, the total being up to No.260 by 1970.

Lodge of the Morning Star No.257 in February 1970

Lodge Salopia No.258 in March 1970

Lodge Bycullah No.259 in June 1970

Lodge Southern Cross No.260 in August 1970

M.W.Bro. Low (front, second from right) with senior Grand Lodge Officers, residents and staff at the opening of Northolme.

Lodge Halcyon No.261 in October 1970

A Home in the North

In 1971 our new Home in the north was opened by the Grand Master at Lytham St. Annes in Lancashire. Called *Northolme*, it was our second home for elderly Brethren who were still

Lodge Ramsey No.262 in November 1970

reasonably mobile and able to look after their own personal needs. Like *Porchway House* at Worthing on the south coast, the home is owned by the Adelaide Litten Trust Fund.

Under the chairmanship of R.W.Bro. Cooper a committee had been formed to consider the 'Home in the North' and the first meeting was held on Friday, 9th January 1970 at the Friends Meeting House, Mount Street, Manchester. Originally it was anticipated the Home in the North would be at Southport, but a beautiful house in Lytham was brought to the notice of the Committee. This house is situated just off the Promenade, with the frontage overlooking Lowther Gardens, in one of the best residential districts and only a short walk from the shops and the picturesque Square in the centre of Lytham.

To enable the Committee to obtain possession it was necessary for the deposit to be paid immediately and to meet the emergency a Worshipful Brother advanced the requisite amount. The acquisition of this house by the Adelaide Litten Trust Fund was a wise decision and has proved a valuable investment. A local House Management

Northolme, *the Order's residential home at Lytham St. Annes.*

Committee was appointed by Grand Lodge under the Chairmanship of R.W.Bro. M.H.P. Sowerby, P.A.G.M., G.M's.G.S. Through her guidance, knowledge and understanding of the work, the Chairman with the assistance of her experienced and keenly interested Committee administered and cared for the Residents and created and established a home in the truest sense of the word.

Lodge Vale Royal No.263 in February 1971

Home and Abroad

Lodge Foreland Light No.264 in March 1971

The consecration took place at Headquarters in May 1971 of Lodge Palm Tree No.267 working at Lagos, Nigeria. Lodge Verity No.7 initiated, passed and raised candidates to work this Lodge. The first Master was W.Bro. T.A. Manuwa, a charismatic tribal chief who for some time had travelled from Nigeria to England to attend meetings of Lodge Tradition of Wigan No.109. The banner of the Lodge - bearing a palm tree - was dedicated by the Grand Master at the same meeting, and in return the Worshipful Master presented the Grand Master with a miniature palm tree emblem to attach to the banner of the Order.

Lodge Gwynedd (I.M.) No.265 in March 1971

Lodge Parvis No.266 in May 1971

The Lodge had problems from the beginning, in that there was no nucleus of experienced Masons in the Lodge, nor anyone in Nigeria to give advice. Distance prevented helpful and constructive supervision. During the period of military rule from 1977 to 1981 it was impossible for the Lodge to meet, and although the Nigerian Brethren tried to revive it in 1981 and very much wanted to continue, M.W.Bro. Frances Hall bowed to the inevitable and suspended their Charter at the end of 1981.

Lodge Palm Tree No. 267 in May 1971

Lodge Cornucopia No.268 in July 1971

In 1972 a purpose-built Temple was finished at Bulawayo in Southern Rhodesia (now Zimbabwe), after eight and a half years of saving and

hard work. Twenty one Brethren from Lodge Zimbabwe at Salisbury (now Harare) made the six hundred mile round trip to be at the first ceremony, a double Initiation. The Grand Master wrote a special prayer to be read before the opening of the Degree. The floor of the

Lodge Fernham No.269 in October 1971

Temple was made of inlaid blocks of white Rhodesian teak and black *panga-panga*, representing the black and white chequers of the Masonic carpet. In the east the dais was carpeted in royal blue, above which was a large stained glass window depicting the Square and Compasses.

Lodge St. Andrew's (I.M.) No.270 in October 1971

Lodge Berkshire Downs No.272 in December 1971

Lodge Kerenza No.273 in December 1971

In September of the same year, a Temple was inaugurated in Salisbury. Lodge Zimbabwe and Lodge St. Kilda both took part in the Opening Ceremony, when the keys of the building were presented to the two Worshipful Masters, who then gave them over to the Tylers of the two Lodges.

Interior of the Temple at Bulawayo.

In October, the Grand Master and other senior Officers attended the dedication of an ecumenical chapel at the Royal Marsden Hospital in Surrey for the benefit of the patients, their families and friends and the hospital staff. The Order had given £1,500 towards the building of this chapel as part of the Diamond Jubilee donations. The Bible was given by Lodge Courageous No.30 at Croydon.

Lodge St. Helena No.274 in April 1972

Lodge St. Chad No.275 in April 1972

In March 1973 the 100th new Lodge of her reign was consecrated by M.W.Bro. Mildred Rhoda Low. It was called Lodge Emarell Centum No.281, so-named from the initials of the Grand Master - Em (M) - ar (R) - ell (L) and the word Centum (100). The Installation which followed was conducted by R.W.Bro. Isabelle Mullen, A.G.M. who installed her daughter, W.Bro. Elizabeth Rutherford, A.G.D.C. in the Chair of King Solomon.

Lodge Westgate (I.M.) No.276 in April 1972

Lodge West Riding (I.M.) No.277 in May 1972

The Doris Jones Fund was approaching £60,000 and the Grand Master informed Grand Lodge that it was hoped to secure the freehold of a small private nursing home which could be converted to our use. The choice of location was a problem. Many people strongly advised against London because the high costs of property, staff and maintenance meant that we should never recoup our money. The suburbs of London or the south were possibilities, so long as the home was easily accessible and within reach of public transport for relatives and visitors.

Further afield, Lodge No.132 - St. Michael and St. George in Malta, consecrated in 1961 - had experienced great difficulties. In early 1972 the British forces withdrew from the island, and as most of the members of the Lodge were from service families, this left only three Brethren, the most senior being the Junior Warden and one of the others only a Fellow Craft. In April 1973 R.W.Bro. Helen Buchmann, S.G.W., care of Malta, visited the island with two other Officers to work the first ceremony since November 1971. Even then it meant taking more than one office each. The Fellow Craft was raised to the Third Degree and three Joining Members balloted for.

The Grand Master was unable to attend the Grand Lodge of October 1973 because of illness. In her Address, read by the Deputy Grand Master, R.W.Bro. Winifred Prior, she mentioned the subject of the Doris Jones Memorial Home:

R.W.Bro. Isabelle Mullen, Deputy Grand Master 1973-1975, G.M's.G.S., care of Northern Counties and Overseas.

"We have yet to realise our biggest venture yet - the Doris Jones Memorial Home for our elderly, incapacitated brethren. We have been working for this since the Albert Hall meeting in October 1968. ... the majority of the Brethren have worked and are working quite wonderfully for the Doris Jones Home, and at the end of September 1973 we now have the magnificent total of £67,709. We are concentrating on buying a private nursing home or Rest Home."

At the January 1974 meeting of Grand Lodge in London, Depute Area Grand Officers were appointed, and were invested by the Grand Master in March. This innovation followed amendments to the Book of Constitutions in October 1973, allowing the Grand Master to appoint Depute Area Grand Officers to assist Grand Inspectors in their respective areas. The number varied according to the size of the Area,

Lodge Tavistock Abbey No.278 in October 1972

Lodge Loyal Cheshire No.279 in November 1972

Lodge Vale of Meon No.280 in December 1972

Lodge Emarell Centum No.281 in March 1973

Lodge Beacon (I.M.) No.282 in April 1973

Lodge Alphege No.283 in April 1973

Lodge Bethania No.284 in May 1973

Lodge Stamford No. 285 in August 1973

Lodge Mazel No.286 in August 1973

but usually included a Depute Grand Inspector, Depute Senior and Junior Grand Deacons, Grand Sword Bearer and/or Grand Standard Bearer. All these ranks had their own regalia. These offices, however, were only filled for a short time - the practice of appointing Depute Area Grand Officers ceased after 1977.

Lodge Temple No.287 in April 1974

Lodge Lucem No.288 in April 1974

Lodge Yeo Valley No.289 in April 1974

M.W.Bro. Low was well enough to attend Grand Lodge in March 1974, when she was nominated Grand Master for the following Masonic Year. Her Proposer commented "Our Grand Master in her unstinting efforts on behalf of our Order has subjected herself to such severe pressure on her personal health and well-being as to give some concern to her immediate associates. We are all delighted to see her here today and to learn that her health has been fully restored". In thanking the Brethren for her Nomination, the Grand Master said she would do her best but unfortunately could not promise to travel much as her doctor would not allow it. If the Brethren found she was beginning to weaken or falter they must not re-elect her because they feel they must; the Order must always come first.

R.W.Bro. Winifred Prior, Deputy Grand Master 1973-1976, G.M's.G.S.

Rhodesia

In May 1974 Deputy Grand Master Mullen and other Officers visited Rhodesia again, journeying to both Salisbury and Bulawayo. They consecrated Craft Lodges and a Chapter. The Aleph Cryptic Council held two Chapter ceremonies to exalt eighteen candidates. The three Principals for each Chapter were then given the secrets of their offices, and Acropolis Chapter No.34 (No.1 Rhodesia) was consecrated. Lodge Sandawana No.290 in the Craft was consecrated in Salisbury, and then St. Christopher No.291 in Umtali.

The Temple at Salisbury was dedicated on 6th May by R.W.Bro. Mullen, assisted by R.W.Bro. D. Hoadley and others. Some of the newly elected Depute Area Grand Officers were also in attendance in their new dark blue and gold regalia. As an eye-witness, V.W.Bro. Marjorie Fern-Ellis, Depute Area Grand Director of Ceremonies, related:

Lodge Sandawana No.290 in May 1974

"The crowning moment of the ceremony was witnessed when the Deputy Grand Master unveiled the Plaque and at the solemn act of dedication the voices of the Brethren rose in a magnificent crescendo 'Glory be to God on high'. What a moment of gratitude - the unison of the work of our hands and our hearts, before the face of the G.A.O.T.U., was now accomplished and dedicated to His name.

Lodge St. Christopher No.291 in May 1974

This wonderful Ceremony was shortly to be followed on the Saturday by the second step in our Expansion - the Consecration of the second Lodge in Bulawayo - Lodge Letaba (the African word for 'Happiness'). The brilliant Rhodesian sun shone through the stained glass window in the East casting beautiful rainbow patterns of colours on the gowns of the Brethren. Again, as at the Dedication of the Temple, greetings were given on behalf of M.W. The Grand Master from many Lodges in all parts of the world - the Masonic Chain binding us with our many Brethren who were rejoicing with us in our happiness.

Lodge Letaba No.292 in May 1974

And finally, on the following Wednesday, our third Ceremony - the Masonic 'Three' was to be completed to climax a wonderful and inspiring week - the Consecration of our Royal Arch Chapter - 'Radiant Light' - a name so aptly chosen for us by M.W. The Grand Master. There was a feeling of mingled pride and humility as we saw our Chapter set out for the first time - the Blue and Gold replaced by glowing Crimson and Gold and the deep warm colours of the Gowns and Sashes. Apart from only two Companions (Comps. Fern-Ellis and Isaacs, whose cherished dream the establishment of this Chapter had been for so many years) the remaining seventeen had only been exalted the previous week by Most Ex. Comp. Mullen.

As the Principals entered, these seventeen Companions were witnessing for the first time the Opening of a Chapter. The pattern of Consecration unfolded again carried out by Most Ex. Comp. Mullen with such sincerity and feeling. Corn, Wine, Oil and Salt were scattered on the Chapter floor and finally the Chapter was constituted

The Lodge Room as it was in 1974 in the Temple at Salisbury,
Southern Rhodesia - now Harare, Zimbabwe.

Lodge Chorley No.293
in June 1974

Lodge Saxon Gate
No.294 in November
1974

in ancient form. Ever-to-be-remembered moments by the first three Principals, Comp. Fern-Ellis, Comp. Donsky and Comp. Tindle as they were Installed in their respective Chairs by Most Ex. Comp. Mullen, Ex. Comp. Hoadley and Ex. Comp. Richley Rutherford. The seventeen Companions, so newly exalted into R.A. Masonry, were all placed in Office, feeling very nervous, but all were inspired to great confidence by the encouraging and reassuring words of Most Ex. Comp. Mullen, Second Grand Principal, when she gave them her blessing".

The report in *The Gavel* ends with the words - now ironic in view of the changed circumstances in Africa: "… we must continue to build and work for the further expansion and establishment of our Order [and] with the help of the G.A.O.T.U.must prove that we will ultimately 'reflect honour on their choice' ". And some words which still endure "… It is a gratifying and comforting thought, that, in spite of the turmoils of the world around us, we are able to join with our Brethren all over the world and that at this time of our great joy so many remembered us and joined with us in thought and prayer".

A simple announcement within a black border appeared in *The Gavel* of November 1974:

"It was the especial wish of the late Past Grand Master, Most Worshipful Brother Mary Gordon Muirhead Hope, that no tributes or obituaries should be printed in *The Gavel*. Hence we have obeyed her last request".

She died on 24th July 1974, aged 80. A Requiem Eucharist was held at the Grosvenor Chapel in London on 11th September. Readings were given from the *Book of Wisdom:* "But the souls of the righteous are in the hands of God ... " and *St. John's Gospel:* "I am the resurrection and the life ... " and the Anthem during the Distribution of Holy Communion was Henry Purcell's *A Funeral Anthem* "Man that is born of a woman hath but a short time to live ... ".

An Order of Service was drawn up for use in all Temples of the Order of Women Freemasons on 5th October, which included the hymn *Dear Lord and Father of Mankind,* the 23rd Psalm and a prayer which began:

"Almighty and Merciful Father of Mankind, Great Architect and Ruler of all Worlds, we Thy humble Servants give thanks for the Sixteen Years of devotion and toil which our dear departed Brother Mary Gordon Muirhead Hope gave so unstintingly to our Order of Women Freemasons. We give thanks to Thee that Thou didst crown her work with success and progress and that Thou didst endue her with the knowledge to comprehend and to expand it and inspire others to enrol under the Order's Banner and thus to spread the benign influence of Freemasonry among Women, here and overseas, to Thy Greater honour and Glory."

The Grand Master's Address to Grand Lodge in October 1975 was still on the same theme of avoiding disagreements during "a very difficult and worrying time" of strikes and economic and industrial unrest during the late 70s:

"Let us look at the foundations of Freemasonry - Brotherly Love, Relief and Truth. Relief and Truth - these are the basic principles of Freemasonry coupled with the qualifications of its Initiates, namely: mature age, sound judgment and strict morals. Working upon these as a foundation and keeping the three tools of our trade, which are the square, the level and the plumb rule, ever in our hands, we are enabled to meet and overcome the vicissitudes of life with honour and fortitude whenever they occur. The Lodge room should be a haven of peace and serenity and every Brother should endeavour to keep all arguments and differences of opinion from marring the pleasant and agreeable atmosphere which should always prevail in it.

In the trying days ahead we must band together to keep the flag of Freemasonry flying high and to see that no-one or nothing shall weaken our endeavours to go forward with high hopes and a determination to win through whatever mishaps may befall us, or any eventuality we may have to face. Never before in peacetime have Freemasons been given the chance to show what they have learned in this wonderful Order and to be able to apply that knowledge to help all mankind.

Now, Worshipful Brethren, you are left with the task of re-organising and getting together in your Lodges to give effect to the various suggestions with the aim of strengthening our Order and achieving economies wherever possible. Broadly, these economies come under the following headings:

    - Economy in postage and printing - Wherever possible to send agendas and notices for different meetings in one envelope; also to distribute mail by hand wherever possible.

    - Economy in refreshments for the festive board - No dinners or formal refreshments, but each Lodge to make its refreshments - such as home-made sandwiches, pastries and cakes, and each Lodge should form a Catering Committee. Members of the Lodge should contribute so much each towards the Catering Fund.

    - Economy and assistance in travel - The Lodges should form groups of those with cars and the Members should pay the driver's contributions towards petrol and running expenses.

We must devote the Order's charitable efforts to concentrate upon the Order's Charities and particularly the Doris Jones Memorial Fund during these difficult times."

Lodge Castell Caernarvon No.295 in February 1975

Lodge Trinity No.296 in March 1975

Lodge Granite City No.271 in April 1975

Lodge Loyal Barum No.297 in May 1975

Lodge Grouville No.298 in June 1975

Lodge De Lovetot No.299 in August 1975

In early 1976 the health of the Grand Master gave cause for further concern. At Grand Lodge R.W.Bro. Frances Hall, A.G.M., G.M's.G.S. addressed the Brethren. She said she was sure everyone was distressed to know that the M.W. The Grand Master was unable to be present.

"The Grand Master herself had hoped to be well enough this time to come. Unfortunately due to inefficient nursing the leg has a *streptococcus* germ, and it has been in a very serious state since. The M.W. The Grand Master is often in great pain and has to keep the leg in one position. She is only able to move about for a very short time. She was very anxious that all the Brethren should know how very sorry she was not to be present, and to assure everyone that she is just as concerned and interested in all the Brethren and the Lodges."

R.W.Bro. Hall said that the M.W. The Grand Master read all the Agendas and discussed every item of news from the Lodges and kept in close touch with all that is going on, still directing everything that has to be done.

R.W.Bro. Hall added that she herself visited the M.W. The Grand Master at least twice a week to discuss matters relating to the Order, and the Grand Secretary also visited her regularly to take papers and get answers to problems. She then read a message from the M.W. The Grand Master to Grand Lodge:

"It is with regret that again I shall not be with you in person and to be able to enjoy the few hours we have together. This is a very important year for our Order, not only because of extraordinary events which are taking place throughout the world, but because pages of history are now being written and are going to be written which may well prove to be some of the biggest changes the world has ever seen taking place. It behoves us as Freemasons to endeavour to struggle and to keep alive all the finest things that man has discovered and striven for throughout the ages; and not let the destruction of present and future episodes swamp those things which are worth while and of beauty."

Further news of the Doris Jones Home came at Grand Lodge in March. With the Grand Master unable to be present through illness, R.W.Bro. Frances Hall, A.G.M. told the Brethren that the purchase of a house for the proposed Home in Woking, Surrey had fallen through because of the high cost of repairs and an increase in the purchase price. After further discussions with the Grand Master, it had been decided that it would be so much better if we could build our own Doris Jones Home from scratch, and we would look again at the freehold plot which we owned at the back of *Porchway House* in Worthing. An architect had drawn up plans. The estimated cost was £110,000 - to include the latest fire precautions, open plan accommodation which can also be made individual, together with single rooms and one or two suites.

R.W.Bro. Hall went on to say that one of the most important considerations was that the Brethren would then have a Temple next to the Home, so that patients could continue their Masonry and share it with others. Also, the Brethren would have noticed that we had recently consecrated Lodge No.299 and then No.301 - this was because No.300 was to be a very special Lodge and the M.W. The Grand Master would like it to be called the Doris Jones Memorial Lodge, to be consecrated in the Temple at Worthing. It was to be a Lodge for Grand Lodge members with the Grand Master as the permanent Worshipful Master, and it would meet twice a year at Worthing to give short papers on Masonic research.

The Doris Jones Memorial Lodge No.300 - jewel of the Permanent Wor. Master, M.W. The Grand Master.

At the same meeting M.W.Bro. Mildred Rhoda Low was again, in her absence, nominated as Grand Master, but she died in office on 19th March 1976.

Her obituary summed up her work for the Order:
"We remember her courage and fortitude during the past several months when her physical ill-health prevented her presence at so many Masonic gatherings, but she was with us in spirit and from her home, controlled and guided the Order, with its many complexities and ramifications.

We pay tribute to her devotion, sincerity and steadfastness to our Order, to which she gave so much of her time and energy through her whole Masonic life and also at a time when she had a busy public and business life, which necessitated constant travelling abroad, and she always gave readily of her business acumen to the finances of the Order.

During the Grand Master's reign, the Order celebrated its Diamond Jubilee in 1968, and through her drive, guidance, encouragement and boundless energy, our London Temple and Headquarters were enlarged, beautified and made more accessible to the Member of the Order, and throughout the Commonwealth where our Lodges exist. Services of Thanksgiving were held in Cathedrals and places of Worship.

Lodge Tamar (I.M.) No.301 in February 1976

During the last few weeks of her life, she knew that that which she had planned for, worked for, and desired for the benefit of the Order was at last coming into being - the Doris Jones Memorial Home - the House for our sick and older members who cannot be cared for under ordinary conditions. The Home named, by edict of the Grand Lodge, after one of its senior members.

Lodge Thetford Priory No.302 in February 1976

We shall always remember Mildred Rhoda Low with affection, call to mind her kindness, her sense of humour, her quiet chuckle, when amused and her approachability by any member who desired to speak to her, which was a wonderful human trait."

Lodge Newton No.303 in August 1976

At a Special Grand Lodge held on Saturday, 10th April 1976 at Headquarters before an assembly of approximately five hundred members, R.W.Bro. Winifrid Prior, Deputy Grand Master, G.M's.G.S. addressed the Brethren saying:

Lodge Glantaf (I.M.) No.304 in May 1976

"You know this Special Grand Lodge has been called today for election of the new Grand Master in accordance with Rule 12 of the Book of Constitutions, for the Masonic Year 1976-77.

Lodge Abbeygate No.305 in June 1976

This should be a happy occasion. It is usually a happy occasion. Today is very far from being so, as we all realise. It is the Grand Master's prerogative and privilege to name her successor. I am sure the Grand Master gave a great deal of thought to this over a very long time as to who she wished to succeed her and she has named R.W.Bro. Frances Hall, Assistant Grand Master, G.M's.G.S., not to take her place, but to try and carry on the wonderful work M.W.Bro. Mildred Rhoda Low did during her years as Grand Master of the Order.

M.W.Bro. Mildred Rhoda Low,
Grand Master of the Order of Women
Freemasons from 1964 to 1976.

I am sure she thought long and carefully because the Order was very dear to her heart and she worked so hard for our Order over many years. When she was head of our Order we all felt that whatever she did was right. Whatever she carried out, though we may not always have agreed in the beginning, we came to realise it was for the good of the Order. It was always something which turned out for the good of everyone, and I know that in nominating R.W.Bro. Hall as her successor in office, she knew all her ideas and plans would be carried through.

"R.W.Bro. Hall has for many years been, as one would say, one of the 'backroom boys' because she has been on the administrative side of our Order and you have heard the Grand Master speak many times of all her efforts and all she has accomplished in making our Headquarters beautiful. Whatever money has been spent has been well spent. Over the years, R.W.Bro. Hall has been the Grand Master's right hand in many things and I know that in choosing R.W. Bro. Hall to succeed her, she knew you would all approve of her choice and help R.W.Bro. Hall in the onerous task that she will take on when she succeeds our late Grand Master.

R.W.Bro. Hall has worked hard for the good of the Order; for several years in very many ways. R.W.Bro. Hall held a very important position in business [*in the multi-national company Unilever*] and has been used to being on the administrative side of a large concern, and to take this office for our Order, I am sure she is well qualified and will do everything she can to help you all."

The Quarterly Communication of Grand Lodge on 5th June 1976 held at Headquarters was preceded by a Memorial Service for Mildred Rhoda Low. The service included the solo anthem *How lovely are Thy dwellings*, St. Paul's words to the Corinthians "Behold I show you a mystery: We shall not sleep but we shall all be changed ... ", the 23rd Psalm and the prayer *God be in my head* ...

Chapter Ten

Frances Hall and the Doris Jones Home

M.W. Bro. Frances Hall was enthroned in October 1976 at the Grosvenor Hotel in London's Park Lane. Her Address at the Enthronement looked forward:

"There will be changes - each decade has changes - but not in our ritual or ceremonies for you have heard in my Obligation that I have solemnly promised to preserve and uphold the true principles and tradition of Freemasonry. You will all identify with that and you know we can only do that if we are absolutely united and absolutely understand the principles we stand for, and do not change them . We cannot be a divided house - I don't think we ever will be again. Remember, we are built on an indestructible foundation of faith, loyalty and love. Our early pioneering brethren gave so much and struggled so hard to this enduring end.

M.W.Bro. Frances Hall, Grand Master 1976-1989

When I say that there will be changes, I want especially to refer to one change. The administration of our Order needs some changes - only because what worked very happily for twenty lodges began to creak a little for one hundred. It carried on because of the experience and dedication of the Officers but it is now very difficult to carry on still in the same way for three hundred and four lodges.

We have at Headquarters a wonderful team of voluntary people helping the Grand Secretary, who works very hard, but I do know, and many of you have told me, that there are times when we do not communicate as we should. I do hope that the changes which I hope to make will streamline those problems and so help you. I speak now to reigning Masters, Treasurers and Secretaries. The changes will not occur too quickly. One of my faults is that I want things to happen too quickly, but when they do come, bear with me and help me. Then they will be pleased with me at Headquarters and everything will be efficient and run smoothly."

During the following week, the Grand Master held a cocktail party at Headquarters for all the visiting Brethren from overseas. It was an ideal opportunity to show the widely scattered Brethren - from Australia, Canada, Malta, the Channel Islands, Ireland, the Isle of Man, Lagos and Rhodesia - that they all had a common bond and belonged to one great family, membership of the Order of Women Freemasons. It also enabled members of Grand Lodge to listen to points of view from overseas, and hear of successes and difficulties.

Lodge St. Agnes No.306 in October 1976

Lodge Red Rose of Lancashire (I.M.) No.307 in February 1977

Lodge Eccles No.308 in February 1977

The Doris Jones Memorial Home

Doris Grace Jones was proposed into Lodge Harmony No.4 by Blanche Ireland, who had worked with her for a long time in the Women's Auxiliary Army Corps. Lodge Harmony had a tradition of membership from the women's services. Progressing through the ranks, she became Master in 1936 and much later Worshipful Master of Lodge Kedron No.75 in Essex in 1956.

Lodge Mosaic (I.M.) No.309 in April 1977

Lodge Rushmere No.310 in April 1977

After leaving the W.A.A.C., Doris Jones joined the American Red Cross. Transferring to the American Relief Society, she became Executive Secretary, a position she held for forty years. She took a similar post with the American Society in London, providing invaluable stability to a changing administrative committee of American bankers, lawyers and businessmen, all in this country for a short time only. She provided social and financial advice to American citizens in the United Kingdom for several decades, and many thousands of people were in her debt.

Lodge Joyous Light No.311 in June 1977

Porchway House, *Worthing - (left) the original house, and (right) the nursing home extension built in 1977, now part of the residential home.*

Lodge Sŵn-y-Gân No.312 in June 1977

Lodge Dunaverty Castle No.313 in May 1977

Lodge Wessyngton No.314 in September 1977

Lodge Fraternal Friendship No.315 in November 1977

Lodge St. Nicholas No.316 in February 1978

Lodge Masonic Joy No.317 in March 1978

Through visiting Lodges, one meets other Brethren with quite different lives, and it was in this way that Doris Jones met Mildred Rhoda Low of Lodge Equity No.16. R.W.Bro. Low was then Grand Treasurer. The two became great friends. Some time earlier, M.W.Bro. Mary Gordon Muirhead Hope had asked Doris Jones to look at properties which might be suitable for a residential Home for our Order, preferably outside London. Following the death of Doris Jones in 1964, the American Relief Society sent a donation of £500 to Rhoda Low, by then Grand Master, which they hoped could be put towards this Home.

Following an unsuccessful search for a suitable property for use as a nursing home, the decision was taken to use the land owned by the Order in Worthing and in 1977 the Doris Jones Memorial Home was in process of being built in the grounds of our retirement home, *Porchway House*.

At the same time, 149 Rowlands Road, next door to *Porchway House* was purchased to provide an annex with several more bedrooms, designed as accommodation for the visiting relatives of patients in the Home. It was known as *Mildred House*, after the late Grand Master, whose dream of such a Home had come true and it was furnished with many of her possessions. *Porchway House* itself was redecorated and refurnished and was now intended as a short holiday or convalescent home for the whole Order, rather than a residential home for a few.

The building of the Nursing Home in the grounds of *Porchway House* had taken two years. "The driving force behind this great building project has been the untiring energy and unceasing planning of M.W.Bro. Frances Hall, who has been making countless visits down to Worthing, and with her great powers of persuasion has kept the builders on schedule and very much on their toes." The Home consisted of a small hospital unit of fourteen beds.

At the same time preparations were being made to fulfil the wish of the late Grand Master to set up a research Lodge in memory of Doris Grace Jones, which would meet at *Porchway House*.

The Doris Jones Memorial Lodge No.300 was consecrated on 22nd April 1978, at Headquarters rather than at Worthing, so that many more Brethren could attend. The ceremony was carried out by M.W.Bro. Frances Hall, assisted by the Deputy Grand Master, R.W.Bro. Olwen Lloyd and the Assistant Grand Master, R.W.Bro. Doris Hoadley. The M.W. The Grand Master was always to be the Permanent Worshipful Master of the Lodge and she was to nominate the Deputy Worshipful Master every two years. The first Deputy Worshipful Master was R.W.Bro. E.V. Smith, P.G.W., the Senior Warden was R.W.Bro. D.E. Smyth, J.G.W., G.M's.G.S., the Editor of *The Gavel* and W.Bro. A. Aldred, D.G.Swd.Br. was Junior Warden - all Brethren noted for their contribution to the history of Freemasonry and of our Order.

Doris Jones Memorial Lodge No. 300 in April 1978

This Lodge works under the banner of Grand Lodge - all those Brethren that are entitled to attend Grand Lodge (Junior Wardens and above) can become members. Its original brief was "to be an unique occasional Lodge which will help to further the important cause of Masonic study and investigation." The Lodge was formed with the idea of encouraging a resurgence of Masonic research, understanding and learning throughout the Order, and the two weekend meetings a year are devoted to the reading of Masonic papers, to be subsequently circulated to all members.

The breast jewel of the Doris Jones Memorial Lodge No.300.

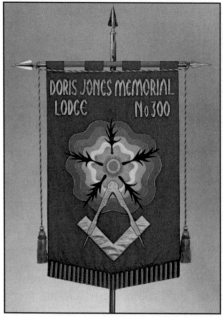

Banner of the Doris Jones Memorial Lodge No.300, meeting at Porchway House.

The Lodge was fortunate in having one thousand Founder Members. The officers of the Lodge wear a distinctive collar of light blue with a stripe of rose pink.

Its first weekend meeting at Worthing included a team of Brethren from Wales who demonstrated a Scottish working of the Third Degree, then lectures and a discussion on the First Degree and an introduction to some Masonic music.

The Banner of the Lodge was presented as a gift by R.W.Bro. Marjorie Ellis, P.A.G.M., and was embroidered by her niece. It was dedicated in 1979 by R.W.Bro. Olwen Lloyd, D.G.M. The design was the inspiration of R.W.Bro. E.V. Smith, first Deputy Worshipful Master of the Lodge. Since the Lodge had such a close association with the Doris Jones Home, and the emblem of this was the red rose of the Doris Jones Charity Jewel, it was thought appropriate that the emblem of the Lodge should also be a rose - in this case the Tudor rose, with five petals reminding us of the five senses. The sprigs of green are emblems of renewal and the Square and Compasses are prominent in gold against the background. The rose also featured on the breast jewel associated with the Lodge.

On 3rd June 1978 the first Grand Lodge to be held in Worthing met at the Assembly Hall with about eight hundred Brethren present. Many of these took the opportunity to inspect and view the new Home. Members of the Worthing Lodges acted as guides and hostesses, supplying over five hundred cups of tea to revive the visitors after the excitement of their tour of inspection.

Seventieth Anniversary Celebrations

For Lodge Golden Rule No.1, Lodge Emulation No.2 and the Lodge of Unity No.3, June 1978 was indeed a landmark, for it was the seventieth anniversary of the Consecration of the three Lodges in 1908. Earlier in the year, the M.W. The Grand Master had expressed the hope that the three premier Lodges would celebrate this event and appointed W.Bro. Dorothy Johnston, G.Supt. of Works, of Lodge Golden Rule No.1, to organise the event.

Accordingly, a Committee was formed consisting of members from the three Lodges. They decided that there should be a Thanksgiving Service and a Celebration Dinner. Permission was given for the Service to be held in the Temple at Headquarters on June 17th. On that day, over seventy members from Lodges 1, 2 and 3 were ranged under their three Banners, together with Brethren from other London Lodges.

R.W.Bro. Marjorie Ellis, P.A.G.M., P.G. Secretary, who gave the banner to the Doris Jones Memorial Lodge No.300.

As the account in *The Gavel* relates "The Service commenced with a Hymn of Praise and an Act of Thanksgiving, which took the form of Prayers giving thanks for our Order, for those courageous founders who with faith and hope started us on our journey, for the work and devotion of our six Past Grand Masters, for the building of the Doris Jones Memorial Home, and for happiness and true brotherly love to remain with us all. This part of the ceremony was conducted by W.Bro. W. Annals, P.G.Purs., of Lodge Golden Rule No.1, who then read two short extracts from *The Builders*, the work of John Ruskin on the theme of 'Therefore, as we build, let us think we build forever'."

R.W.Bro.Olwen Lloyd,
Deputy Grand Master 1977-1984,
care of Wales, G.M's.G.S.

Lodge Northgate
No.318 in March 1978

Lodge Guestling
No.319 in October
1978

Lodge Ashridge
No.320 in November
1978

Lodge Lancaster
No.321 in December
1978

Lodge Mole Valley
No.322 in March 1979

Lodge Blendon Wood
No.323 in March 1979

More hymns followed and a Scripture Reading by W.Bro. Gillies, L.G.R., the Chaplain of Lodge Emulation No.2, from *Chronicles II,* Chapters 2 and 5, giving the account of the preparation for the building and dedication of the first Temple at Jerusalem. R.W.Bro. M. V. Ellis, P.A.G.M. read a Prayer:

'Great Architect of the Universe, send down Thy Blessing upon the Grand Master of our Order, and upon those whom she has set in authority under her.
Grant her Light, that it may guide her in her charge;
Grant her Courage, to support her in the daily duties committed to her care;
Grant her Love, that she may teach us to act in Brotherly Love;
Grant her Strength, that she may never tire in her work for the good of Freemasonry for Women'.

"After this, all the Brethren stood to recite the Dedication Prayer which was followed by the Family Prayer by Robert Louis Stevenson:

'Lord, behold our family here assembled. We thank Thee for this place in which we meet; for the love that unites us; for the peace accorded this day; for the hope with which we expect tomorrow; for the health, the work, the food, and the bright skies, that make our lives delightful; for our friends in all parts of the earth.
Let peace abound in our small company. Purge out of every heart the lurking grudge. Give us the strength to forbear and to persevere. Offenders, give us the grace to accept and forgive offenders. Forgetful ourselves, help us to bear cheerfully the forgetfulness of others. Give us courage and

gaiety and the quiet mind. Spare us to our friends, soften us to our enemies.

Bless us, if it may be, in all our innocent endeavours. If it may not, give us the strength to encounter that which is to come, that we may be brave in peril, constant in tribulation, temperate in wrath, and in all changes down to the gates of death, loyal and loving one to another. As the clay to the potter, as the windmill to the wind, as children of their sire, we beseech of Thee Thy help and mercy'.

W.Bro. Gillies, L.G.R. sang the anthem *God be in my head*, accompanied by the Grand Organist. R.W.Bro. D.E. Smyth, J.G.W., G.M's.G.S. then gave an interesting and inspiring Address, in which she traced the history of the past seventy years in our Lodges. She had so much to relate, and in her own inimitable way, made the past come alive, encouraged us in the present and inspired us for the future. The Service concluded with a further hymn of praise and Thanksgiving ... a memorable occasion, conducted in Peace and closed in Harmony."

Lodge Clwyd (I.M.) No.324 in April 1979

Lodge Norton Priory (I.M.) No.325 in June 1979

Lodge Pennine No. 326 in March 1980

Lodge St. Aidan No. 327 in November 1980

Travels Overseas

September 1979 saw M.W.Bro. Frances Hall and R.W.Bro. Hoadley in Canada to celebrate the silver jubilee of the Lodges there. They attended the Installation ceremony of the newly-merged Lodge Pioneer Hope of Toronto/Trillium of York and re-dedicated their banner. A Silver Jubilee Dinner was held the following night in the Library of the Royal York Hotel. A Silver Jubilee Temple Fund was inaugurated to raise funds for a permanent centre in Canada.

Lodge Viking No.328 in January 1981

Lodge Deira No.329 in April 1981

Lodge Marcellus No.330 in May 1981

Three years later - in 1982 - the Grand Master and Assistant Grand Master visited Zimbabwe and South Africa, together with R.W.Bro. Lilian Chapman, P.G.W., Grand Registrar, G.M's.G.S. When Brethren from England and Zimbabwe began to take up residence in South Africa, the prospect of continuing their Masonic interests was very remote. Whilst there were Lodges in Zimbabwe working under difficult conditions, there was no Lodge belonging to our Order in South Africa.

After months spent in establishing contact with Brethren exiled from Zimbabwe and then spread far and wide through South Africa, constant searching for the right premises and the acquisition of furnishings and regalia, nearly two years later the dream became a reality and in September 1982 the Grand Master consecrated Lodge Protea No.337 (No.1 South Africa) at Johannesburg (*protea* is the national flower of South Africa). There were one hundred and eleven Founder Members from England, Zimbabwe and South Africa and over sixty were present at the Consecration. The first Master, W.Bro. Kitty Harris, belonged to Lodge Albanus No.68 and W.Bro. Vera Clare of that Lodge installed her in the Chair.

The following week Lodge Flame Lily No.338 (No.2 South Africa) was consecrated in Durban by the Grand Master, after just eight months of hard work.

Worthing

Returning home, 1980 had seen changes at the Doris Jones Memorial Home. The Matron left and eventually W.Bro. Freda Pearce, an experienced Matron and Administrator, took up the permanent appointment. There was some criticism over the fees charged to patients, but the Grand Master stressed that nobody would be refused because of inability to pay the fees, the amount of which in each case was confidential. The Health Authority obliged us to make a minimum charge of £60 for a bed in a ward, and more for a private room. This contrasted with the real cost per patient per week, which was estimated to be at least £300. The aim and purpose of the Home was to admit patients needing nursing convalescence after hospitalisation and patients in need of short-term medical care.

By January 1989 pressing problems had arisen at Worthing. A close inspection had been made by the District Fire Officer which resulted in very detailed alterations which had to be made, such as the lowering

Lodge Alpha (I.M.) No.331 in August 1981

Lodge Menorah No. 332 in February 1982

Lodge Sussex Masters (I.M.) No.333 in March 1982

Lodge Holmvalia No. 334 in April 1982

of ceilings, fitting additional smoke detectors and improving the alarm system. These alterations affected both parts of the building and was the reason for the suspension of Lodge No.300 meetings that year. Our Nursing Home had always been acknowledged by the Health Authority as of a very high standard and one of the best of its kind in the area. However, rules had changed and we had to abide by them. Work had to be done to bring our Home up to the standard required by the Health Inspector.

Much difficulty was being experienced in obtaining fully qualified nurses for the Home. In accordance with the regulations it was essential to have two qualified S.R.N.s on duty day and night. Worthing was one of the worst areas for obtaining nursing staff, as there were so many Nursing and Rest Homes in the area.

Lodge Shropshire I.M. No.335 in May 1982

The Grand Master asked that if there were any Brethren who were nurses and who could give some staffing help. The cost of running the Nursing Home was very high, but because of the shortage of nursing staff we could only have a small number of patients.

Lodge Ludlow Castle No.336 in May 1982

A recurrent theme in M.W.Bro. Hall's addresses to the Brethren is that of encouraging younger women to enter the Order and to progress within it, thus providing a firm foundation - the strength of our Order was in the present and the future. The appointment of Grand Officers and the conferment of Honours also looked to the future in acknowledging the talents and abilities of individual Brethren.

M.W.Bro. Frances Hall will also be remembered for widening the base on which our work is set and she carried out a programme of

R.W.Bro. Edna Shepherd, D.G.M., G.M's.G.S., care of East Lancashire and Cheshire.

Lodge Protea No.337 in September 1982

Lodge Flame Lily No. 338 in September 1982

expansion in some of the additional Degrees bringing them more into line with the progress made in the Craft. In particular, during her reign twenty Mark Lodges were consecrated. Over most of this period R.W.Bro. Edna Shepherd, then Assistant Grand Master, had care of the administration of the Mark Degree.

The Grand Mastership

Lodge Kelso Abbey No.339 in October 1982

Lodge St. Francis No. 340 in October 1982

Lodge Northolme (I.M.) No.341 in April 1983

Item No.6 on the Agenda of Grand Lodge in June 1988 was to nominate the M.W. The Grand Master for the ensuing year. The Grand Master addressed the Brethren, saying that since the last Quarterly Communication of Grand Lodge in March when she had been nominated, she had unfortunately realised she would be unable to carry on and accept the office of Grand Master because as the Brethren will have noticed there was something very wrong with her sight, and she had also been having sudden black-outs. The Grand Master said she had consulted several specialists, who had told her that apart from the eye trouble she also had very high nervous tension and blood pressure. Urgent treatment was needed on one eye and she could only be convinced the sight would remain in the other eye if she retired and had complete rest. She had been warned five years ago that she must give up as her sight was affected, but of course she had remained.

Lodge Chiltern Hills No.342 in September 1984

Belmont Lodge of I.M. No.343 in October 1984

M.W.Bro. Frances Hall

Although it was sad for her and a surprise for the Brethren, she had foreseen some time ago that it was her duty to nominate her successor. After careful thought the Grand Master said she was now nominating R.W.Bro. Daphne Cudmore, S.G.W. to be elected as Grand Master. She outlined R.W.Bro. Cudmore's career in the Order and the work she had done at Headquarters and in connection with the Higher Degrees. To assist her, the Grand Master would continue to oversee the Adelaide Litten Trust and the Doris Jones Home, and to help her even further, R.W.Bro. Hoadley would continue as Deputy Grand Master in order to introduce the Grand Master Elect to her many commitments.

Grand Lodge stood in unanimous approval of the Nomination and Election. R.W. Cudmore acknowledged the work of the Grand Master:
"She has given of herself unstintingly over the past twelve years carrying out all the duties with complete dedication and devotion. We are fully aware of the vast expansion of the Order during the time she has served as Grand Master and her untiring efforts for the Order we love are an inspiration to us all."

Lodge Causeway No. 344 in September 1985

The Grand Master's deteriorating sight meant that in October 1988 she was unable to attend Grand Lodge for the first time in the twelve years of her tenure. An operation on her eye had not been as successful as had been hoped and she was generally not at all well.

Lodge Balloch No.345 in September 1985

But the transfer of power was not to be straightforward - *The Gavel* of November 1988 merely states briefly "unhappily fate has decreed that the election of R.W.Bro. Daphne Cudmore to the office of Grand Master has now been cancelled due to the serious nature of her illness, and the fact that she has to continue as an out-patient at hospital and must be spared any undue strain or stress. Fortunately our reigning Grand Master is now recovering from her eye operation and will continue as Grand Master for the foreseeable future and until she again decides to exercise her right and privilege to nominate and install a successor."

Lodge Obedience No. 346 in March 1987

Lodge Liskerrett No.347 in December 1987

In January 1989 R.W.Bro. Cudmore was unable to be present at Grand Lodge as she was still attending hospital following a serious operation for cancer.

M.W.Bro. Hall did exercise her right in March 1989 by nominating R.W.Bro. Brenda Fleming-Taylor, P.J.G.W., G.M's.G.S., Grand Registrar, as her successor. R.W.Bro. Fleming-Taylor was the Secretary of the Doris Jones Memorial Lodge No.300 and also did valuable work at Headquarters, where she was a very efficient secretary and administrator. As the Grand Master said "As she is still only in her fifties she is young enough and ardent enough to take our

Order into the next century. This is important as we have a growing and wonderful Order and we must have continuity ... she is a wonderful person with tenacity and courage."

The Deputy and Assistant Grand Masters endorsed the Nomination. The Election Meeting of Grand Lodge would again be held in Newcastle in the next June and arrangements had been made for the Enthronement to be held at the New Connaught Rooms in London in October.

At the same meeting M.W.Bro. Hall explained that it had been necessary to sell 149 Rowlands Road (*Mildred House*) in Worthing.

R.W.Bro. Doris Hoadley, O.B.E.,
Deputy Grand Master

It was not used very much. It was originally intended to accommodate relatives of patients in the Nursing Home but there had not been sufficient need, and even as holiday accommodation it was used very little. It was unsuitable for housing the nursing staff as they had to be within three minutes of their patients in case of fire. All properties came under the Adelaide Litten Trust and the money for 149 Rowlands Road would help towards the heavy bills for the statutory alterations necessary to 151.

The Election of R.W.Bro. Brenda Fleming-Taylor as Grand Master took place in June at Newcastle. Item 11 on the Agenda was "That the future of the Doris Jones Memorial Home, temporarily closed due to statutory requirements, be fully discussed." After outlining the circumstances leading up to the temporary closure of the Home - staffing, extensive necessary alterations, pressure from the Health Authority resulting in the transfer of the three patients to other homes - the Grand Master said we were now moving into another era, where the trend was to care for elderly and sick people in their home environments. Possibilities to be considered were a change in function to a convalescent short-stay home, or the Home could be sold and the money used for a Fund for sick and needy Brethren all over the country.

The Gavel of May 1989 included a personal announcement from R.W.Bro. Cudmore:

"R.W.Bro. D.S.E. Cudmore, P.G.W., wishes to thank Brethren throughout the Order, in individual Lodges, Mark, Chapter, and Chivalric Degrees, for the vast numbers of 'Get Well' cards, flowers and telephone calls she received when news of her illness became known. Also for the hundreds of Christmas cards conveying fraternal love and good wishes for a speedy return to full health, which she regrets were far too numerous to reply to individually.

The brotherly love and affection they represented together with thoughts and prayers have been quite overwhelming and have given her strength, courage and hope for the future. She would like you all to know that she is making a very good recovery and already attendance at Meetings has done so much for her both spiritually and mentally.

She sends greetings and fraternal love to all the Brethren in the Order and wishes them every happiness and success."

M.W.Bro. Frances Hall.

Chapter Eleven

Brenda Fleming-Taylor, Headquarters and the Trust Funds

On Saturday 7th October 1989 an Especial Grand Lodge was opened in the Great Hall of the New Connaught Rooms in London to enthrone the eighth Grand Master of the Order. The grandeur of the occasion was heightened by the setting which lent much dignity to the proceedings. The pale blue and silver, the dark blue and gold of regalia - the Masonic ambience was enhanced by the classical surroundings of columns and pilasters and chandeliers glittering overhead.

M.W.Bro. Brenda Fleming-Taylor after her Enthronement in 1989.

The entrance of the Grand Master Elect was preceded by that of the Grand Director of Ceremonies, with two Grand Deacons, two Assistant Grand Standard Bearers and the Deputy Grand Director of Ceremonies who carried the regalia of the Grand Master.

Following the Dedication Prayer *Lord, be Thy word my rule ...,* spoken by the Grand Chaplain, the Grand Master Elect took her Oath of Office after which she was clothed and enthroned in the Chair of King Solomon by M.W.Bro. Frances Hall. The Grand Director of Ceremonies then proclaimed "Be it known that this day M.W.Bro. Brenda Fleming-Taylor has been enthroned as the Most

Worshipful The Grand Master of the Order of Women Freemasons, whom may the Great Architect of the Universe long preserve." The Brethren saluted the Grand Master with eleven. Then came the solo, the prayer of St. Patrick *God be in my head,* after which the Deputy Grand Master, R.W.Bro. Edna Shepherd, G.M's.G.S., care of East Lancashire and Cheshire and the Assistant Grand Master, R.W.Bro. Marion Kennedy, G.M's.G.S., care of Northern Counties and Scotland, were invested and saluted.

The Grand Master then appointed and invested her Grand Lodge Officers and conferred Past Grand Honours.

R.W.Bro. Marion Kennedy,
Assistant Grand Master, G.M's.G.S.

In her Address M.W.Bro. Brenda Fleming-Taylor set the tone for the early part of her reign:

"… it cannot be denied that in recent years we have enjoyed great expansion - perhaps it could even be argued that such expansion was too rapid because we have Lodges struggling to survive. I feel now is an opportune time to take stock of that which we already have, and try where necessary to build up those Lodges where support is badly needed and so, by strengthening them, strengthen the Order as a whole."

The Grand Master asked the Brethren for tolerance and time in dealing with outstanding problems so that the best solutions might be found. In the immediate future, Supreme Grand Chapter would once more be held in November and Lodge Voyagers No.40 would meet in December - the first time for two years.

The Quarterly Communication of Grand Lodge was held the following week at Headquarters. R.W.Bro. Daphne Cudmore was able to be present (sadly, she died in July 1990, days before she was due to be admitted to a Hospice). Regarding the fate of the property at

Worthing, the Grand Master asserted that the purchase or sale of property by the Adelaide Litten Trust Fund could only take place on the recommendation of the Trustees, with the decision referred to Grand Lodge for ratification. She believed that whilst the premises in Rowlands Road were unoccupied, the opportunity should be taken to make a thorough appraisal of the situation and to examine every alternative in an effort to keep this valuable asset.

The policy to publish the Grand Master's speeches in *The Gavel* was welcomed as a sign of the new style of leadership - as the Editor summed it up:

"The Grand Master's recently published speeches have been read with great interest and applauded for their straight-forward and business-like approach, which has reassured and enlightened the Brethren on several major issues affecting the Order's future. Openness and common sense seem to be the order of the day in Freemasonry and members are grateful for the free and honest exchange of ideas and information which has been imparted rather like a breath of fresh air reviving the Order with hope for the future…".

Worthing and the Adelaide Litten Trust Fund

The Grand Master very quickly formed a committee to consider fully all aspects of the Trust Fund and its properties, including the suggestion that *Porchway House* and the Temple area should be separated from the nursing home part. It was necessary to keep within the terms of reference imposed by the Charity Commissioners in the Deed of Trust relating to the Adelaide Litten Trust Fund. The Grand Master proposed that - with minimum refurbishment - the Nursing Home extension could be converted into a short stay or holiday home, with a management committee and a resident housekeeper.

The Charity Commissioners wanted to revise the constitutional and administrative framework of the Trust under a detailed new Scheme of Administration. They also appointed new Trustees. The resources in the Fund were invested by a firm of independent stockbrokers to provide income and capital growth to allow regular payments to be made to needy members of the Order. Major improvements were made at the other property - *Northolme* - and the slow process of converting the new wing of *Porchway House* from a nursing home and re-opening the whole property was under way. It was hoped to use it firstly as a holiday home but ultimately as the residential home for which it had always been intended.

Trust managers were appointed to provide legal and accountancy services. This led to an Annual Report outlining the activities of the previous year and including accounts, providing every member with an insight into how the Trust is run and how their money is being spent. Chartered surveyors were also appointed to manage the properties at Worthing and Lytham and the freehold of *Northolme* was purchased.

The Grand Master took her place as a Trustee. All nominations for Trustees in the future would be from within the Order, and appointments would be made by the Trustees themselves. The name of the Trust was changed slightly to

R.W.Bro. Margaret Masters, Deputy Grand Master, care of N. Counties and Scotland, G.M's.G.S.

reflect its charitable nature, and it became the Adelaide Litten Charitable Trust.

The following year - 1996 - the Doris Jones Memorial Lodge No.300 returned to *Porchway House* for their August meeting, and the House was opened for holiday breaks. There were six en-suite apartments with work in progress on further rooms, and a resident Housekeeper. A year later, with decoration complete and all the staff and equipment necessary, applications were invited for permanent residence. It was not, however, until 2000 that the first resident came to *Porchway* -

R.W.Bro. E. Parker, P.G.W., G.M's.G.S., former Grand Secretary, who enjoyed several happy years there until her death in 2005. In 2008 there are five residents at *Porchway House* and two at *Northolme*.

Over the years considerable work has been done at both properties, both in maintenance and on improvements. More rooms have been redecorated and made habitable and double glazing has been installed.

Further and Higher Degrees

Several of the Degrees beyond the Craft had been in abeyance for some years. R.W.Bro. Monica Oktabcova, P.D.G.M., assisted by R.W.Bro. Joan Abbott, P.G.W., Grand Registrar were entrusted with their re-introduction. Their experience, together with much research into the history, ceremonial, ritual and administration of the Higher and Further Degrees, led to the re-introduction of several Degrees which had not been worked for some time. These included in 1990 the Chivalric Degree of the Holy Sepulchre and St. John of Jerusalem (Pillar of Light Conclave No.1), followed later by meetings of Rose Croix Chapters, Knight Templar Priest (1999) and the Order of the Secret Monitor in 2001. Several of these Degrees expanded into the provinces.

Other Degrees grew in a controlled and sensible manner. The ritual of the Allied Masonic Degrees was expanded to include all the five Degrees, in line with the men's working. The 30th and higher Degrees of the Ancient and Accepted Rite were worked again after many years, as and when sufficiently qualified officers became available.

At Grand Chapter in 1997 the ranks of Chapter Grand Steward and Grand Rank were introduced, and at Mark Grand Lodge those of Mark Grand Steward and Grand Rank.

R.W.Bro. Monica Oktabcova, P.D.G.M. in the Craft, G.M's.G.S., in the office of Deputy Supreme Ruler of the Order of the Secret Monitor at the Consecration of Seal of Solomon Conclave No.6 in 2007.

In 2001, a Grand Imperial Conclave was established for the first time. The Grand Master is Grand Sovereign, with R.W.Bro. Monica Oktabcova as Grand Viceroy. 2007 saw the introduction of the Great Priory, the Grand Lodge of the Knights Templar Degree.

Essex Lodge of Installed Masters No.348 in May 1992

As a completely new venture, in 2006 two Chapels of the Commemorative Order of Knights of St. Thomas of Acon were consecrated, Londinium Chapel No.1 and Becket Chapel No.2. This Order is linked to that of Knights Templar and takes as its historical basis the work of warrior monks who buried the bodies of Christian knights in the Holy Land during the Third Crusade and also ransomed the captives of the Saracens. The ritual mainly centres on Gilbert Becket and his son Thomas, who was martyred at Canterbury in 1170.

White Rose (I.M.) Lodge No.349 in November 1998

Membership

At her Enthronement the Grand Master had spoken of the need to consolidate and strengthen our weaker Lodges where necessary. There was a decline in membership in the early 1990s. Some Craft Lodges experienced great difficulty in surviving because of lack of candidates or the unwillingness of members to progress. As the Grand Master said:

" ... we must ask ourselves why this is happening. Greater care must be exercised in the selection and admission of candidates - we must be absolutely sure that they wish to join for the right reason - not just because they view the Order from a social aspect, and they must be made aware that social events were originally, and still are, incidental to our purpose. A lodge will not survive if too much emphasis is placed on social activities. Survival depends solely on the ability of Lodge officers to learn the ritual, to progress from office to office and ultimately the Chair of the Lodge. Without this dedication of purpose, the Lodge will, sooner or later, fail."

Norfolk & Suffolk Lodge of Installed Masters No.350 in December 2000

Where possible, Lodges with an insufficient number of working members were encouraged to amalgamate, but if this proved impossible or undesirable, Warrants were surrendered or Lodges suspended. The London Lodges also suffered, due mainly to travelling and transport problems, and the ever-present threat of crime and

Lodge Solent (I.M.) No.351 in January 2001

R.W.Bro. Barbara Whittingham, A.G.M., care of Outer London, Bedfordshire, Hertfordshire and Cambridgeshire, G.M's.G.S.

terrorism in the capital. They were the pioneers, the foundation stones on which the rest of the Order was constructed and without which it would not exist. Brethren in the outer suburbs were encouraged to become Joining Members in order to keep these old Lodges going.

Further evidence of the Grand Master's more open approach regarding the position of women's Freemasonry in the outside world was shown by her attitude to recruitment:

"It could be suggested that we have been hiding our light under a bushel and that the time is now right to take steps to redress that deficiency. You will I am sure remember the words addressed to every newly installed Master '*that the world may know*' and I feel that each one of us has, at some time, asked the question how can the world know if we do not tell them. In short, Brethren, there can be nothing wrong, if you have a friend whom you are convinced would make a good Mason, in gently introducing the subject of Freemasonry."

Lodge Millennium No.352 in March 2001

Lodge Solway No.353 in September 2001

East Kent Lodge of Installed Masters No.354 in December 2001

The decline in membership started slowly to reverse around 1996. In the early part of the Grand Master's reign only three Lodges (all Installed Masters) were consecrated, in 1992, 1998 and 2000. It was not until 2001 that two new Craft Lodges, Lodge Millennium No.352 in Somerset and Lodge Solway No.353 in Scotland, were founded.

To help this cautious expansion, in 2002 collections for the Expansion Fund were revived, which not only defrayed the considerable expenses associated with the Consecration of a new Lodge but also helped towards the cost of journeys overseas by senior Grand Lodge Officers.

Headquarters and the Grand Temple

Storm damage over the winter of 1989-90 affected the Temple at Headquarters. Many parts of the flat roof were no longer weatherproof and the whole of it needed re-roofing. Damp was coming through the brickwork of the Tyler's room, the dining room needed redecoration and there were various cracks needing attention in other areas. It was our responsibility to maintain the Grade II listed building and restore it to its former glory. Whilst the re-roofing was in progress it was found that the electrical wiring was in a dangerous condition, resulting in its having to be repaired and repositioned. The exterior also needed decorating.

A central heating system was installed for the fourth floor, to replace the various costly electric heaters. The first, second and third floors were rewired, and at the same time, the existing lift was upgraded. During the external painting over the summer of 1990 many window frames were found to be needing work. The house was owned by the Order rather than by the Adelaide Litten Trust Fund and so had not received the financial help necessary to maintain such a listed building. An extensive programme of refurbishment and redecoration would be necessary to bring the house up to standard and compensate for years of neglect. A regular maintenance programme was also needed. The Grand Master suggested the creation of a Building Restoration Fund, with a jewel awarded annually to the Worshipful Master of each Lodge that raised a minimum amount. The jewel took the form of a miniature gilt trowel suspended from a pale blue ribbon and was subsequently awarded not only to the Worshipful Master of a Lodge but any Brother who donated a minimum of £100 to the Fund.

The Building Restoration Fund jewel.

Also in 1990 a 'new' second-hand organ was bought for the Temple, replacing the one which had been donated in memory of Marion Lindsay Halsey by her daughter in 1925. It was our Grand Master's wish that all Grand Lodge meetings held there should open and close with the traditional Opening and Closing Hymns.

In 1992, during external decoration of the building, it was discovered that the roof over the crush area leading to the Grand Temple, as well as the roof of the Grand Temple itself, was in a poor state of repair and in spite of work carried out in 1990 it had to be re-roofed in part. This involved the extra cost of scaffolding.

An inspection of Headquarters in 1993 by civil engineers appointed by the insurers revealed several serious cracks causing major structural defects, principally on the south side of the building in the Temple. These had to be monitored and measured to see how they developed before appropriate remedial work could be implemented. In 1929, just five years after the construction of the Temple in the garden of 27 Pembridge Gardens, engineers had reported a subsidence problem in this area, but had decided that it would not cause problems in the future. The subsidence was apparently caused by the roots of trees in the gardens of the adjoining properties. It would, however, cause further problems if these trees were removed altogether.

The engineers recommended to the insurers that the south wall needed underpinning. This took place in the summer recess of 1994, when a concrete base was constructed below the Temple to support it.

The redecorated Grand Temple at Headquarters, following the works in 1994.

The completion of the underpinning was followed by the redecoration of the Temple. There was also a lack of adequate fire precautions and equipment, which was rectified and brought up to the required standard. An up-to-date central heating system was installed. The administration areas were redecorated, with a new telephone system and a photocopier. The decoration and refurbishment of the Library and the top floor were completed and chandeliers and new curtains installed in the Dining Room. New chairs, paid for by the Doris Jones Memorial Lodge No.300, were placed in the Temple and the Dining Room. The external brickwork of the building was waterproofed and new guttering installed. Thanks to the Building Restoration Fund, this listed Grade II building was put back into good repair and will be well maintained in the future.

Unfortunately, as the Grand Master announced some time later in October 2006, the subsidence problem proved not to have been rectified and further cracks were to appear in the building.

The Building Restoration Fund also allowed the installation of a sound system in the Temple, which was a great advantage for large gatherings such as Grand Lodge. In 2002 the exterior of the whole building was redecorated, with further work on the Temple roof. The following year, the interior paper and paintwork was renovated. The lift was again overhauled and upgraded in 2004.

The Grand Lodge regalia kept at Headquarters also needed attention. After eighty years of use, with very few interim purchases, much of it needed to be replaced. As the Grand Master said: "We must never lose sight of that pageantry which forms such an important part of our ceremonial occasions and the striking gold and dark blue of a Grand Lodge Officer's regalia can prove not only a thing of beauty when first seen by a new member, but can also provide stimulus and encouragement to progress."

Journeys Overseas

Less than a year after her Enthronement, the Grand Master made her first official visit overseas to Canada. At the beginning of September she travelled to Toronto to meet the Canadian Brethren and visit three

Lodges working in that Area. She was accompanied by the Grand Director of Ceremonies, V.W.Bro. Barbara Pickett and V.W.Bro. Barbara Whittingham, Grand Inspector for Oxfordshire, Berkshire and Buckinghamshire.

Under the leadership of their Grand Inspector, V.W.Bro. Ruby Boersma, P.G.D.C., the Canadian Brethren had given much time, effort and forethought to planning the Grand Master's visit. During an action-packed week she was able to meet many of the Brethren both formally and informally, thus hearing at first hand of their difficulties and learning of their successes.

In a break from tradition, the Grand Master attended meetings of Lodge Pioneer Hope/Trillium of York No.72/79 and Lodge Keele Gate No.172, when they were working Degree Ceremonies. The climax of the visit came when the Grand Master attended a meeting of Lodge Heritage No.84 and, in a very dignified and moving ceremony, dedicated their beautiful Banner. The Grand Director of Ceremonies gave an interesting talk on *Grand Lodge Jewels and Protocol* and then invited questions.

In early 1991 M.W.Bro. Fleming-Taylor fulfilled a promise made by her predecessor to consecrate a Mark Lodge in Zimbabwe. At Bulawayo eighteen Brethren were advanced into the Mark Degree before the actual consecration of Matopos Mark Lodge No.55 on 30th January. The party moved to Johannesburg, where the Warrant was restored to Lodge Protea No.337 which had temporarily been in abeyance.

The Deputy Grand Master accompanied by the Grand Director of Ceremonies and other senior Brethren visited Australia to introduce Brethren there to the Mark Degree. Twenty Brethren were advanced into the Degree, and on 30th April 1992 Austral Mark Lodge No.56 was consecrated.

Zimbabwe and South Africa were revisited in June 1997. The Grand Master and her Deputy, accompanied by R.W.Bros. Oktabcova and Abbott and V.W.Bro. Penn - all very experienced in the Higher Degrees - advanced Mark Masons and consecrated two Mark Lodges, Msasa No.58 and Mount Horeb No.59. The Conclave and Knights

Templar Degrees were introduced to the Brethren there - Byzantium Conclave No.24 and Peace and Harmony Preceptory No.7 were consecrated in Bulawayo. An Ark Mariner Lodge was consecrated and moored to Matopos Mark Lodge No.55. In South Africa, Circle of Light Chapter No.49 was consecrated and the banners of Lodge Protea No.337 and Lodge Flame Lily No.338 dedicated.

Unfortunately the political and economic situation in Zimbabwe in the succeeding years deteriorated to the point where it was very difficult for our members to keep their Freemasonry alive. The shortage of staple foods and of oil and petrol, coupled with a ban on group meetings, meant that all Degrees beyond the Craft were placed in abeyance for the time being, whilst Brethren struggled to keep in contact with each other even if they could not officially hold a Lodge meeting. Many members living in Zimbabwe chose, or were forced, to emigrate.

The Deputy Grand Master, R.W.Bro. Margaret Masters, accompanied by V.W.Bro. Zuzanka Penn, Grand Director of Ceremonies, visited South Australia in May 2001 and attended Austral Mark Lodge No.56 and Lodge Pathana No.96, as well as having the opportunity to meet

The Deputy Grand Master and Grand Director of Ceremonies
at Austral Mark Lodge No.56 in 2001.

the Grand Master of the men's Southern Australian Constitution and Northern Territories at their Grand Lodge Headquarters in Adelaide. Later in 2004 R.W.Bro. Monica Oktabcova, Past Deputy Grand Master, and R.W.Bro. Zuzanka Penn, Grand Director of Ceremonies, visited Ontario where they attended the Installation meetings of Lodge Heritage No.84 and Lodge Pioneer Hope/Trillium of York No.72/79, as well as holding an Instruction Session for the Ontario Lodges.

Lodge La Rama Primera No.355 in February 2005

The banner of Lodge La Rama Primera No. 355, the first Lodge of the Order of Women Freemasons in Spain.

In 2005 the Order of Women Freemasons moved into new territory. The increasing number of members with holiday homes overseas and the trend to move abroad on retirement led to a petition by some of these Brethren to start a Lodge in Spain. Lodge La Rama Primera *[the first branch]* No.355 was consecrated on 5th February 2005 at 27 Pembridge Gardens. There were one hundred and forty Founder Members and also enquiries from ten potential Initiates. The home of the Lodge is at Fuengirola, near Malaga in Southern Spain. It was also hoped to introduce Freemasonry for women to other English expatriates in Spain. The Lodge goes from strength to strength and has a waiting list of Candidates.

Grand Lodge

In October 1991 Grand Lodge was at its usual venue of Porchester Hall in Bayswater but accommodation was very cramped with only five hundred people allowed. This meant that admission to the Enthronement meeting was restricted by ticket and initially to those receiving reigning or Past Grand Lodge Honours. A second meeting would be necessary the following week at Headquarters for the conferment of London, Provincial, Scottish and Overseas Grand Ranks. A new and larger venue for October 1992 was investigated, where it would be possible to follow the meeting with a formal dinner. The Enthronement and conferment of Honours meeting of Grand Lodge was subsequently held at various hotels in Earl's Court, London until 1998, when a more permanent home was found at the Hilton Metropole Hotel at the National Exhibition Centre, Birmingham. In that year, for the first time, the Enthronement of the Grand Master took place outside London.

Since then, the June and October Quarterly Communications of Grand Lodge - the October meeting including the Enthronement of the Grand Master, the investiture of Grand Lodge Officers and the award of Honours - have taken place at this Birmingham venue.

A New Sword

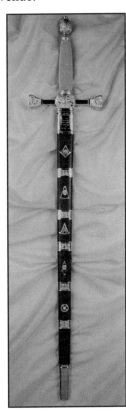

In June 1996, following the death of the Assistant Grand Master, R.W.Bro. Marion Kennedy, P.D.G.M., G.M's.G.S., the Grand Master announced that a specially designed Masonic Ceremonial Sword would be commissioned in her memory, and known as the Kennedy Sword. It was to be similar to the sword which is on display in the No.1 Royal Court of Justice and which bears the Coat of Arms of the City of London. The Senior Sword Adviser of the Wilkinson Sword Company was consulted and confirmed that it was possible to design a similar sword for the Order, suitably modified so that it could easily be carried by the Order's Sword Bearer. The scabbard was decorated with enamelled plaques on which were depicted the various emblems of the Craft, Mark and Royal Arch Degrees, so that it could be used at every Grand Lodge Meeting of those Degrees.

The Kennedy Sword.

A New Trust Fund

When problems began to arise with the Adelaide Litten Trust Fund, all monies raised by Brethren for charity and sent to Headquarters were banked in a separate interest-bearing bank account, pending resolution of the difficulties. This money had to be administered by a properly regulated Trust registered with the Charity Commissioners. The Board of General Purposes agreed in 1996 to recommend the formation of a new Trust, called *The Order of Women Freemasons Grand Charitable Trust,* to do this.

The new Trust dealt with aspects of relief other than the payment of annuities, pensions, elderly allowances and similar, or any such items which would require constant funding. A new Charity Allocation Form was introduced which allowed each Lodge to qualify for the Charity Sash and Jewel, as well as donating to an approved outside charity with an equal amount being allocated by the Lodge to one of either the O.W.F. Grand Charity, *Northolme, Porchway House* or the Adelaide Litten Trust Fund.

A public Annual General Meeting of the new Trust, with published Accounts, took place following the March Quarterly Communication of Grand Lodge, and has done every year since.

Publications

From 1997 onwards the Library at Headquarters was extensively re-organised, catalogued, and the stock updated. In order to encourage use of the facilities by more members, a lending and enquiry service for Brethren who can get to Headquarters was started. Brethren outside London were encouraged to contact the Librarian at any time and queries would be dealt with by post.

Our journal, *The Gavel,* has been published since 1909, with one gap between 1912 and 1929. As it is the most important source for the history of the Order, it was felt that a subject index to the main articles would help Brethren wishing to find information on different topics and this was compiled by the Librarian in 1996.

R.W.Bro. Betty Wildman,
Assistant Grand Master since 2001,
care of Shropshire, G.M's.G.S.

At the same time a plea was made by the Librarian for any material suitable for our Archives - old Agendas, programmes, rituals, photographs and similar items - which Brethren would be willing to donate. The complete lack of any Archive relating to the Order's history and the indiscriminate disposal of historical records was - and still is, particularly at the time of our Centenary - a cause for great concern. In order to raise awareness of the importance of keeping past records such as Minute Books and other material which may seem to have little relevance to the present, an Archive Survey was instigated in 2003. Each Lodge Secretary was asked to list all the books kept by the Lodge and describe how they were stored. This awareness-raising exercise was successful and prompted several Secretaries to investigate (and find) the whereabouts of their early Minute Books. A small Archive Room at Headquarters now houses some of the papers, books and Warrants of Lodges which are no longer working, together with a catalogued collection of other historical material. The Agendas of all Lodge meetings held at Headquarters since 2002 are kept on CD in the Archive as a permanent record

For some years the Order published a diary cover with annual refill pages, giving the dates of all the meetings held. In 1997 the Board of General Purposes approved the format of a slimline diary. As well as the usual personal details and pages of general information; the left hand page functions as a standard diary whilst on the right hand page a list of Lodges and other Degrees meeting on that day is shown. The diary commences at the beginning of the Masonic year in September.

Towards the end of the 1990s concern was expressed over a decrease in orders for *The Gavel*. There had been a deficit on the cost of the publication for some years. The format had been the same since its re-appearance in 1929, although over the years black and white photographs and later a few colour plates had been included. The content had changed, in that alongside Grand Lodge business and addresses by the Grand Master and senior Officers, Brethren were invited to contribute articles and news of their Lodge activities. The size of each issue was also much larger than the slim publication of the early years. For twenty-

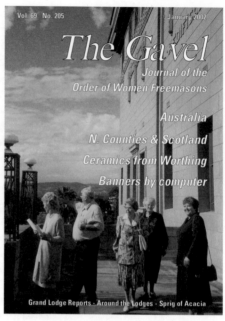

The first full-colour issue of The Gavel *in January 2002.*

five years the journal was edited by R.W.Bro. Doris Smyth, P.A.G.M., G.M.'s.G.S., who frequently wrote papers for it herself, and who made an enormous contribution to the recording of the history of the Order.

But times move on - the decreasing subscriptions together with changes in the world of printing suggested that the format of *The Gavel* should be reviewed. In 2001 a new Editor was appointed, V.W.Bro. Ann Pilcher-Dayton, who had worked for some time with R.W.Bro. Smyth. Although computerised typesetting had been in use for some years, the design potential of this opened up exciting possibilities. A look at current popular magazines showed how pages could be made more visually interesting. A two-column format - easier to read - of a standard sixty-four pages, with colour pictures included in the text and a coloured cover was approved by the Board of General Purposes in May 2001. It was decided that the publication dates be changed to January and June, so that the full proceedings of the Enthronement and Honours Quarterly Communication of Grand Lodge could be included and as many copies as possible could be collected by Brethren themselves at Grand Lodge to save postage. The cost of the new *The Gavel* would remain the same.

Still in A5 format, each issue has a centre-fold *Around the Lodges* entirely of pictures. Regular features include *O.W.F. in the Regions*, where each Area and their Grand Inspector produce an illustrated survey of their region, Grand Lodge information and *Sprig of Acacia* (obituaries). Each issue usually contains one or two longer articles.

In 2003 the first step was taken towards introducing computerised records. All the forms normally sent to a Craft Secretary at the time of their Lodge's Installation were produced in an interactive format on computer disk or CD. This was designed to simplify the procedures and make life easier for both Secretaries and Headquarters. It also ensured standardisation of forms. A pilot scheme was put in operation before the disks became generally available.

This small advance led to the momentous decision, taken by the Board of General Purposes in 2007, to computerise the membership records at Headquarters. The introduction of a computerised database has inevitably been a slow one, as there are so many factors to be considered and processes to be evaluated, but it should be completed during 2008.

The importance of electronic communication today indicated that the Order should develop a website as part of its interaction with the outside world, as a source of accurate information about the Order and as a means of enquiry. The Board of General Purposes approved this initiative in May 2007 and it was put online in its final form in 2008.

Board of General Purposes

In 1998 the Most Worshipful The Grand Master invited several senior Brethren who were members of the Board of General Purposes to look into the possibility of Area nomination and voting for Board members, an exercise which has been attempted in the past and abandoned for various reasons. Delegates from all Areas would help to ensure that the interests of all Brethren throughout the country would be represented in the recommendations made to Grand Lodge for the welfare of the Order. The committee reported back and its conclusions were approved by the Board to go forward to Grand Lodge for ratification, so that the necessary alterations to the Book of Constitutions could be made.

The recommendations were that the members of the Board should be elected on an Area basis and representation would be proportional to the number of Lodges in each Area. This ensured that all Areas were represented, which was not the case up to then. Furthermore voting would take place within the Areas concerned. Hitherto voting for the Board was at the October meeting of Grand Lodge, and so was restricted to those able to attend. The candidates for election in the past were probably not well-known to most of the Brethren - in future members would find it easier to vote for people whom they knew. The hope was also that this change would inspire more interest in the Board at the grass roots level and that the occasional dearth of nominations would be avoided.

As the Grand Master said:

"We have many young, capable and enthusiastic Masters and Past Masters who could contribute much to the deliberations of the Board. By 'opening-up' the eligibility to vote, the introduction of Area nomination of candidates, voting within each Lodge and the counting of votes on an Area basis, we hope to ensure a greater selection of candidates, easier voting facilities to those so qualified, and thus a fairer system of election to the Board."

Voting takes place in a different group of Areas each year. Brethren interested in standing for a vacancy on the Board must first complete a nomination form which is returned to Headquarters to enable ballot forms to be raised. Balloting in each Lodge (with the exception of Installed Masters' Lodges) takes place at a Regular Meeting with the Grand Inspector or a Senior Grand Lodge officer in attendance. When all Lodges in an Area have voted, an official count takes place and then the result is communicated to the Grand Secretary. The minimum qualification for voting is that a Brother must be a Master Mason of at least three years standing and Brethren are allowed to vote once only.

Relations with United Grand Lodge

The Board of General Purposes of the men's United Grand Lodge of England included in their report of February 1999 - without further comment of any kind - a section headed *Women and Freemasonry*:

"There exist in England and Wales at least two Grand Lodges solely for women. Except that these bodies admit women, they are, so far as can be ascertained, otherwise regular in their practice. There is also one which admits both men and women to membership. They are not recognised by this Grand Lodge and intervisitation may not take place. There are, however, informal discussions from time to time with the women's Grand Lodges on matters of mutual concern. Brethren are therefore free to explain to non Masons, if asked, that Freemasonry is not confined to men (even though this Grand Lodge does not itself admit women)."

This was at a time when our senior members were increasingly being asked to give talks about our Order to male Masons. These talks were well received and helped to dispel many former negative and inaccurate ideas about us.

With this formal statement and acknowledgement of the existence of female Freemasons by United Grand Lodge, there have been several offers of the use of premises - both for meetings and for Festive Boards - which are owned and supported by male Masons. However, the Grand Master reminded Brethren that:

R.W.Bro. Zuzanka Penn,
Assistant Grand Master, G.M's.G.S.

"In using such accommodation it must be remembered that we do nothing which would cause any form of embarrassment to any member of United Grand Lodge. We have existed quietly, independently and with dignity, with little or no contact with United Grand Lodge as a body for almost one hundred years. We have been more than happy in recent times to offer our unqualified support against the ruling that members of the Police Force and Judiciary, and even other public bodies, be forced to disclose membership of a Masonic organisation and we shall continue such support whenever called upon to do so."

The following year, in June 2000, at Grand Lodge the seconder of the Grand Master's election said in her speech: "We are no longer a society hidden behind closed doors, because the Grand Master has made it quite clear that we are to be proud of who we are and what we do." At the same meeting the Grand Master summarised the change in the relationship between our Order and the men's, but added a note of warning:

"I believe the Order is enjoying a period of greater enthusiasm, not only within the organisation, but from a much wider spectrum. As a result of more open publicity we are receiving more enquiries about possible membership, many instigated by members of the 'Older Obedience'. Our plea to United Grand Lodge in 1920 for recognition has in recent years been unofficially accepted; many of our Lodges are being offered the use of accommodation in Masonic premises, and we are now being asked to address gatherings of our male counterparts on the subject of the Order ... However, as Women Freemasons, we must always exercise caution. The days of ridicule are coming to an end, but there will always be those who will not accept us - we must be generous in our treatment in such cases, remembering everyone has a right to their own opinions and beliefs."

Millennium Jewel

The Millennium was celebrated by the striking of a Millennium Jewel. This was similar to the Building Restoration Fund jewel but with the figure 2000 on the lower bar and with Albrecht Durer's *Praying Hands* motif, acknowledging 2000 years of Christianity, in gold suspended

The Millennium Jewel.

from the lower bar. The jewel was available to all members of the Order. It was suggested that the profits from the sale of these jewels should go to support the Hospice Movement, and Areas were asked to submit a list of hospices in their localities, one for adults and one for children.

The Board of General Purposes agreed in September 2002 to the issue of a certificate commemorating fifty years continuous membership of the Order, and another for twenty five years.

Plans for the Centenary

In 2004 the Grand Master set up a Centenary Committee to plan for the Centenary. The June Quarterly Communication in that special year will take place at 27 Pembridge Gardens on Friday 6th June 2008, whilst the major celebration of the centenary is at the Royal Albert Hall on Saturday 7th June. All members will be welcome at the Royal Albert Hall and Brethren will be able to bring a non-Masonic guest. The arrangements for the meeting are mainly in the hands of the two Assistant Grand Masters, R.W.Bro. Betty Wildman, G.M's.G.S. and R.W.Bro. Zuzanka Penn, G.M's.G.S.

Lodge Royal Derby No.356 in July 2005

Centenary Gown Clips and Pendant, designed by R.W.Bro.I.M. Oktabcova, P.D.G.M.

A Centenary Festival Charity was set up in 2004 with the objective of raising £100,000 by 2008. In the interim, Brethren voted to select two or three national charities. A representative of each charity is invited to the celebrations at the Albert Hall to receive their cheque. At the beginning of 2008, the Centenary Charity has already received £307,000 through the fund-raising and contributions of the Brethren. The highlight of the year will be the celebration at the Royal Albert Hall - following in the tradition of the Golden and Diamond Jubilees. The meeting will include a procession of Lodge banners, a procession of representatives of the other Degrees and Orders in regalia and a Thanksgiving Service. Following an interval, there will be a presentation of cheques to the charities nominated by the Brethren to receive the proceeds of the Centenary Charity Appeal. The meeting will conclude with a spectacular show of music, song and dance on the theme of one hundred years of Freemasonry for women in the setting of national and world events.

Postscript

Two years after the Centenary M.W.Bro. Brenda Fleming-Taylor chose as her successor as Grand Master R.W.Bro. Zuzanka Daniella Penn, A.G.M., G.M's.G.S. She was enthroned at the Quarterly Communication of Grand Lodge at Birmingham in October 2010.

The Grand Master with the Deputy Grand Master, R.W.Bro. M. Masters G.M's.G.S.;
Assistant Grand Master, R.W.Bro. I.M. Oktabcova P.D.G.M., G.M's.G.S.;
Senior Grand Warden, R.W.Bro. E.J. Keitch
and Junior Grand Warden, R.W.Bro. M.J. Harwood.

Epilogue

The century that has passed since 1908 has not only seen the Honourable Fraternity of Antient Masonry develop and alter as an organisation into the Order of Women Freemasons but it has also seen changes in attitudes towards Freemasonry, both on the part of its members themselves and of society. This history, the words of which have for the most part been taken from contemporary accounts, traces the events more easily than the thoughts.

It is therefore fitting that it should conclude with these words of the eighth and present Grand Master, speaking to Grand Lodge in 2007:

"Brethren, today marks the beginning of our one hundredth year as a Masonic organisation for women. During this period of time, we have cautiously navigated our chosen destiny with what I believe to be unqualified success. Our membership has remained steady for some years now but we have created expansion in new areas both from a geographical and ceremonial point of view. Our knowledge and, more importantly, our understanding of the true meaning of Freemasonry are increasing as we put into practice all that we preach. We are initially taught the virtues of humility, which we should all accept without question, and charity for the benefit of all mankind and although we did not, during part of our history, disclose or publicise our existence as a female Masonic organisation, we have pride in what we do and why we do it. Therefore, Brethren, don't ever be afraid to stand up and be counted as one of those uniquely privileged women, a member of the Order of Women Freemasons - an institution which promotes the general good of society and a society which offers so much, to so many, for so little."

Appendix I

The Petition of 1920

(i) The text of the Petition

To the Grand Secretary, United Grand Lodge of England.

Sir, We, the undersigned, being the Grand Master, Deputy Grand Master, the Grand Treasurer, and the Grand Secretary of, and on behalf of the Honourable Fraternity of Antient Masonry beg leave to present this our humble and respectful Petition to the United Grand Lodge of England, praying, for the reasons hereinafter set out, favourable reception, consideration, and acceptance of this our prayer the same being made with due submission to, and in the most sincere regard for, your august Body.

The Honourable Fraternity of Antient Masonry would respectfully direct the attention of the United Grand Lodge of England to the fact that everywhere throughout the world doors hitherto closed to women are opening before them, admitting them to a participation in much of the work and responsibilities of men.

These newly acquired privileges are largely the outcome of women's public work during the last six years. Is it therefore too much to hope that with these heavy responsibilities upon them, women should also gain the privileges of Masonic Brotherhood in which men have found so much help and inspiration.

The Honourable Fraternity of Antient Masonry further humbly prays for a full examination into its *bona fides* as a genuine Masonic Organisation, working on strictly orthodox lines both in regard to its Constitution and Ritual which are modelled upon those of the United Grand Lodge of England, and departing from them only in the one matter of the admission of women.

The Honourable Fraternity of Antient Masonry, after twelve years of quiet and unobtrusive work, is very desirous of regularising its existence in the Masonic world by receiving (should examination prove them worthy) the imprimatur of the United Grand Lodge of England. Not by soliciting that its women members should be permitted entrance to the Lodges under the rule of the United Grand

Lodge of England - this is neither sought nor desired - but by a removal of the ban of 1910 and 1919, thereby giving to Masons who owe obedience to the United Grand Lodge of England the liberty, if desired, of extending to us their fraternal association and support, without compromising their honour or allegiance.

The Honourable Fraternity of Antient Masonry would respectfully remind the United Grand Lodge of England that the number of women who are given possession of the genuine Masonic secrets is daily increasing. The illegitimacy, masonically speaking, of the bodies communicating these secrets is not denied, but an organisation such as the Honourable Fraternity of Antient Masonry existing side by side and under the protection of the United Grand Lodge of England, would afford an orderly, dignified, and legitimate vehicle, for securing an acceptable Masonic standing to all women conforming thereto.

The Book of Constitutions, and the two pamphlets accompanying this Petition may serve to show the foundation upon which we have builded, and although we can in no way presume to dictate the measure of your acceptance of our prayer we do (should examination into our aims and working be granted) look with confidence to your recognition that the men and women comprising this Order, who are striving to inculcate and practice the high principles of Craft Masonry, are worthy of your generous and careful consideration.

And your Petitioners will ever pray, So mote it be.

(Signed) MARION LINDSAY HALSEY, Grand Master
PETER BIRCHALL, Deputy Grand Master
ADELAIDE D. LITTEN, Grand Treasurer
P.W. SLINGSBY, Grand Secretary

November 1920.

(ii) Letter from Marion Lindsay Halsey accompanying the Petition.

14, South Audley Street, W.1.

The Grand Secretary, United Grand Lodge of England.
November, 1920.

Sir, In sending you the accompanying Petition, and begging you to lay it before the Board of General Purposes, I venture to add a few words of further explanation which could not find a place in the formal document.

Firstly, we want to make it clear that our prayer is for examination, with a view to possible recognition; recognition which would enable members of Lodges working under the United Grand Lodge of England to visit the Lodges of our Order.

Secondly, may I also explain why such a small organisation as ours should take the (to us) momentous step of petitioning your Honourable Board to-day.

It might be thought that we should have had a far better chance of consideration, had we waited till our numbers had grown, and our position generally had consolidated. Many reasons have decided us to move to-day in a matter which is so near our hearts, and as one consideration has weighed with us beyond the rest, I ask your forbearance while I explain it in a very few words.

In the printed "Open Letter", which I am sending for your consideration and that of your Board, mention is made of a piece of pioneer educational work which has been undertaken by our Order, under the name of the "Guild of Education as National Service."

This Guild embraces amongst its other activities a Training College which is known as the "Halsey Training College", and which has been recognised by the Board of Education.

The College trains Teachers for the Continuation Schools under the new Education Act, and the Board of Education gives us certain grants for our students. [*]

Should our prayer for examination be happily granted, and should recognition follow, the sphere of influence of our Order would rapidly increase, and our chance of successfully carrying on our educational scheme would be assured; in spite of the many difficulties which beset such privately supported schemes to-day.

In conclusion may I say that we are quite aware of the magnitude of what we are asking. May we plead in excuse the sincere love we have for our Masonic work, and our deep sense of what Masonic discipline and Masonic teaching can do for women. Among the large armies of women existing to-day - doctors, nurses, teachers, and social workers - there is no one Organisation which can establish a close link between them all, while embracing every shade of religious opinion.

Masonry alone can supply this want, which is every day making itself more felt in our midst.

We would appeal to your Honourable Board with all the persuasion of which we are capable, seriously to consider the whole question of women's possible place in Freemasonry, in the light of recent events; and to that end to allow the Honourable Fraternity of Antient Masonry to give some account of its aims and working.

Believe me, Sir, Yours very faithfully,
MARION LINDSAY HALSEY

[*] Subsequent educational Legislation made necessary the absorption of these activities into another body outside our control.

(iii) Reply from United Grand Lodge of England

United Grand Lodge of England,
Freemasons' Hall, Great Queen Street, London, W.C.
February, 1921.

Dear Madam,
I have laid before the Board of General Purposes your communication of November last, enclosing a petition from a body styling itself the Honourable Fraternity of Antient Masonry, praying recognition from the United Grand Lodge of Antient, Free and Accepted Masons of England.

The Board, after giving full consideration to this petition and the explanatory statement from yourself with which it was accompanied, directs me to state that it cannot recommend the prayer of the petition for acceptance by Grand Lodge. The body from which that document emanates, claims, in the words of the petition, to be "a genuine Masonic Organisation ... working on strictly orthodox lines ... and departing from them only in the one matter of the admission of women." This "one matter" affects a principle on which the United Grand Lodge of England has always stood firm, and concerning which it admits no compromise. No woman can be a Freemason, according to the original Plan of Freemasonry to which English Freemasons have from time immemorial adhered. Every Brother among them is pledged, while respecting genuine and true Brethren wherever they are to be met, to discountenance all dissenters from that original Plan, and to admit that it is not in the power of any man or body of men to make innovation in the Body of Masonry. In these conditions, it is impossible for the Board of General Purposes to recommend to Grand Lodge the prayer of the petition, and it will continue to exercise its disciplinary powers towards any member working under the English Jurisdiction who violates his obligation by being present at or assisting in assemblies professing to be Masonic, which are attended by women.

Yours faithfully,
(signed) P. COLVILLE SMITH,
　　　Grand Secretary.

Mrs. Reginald Halsey,
14, South Audley Street, W.

(iv) Grand Secretary's acknowledgement.

4, Southampton Row, London, W.C.1.
February 25th, 1921.

P. Colville Smith, Esq., Grand Secretary,
United Grand Lodge of England,
Freemasons' Hall, Great Queen Street, W.C.

Sir , M.W.Bro. Marion L. Halsey, Grand Master of The Honourable Fraternity of Antient Masonry, desires me to acknowledge your letter of the current month and to express her gratitude to you for the very kind and courteous way in which you received her on the two occasions on which she came to your office.

She and her Officers regret the answer of your Honourable Board to the petition handed to you in November of last year, an answer containing a refusal basing the exclusion of women solely upon adherence to the "original Plan of Freemasonry", but feeling as she and her Officers do, that the recognition of women's place in Freemasonry is nevertheless only a question of time and patience, they will continue to devote their best energies to developing their part of the Movement in the true spirit of Masonry; so that, when recognition is finally granted, The Honourable Fraternity of Antient Masonry will be seen to be securely founded upon the three grand principles of Brotherly Love, Relief, and Truth.

I am, Sir, Faithfully yours,
(Signed) P. W. SLINGSBY, Grand Secretary.

Appendix II

List of Craft Lodges and other Degrees

(i) Craft Lodges

* Suspended   ** Amalgamated   *** Installed Masters

Number:	Name:	Consecration:	Original location.	
1	Golden Rule	1908	London	
2	Emlulation	1908	London	
3	Lodge of Unity	1908	London	
4	Harmony	1910	London	S*
5	Stability	1910	London	S
5	Stability & Peace	1951	London	S
6	Installed Masters	1912	London	
7	Verity	1928	London	S
8	Fidelity	1926	London	
9	Loyalty	1927	London	
10	Marion Halsey	1928	London	
11	Mercury	1928	travelling	S
12	Fraternity	1930	Leigh-on-Sea	
13	King Solomon	1958	travelling	S
14	Sanctuary	1930	Newcastle	
15	Perseverance	1930	Sunderland	
16	Equity	1931	London	
17	Sincerity	1932	Manchester	
18	Joyous	1933	Liverpool	
19	Progress	1933	Worthing	A** +90
20	Fellowship	1938	Cardiff	
21	Hope & Integrity	1943	Wouldham	
22	Stone of Foundation (I.M.***)	1944	Manchester	
23	Adelaide Litten	1945	London	
24	Inspiration	1945	Liverpool	S
25	Faith & Friendship	1945	London	
26	Concord	1947	Wolverhampton	
27	Argosy	1948	Bradford	
28	Meridian	1948	London	S

29	St. Mungo	1948	Glasgow	
30	Courageous	1949	Croydon	
31	Sirius	1949	Bournemouth	
32	Herakles	1949	Southgate	
33	Constancy & Faith	1949	Barnsley	
34	Duegarde	1949	Bognor	
35	Endeavour	1949	Manchester	A+87
36	Felicity	1949	Norwich	
37	Fortitude	1950	Aberdeen	S
38	Herewe	1950	Ickenham	
39	Adherence	1950	Swansea	
40	Voyagers	1950	London	
41	Granta	1950	Cambridge	
42	St. Mary's	1950	Sunderland	
43	Phoenix	1951	Bolton	
44	Tranquillity	1951	Choppington	
45	Valiant	1951	Manchester	
46	Good Report	1952	Aberdeen	
47	Mystic Tie	1952	Leeds	
48	Bond of Friendship	1952	Rochdale	
49	Gordon	1952	Stoke	
50	Isle of Sarnia	1952	Guernsey	S
51	Tyrian	1952	Hove	S
52	Anchorage	1952	Jersey	S
53	Faith & Zeal	1953	Sheerness	
54	Radiant	1953	Gillingham	
55	Corinthian	1953	Liverpool	A+104
56	Orion	1953	Birmingham	
57	Doric	1953	Stockport	
58	Peace & Harmony	1953	Birmingham	
59	Contemplation	1953	Newcastle-on-Tyne	
60	Arbitrium	1953	Birmingham	
61	Loyal Ulster	1953	Belfast	
62	Ashlar	1954	Birkenhead	
63	Steadfast	1954	Liverpool	A+161
64	Ionic	1954	Southport	
65	Justice	1954	Blackpool	A+275
66	Tuscan	1954	Glasgow	
67	Western Light	1954	Chiswick	

68	Albanus	1954	St. Albans	
69	Vigilance	1954	Nottingham	
70	St. Barbara-in-Teesdale	1954	Barnard Castle	
71	Patience & Industry	1954	Darlington	
72	Pioneer Hope of Toronto	1954	Toronto	A+79
73	Pillar of Strength	1954	Enfield	A+120
74	De Laci	1955	Elland	
75	Kedron	1955	Woodford	
76	St. David	1955	Cardiff	
77	Portsmouth L.of Duty	1955	Southsea	
78	London L. of Accord	1955	London, Ontario	S
79	Trillium of York	1955	Toronto	A+72
80	Enterprise	1955	Northampton	S
81	Staffordshire Knot	1956	Wolverhampton	
82	Serenity	1956	Ryde, I. of W.	
83	Acacia	1956	Warrington	S
84	Heritage	1956	Oshawa, Ontario	
85	Amethyst	1956	West Kirby	S
86	York	1956	York	
87	Mancunian	1957	Manchester	A+35
88	Bury L. of Goodwill	1957	Bury	
89	St. Wilfred	1957	Hassocks	S
90	Sussex Downs	1957	Worthing	A+19
91	St. Anne	1957	Lytham St. Annes	
92	Wharfedale	1957	Ilkley	
93	St. Edmundsbury	1957	Bury St. Edmunds	
94	Assheton	1957	Ashton-u-Lyme	A+285
95	Thorpe	1957	Thorpe Bay	
96	Pathana	1957	Adelaide	
97	Courtesy	1957	Newport	
98	Zimbabwe	1957	Salisbury, S.Rhod.	A+180
99	Lucy O'Hea	1958	Liverpool	A+173/S
100	Elizabethan	1958	Stratford-on-Avon	
101	Three Lights	1958	Liverpool	A+202
102	Cornerstone	1958	Eton	
103	Pentagram	1958	Beaconsfield	
104	Acanthus	1958	Liverpool	A+55
105	City of Durham	1958	Durham	
106	Prudence	1958	Seaton Carew	

107	Golden Jubilee	1958	Wakefield	
108	Crusader	1959	Leicester	
109	Tradition of Wigan	1958	Wigan	
110	Edinburgh Castle	1959	Edinburgh	
111	Mercury North	1959	travelling	
112	St. Thomas of Canterbury	1959	Canterbury	
113	Meditation (I.M.)	1959	Cardiff	
114	Southern Light	1959	Southampton	
115	Ewenny	1959	Bridgend	
116	Hampton Court	1959	Hampton Court	
117	Cedar & the Olive	1959	Belfast	
118	Farley	1960	Luton	
119	Integrity	1960	Huddersfield	S
120	Three Pillars	1960	Enfield	A+73
121	Honour	1960	Skipton	
122	St. Seiriol	1960	Llandudno	
123	Reading Abbey	1960	Reading	
124	Victoria	1960	Victoria, B.C.	S
125	Vanguard	1960	Vancouver, B.C.	S
126	Achievement	1960	Harrogate	
127	Northern Light	1960	Whitley Bay	
128	Milestone	1960	Bromley	
129	St. Andrew	1961	Plymouth	
130	Stronghold	1961	Ilford	
131	Alnwick	1961	Alnwick	
132	St.Michael & St.George	1961	Malta	S
133	Courage & Hope	1961	Oswestry	
134	Tudor Manor	1961	Richmond	S
135	City of Rochester	1961	Rochester	
136	Calder Vale	1961	Pontefract	
137	Sir Fon	1961	Anglesey	
138	Danum	1961	Sheffield	S
139	Tolerance	1961	Margate	
140	Cartref	1961	Cardiff	
141	Priory L.of Christchurch	1961	Christchurch	
142	Curtana	1961	Consett	
143	Le Boleyn	1961	Alderley Edge	
144	Lodge of Freedom	1961	Balham	
145	North Cestrian	1962	Altrincham	

146	St. Crispin	1962	Walsall	
147	Dyffryn	1962	Cardiff	
148	Venturer	1962	South Shields	
149	Remembrance	1962	Manchester	A+332
150	Landmark	1962	Upholland	A+233
151	Barrule	1962	Douglas, I of M.	
152	Amity	1962	Wallasey	A+246
153	Pilgrim	1962	Widnes	
154	L. of the Golden Portal	1962	Dunmurry	S
155	Colchester Priory	1962	Colchester	
156	Dwr-y-Felin	1962	Neath	A+183
157	St. Cecilia	1962	Maidstone	
158	Aqua Sulis	1962	Bath	
159	Offa	1963	Leamington Spa	
160	East Gate	1963	Chester	S
161	Mariners	1963	Liverpool	A+63
162	Perpendicular	1963	Ormskirk	S
163	Blyth Harbour	1963	Blyth	
164	Exonian	1963	Exeter	
165	Bryn Golau	1963	Flint	A+284
166	Pambili	1963	Bulawayo	A+292
167	Haven	1963	Scarborough	
168	Masonic Pioneers	1964	Reigate	S
169	Friendship	1964	Bournemouth	
170	Shalom	1964	Liverpool	S
171	Gothic	1964	Barnet	
172	Keele Gate	1964	Toronto	
173	Fealty	1964	Liverpool	S
174	Hospitality	1964	Middlesborough	
175	Clemency	1964	Halifax	S
176	Composite of Shrewsbury	1964	Shrewsbury	
177	Lodge of Truth	1964	Bedford	
178	St. Cuthbert	1964	Chester-le-Street	
179	Diligence	1964	Loughton	
180	St. Kilda	1964	Salisbury, S.Rhod.	A+98
181	Humility	1964	Liverpool	A+237/S
182	Grand Design (I.M.)	1964	Liverpool	
183	Caredig	1964	Llanelly	A+156
184	Avenham	1964	Preston	

185	Harbour	1964	Scarborough	
186	Runnymede	1964	Staines	
187	Invicta	1965	Whitstable	
188	Carmel	1965	Cookstown, N.I.	
189	Gateway	1965	Oakengates	A+318
190	Cheviot	1965	Wooler	
191	Burnley	1965	Burnley	
192	Lodge of Peace	1965	Hollywood, N.I.	
193	Mercia	1965	Runcorn	
194	Rectitude	1965	Paisley	S
195	Coeur de Lion	1965	Leicester	
196	St. John Prescot	1965	Liverpool	S
197	Lodge of St. Peter	1965	Woolton	A+254
198	Airedale	1965	Bingley	
199	Wyndleshora	1965	Windsor	
200	Torbay	1965	Paignton	
201	St. Gwynllyw	1965	Newport	S
202	Queensway	1965	Liverpool	A+101
203	Croeso	1965	Wrexham	
204	St. Clare	1966	Warrington	
205	Tudor Rose	1966	Todmorden	
206	St. Lawrence (I.M.)	1966	Toronto	
207	Carreg Harlech	1966	Harlech	
208	Horizon	1966	Downpatrick	
209	Kingdom of Fife	1966	Kirkaldy	S
210	Cabot Tower	1966	Bristol	S
211	Emerald	1966	Dublin	S
212	Sussex Martlets	1966	Crawley	S
213	Allegiance	1966	Oldham	
214	Bedale	1967	Bedale	
215	Faversham Abbey	1967	Faversham	
216	Cefnllys	1967	Llandrindod Wells	
217	Aspiration	1967	Chesterfield	
218	Endurance	1967	Epping	A+219
219	Connaught	1967	Chingford	A+218
220	Sarum	1967	Salisbury	S
221	Whytchurche	1967	Shrewsbury	
222	Hala	1967	Halesowen	S
223	Cashio	1968	Watford	A+320

224	Lodge of Grace	1968	Little Sutton	
225	Diamond Jubilee	1968	Sunderland	
226	Algum Tree	1968	Harwich	A+330/S
227	St. Mildred	1968	Leyland	A+293
228	Taunton Dene/Quantocks	1968	Taunton	S
229	Pen Dinas	1968	St. Asaph	
230	Brawdgarwch (I.M.)	1968	Cardiff	
231	St. Dorothea	1968	Grimsby	
232	Alliance (I.M.)	1968	Birmingham	
233	Dormer Light	1968	Hindley	A+150
234	St. Barnabas	1968	Barnsley	
235	Hestenga	1968	Hastings	A+319
236	Glaslyn	1968	Port Madoc	S
237	Jasper	1968	Formby	S
238	Vinovium	1968	B.Auckland	
239	Revelation (I.M.)	1968	Sunderland	
240	Oxford Temple	1968	Oxford	
241	Prescelli	1969	Haverfordwest	
242	True Light	1969	Liverpool	A+243/S
243	Semper Fidelis	1969	Liverpool	S
244	Ribble Valley	1969	Blackburn	S
245	Perfect Ashlar (I.M.)	1969	N.Wales/Midlands	
246	Simplicity	1969	Moreton	A+152
247	Resolution	1969	Rotherham	
248	Montpellier	1969	Cheltenham	
249	Minerva	1969	Widnes	
250	Brig O'Doon	1969	Ayr	
251	Durnovaria	1969	Dorchester	
252	St. Martin (I.M.)	1969	Bournemouth	
253	St. Mary's Priory	1969	Bridlington	
254	Ner Tamid	1969	Liverpool	A+197
255	White Cliff	1969	Dover	
256	Anwyl	1969	Mold	
257	L. of the Morning Star	1970	Basingstoke	
258	Salopia	1970	Newport	A+336
259	Bycullah	1970	Enfield	
260	Southern Cross	1970	S.Australia	
261	Halcyon	1970	Eastbourne	
262	Ramsey	1970	Isle of Man	

263	Vale Royal	1971	Weaverham	
264	Foreland Light	1971	Broadstairs	
265	Gwynedd (I.M.)	1971	Llandudno	
266	Parvis	1971	Hounslow	
267	Palm Tree	1971	Lagos, Nigeria S	
268	Cornucopia	1971	Crewe	
269	Fernham	1971	Fareham	
270	St. Andrew's (I.M.)	1971	Glasgow	
271	Granite City (I.M.)	1975	Aberdeen	S
272	Berkshire Downs	1971	Newbury	
273	Kerenza	1971	Truro	
274	Saint Helena	1972	Ryton	
275	St. Chad	1972	Poulton/Fylde	A+65
276	Westgate (I.M.)	1972	Preston	
277	West Riding (I.M.)	1972	Leeds	
278	Tavistock Abbey	1972	Tavistock	
279	Loyal Cheshire	1972	Crewe	
280	Vale of Meon	1972	Chawton	
281	Emarell Centum	1973	Chester-le-Street	
282	Beacon (I.M.)	1973	Wolverhampton	
283	Alphege	1973	Solihull	S
284	Bethania	1973	Flint	A+165
285	Stamford	1973	Ashton/Lyne	A+94
286	Mazel	1973	Prestwich	
287	Temple	1974	Bootle	S
288	Lucem	1974	St. Helens	S
289	Yeo Valley	1974	Yeovil	
290	Sandawana	1974	Salisbury, Rhodesia	S
291	St. Christopher	1974	Umtali, Rhodesia	
292	Letaba	1974	Bulawayo, Rhod.	A+166
293	Chorley	1974	Chorley	A+227
294	Saxon Gate	1974	Wokingham	
295	Castell Caernarvon	1975	Caernarvon	
296	Trinity	1975	Warrington	
297	Loyal Barum	1975	Barnstaple	
298	Grouville	1975	Runcorn	
299	De Lovetot	1975	Worksop	
300	Doris Jones Memorial	1978	Worthing	
301	Tamar (I.M.)	1976	Devon & Cornwall	

302	Thetford Priory	1976	Norfolk	
303	Newton	1976	Newton-le-Willows	
304	Glantaf (I.M.)	1976	Cardiff	
305	Abbeygate	1976	Abingdon	
306	St. Agnes	1976	Scunthorpe	
307	Red Rose of Lancs.(I.M.)	1977	Bootle	S
308	Eccles	1977	Eccles	
309	Mosaic (I.M.)	1977	Belfast	
310	Rushmere	1977	Ipswich	
311	Joyous Light	1977	Gravesend	
312	Sŵn-y-Gân	1977	Cardiff	
313	Dunaverty Castle	1977	Campbeltown	S
314	Wessyngton	1977	Birtley	
315	Fraternal Friendship	1977	Sittingbourne	
316	St. Nicholas	1978	Harpenden	S
317	Masonic Joy	1978	Tonbridge	
318	Northgate	1978	Bridgnorth	A+189
319	Guestling	1978	Hastings	A+235
320	Ashridge	1978	Hemel Hempsted	A+223
321	Lancaster	1978	Lancaster	
322	Mole Valley	1979	Leatherhead	
323	Blendon Wood	1979	Bexleyheath	
324	Clwyd (I.M.)	1979	Flint	
325	Norton Priory (I.M.)	1979	Runcorn	
326	Pennine	1980	Littleborough	S
327	St. Aidan	1980	South Shields	
328	Viking	1981	Ramsgate	
329	Deira	1981	Driffield	
330	Marcellus	1981	Holland-on-Sea	A+226/S
331	Alpha (I.M.)	1981	Harare, Zimbabwe	
332	Menorah	1982	Manchester	A+149
333	Sussex Masters	1982	Worthing	
334	Holmvalia	1982	Barnsley	S
335	Shropshire I.M.	1982	Shrewsbury	
336	Ludlow Castle	1982	Ludlow	A+258
337	Protea	1982	Johannesburg	
338	Flame Lily	1982	Kloof, Natal	
339	Kelso Abbey	1982	Kelso	
340	St. Francis	1982	Sunderland	

341	Northolme (I.M.)	1983	Lytham St. Annes
342	Chiltern Hills	1984	Thame
343	Belmont (I.M.)	1984	Manchester
344	Causeway	1985	Portrush
345	Balloch	1985	Keith
346	Obedience	1987	Witham
347	Liskerrett	1987	Liskeard
348	Essex I.M.	1992	Leigh-on-Sea
349	White Rose (I.M.)	1998	Driffield
350	Norfolk & Suffolk I.M.	2000	Attleborough
351	Solent (I.M.)	2001	Titchfield
352	Millennium	2001	Minehead
353	Solway	2001	Castle Douglas
354	East Kent I.M.	2001	Faversham+Wouldham+Westgate
355	La Rama Primera	2005	Fuengirola, Spain
356	Royal Derby	2005	Ripley
357	Centennial Magna Carta	2008	Lincoln
358	Fleming-Taylor	2009	Sheringham
359	Lady Isabella	2011	Onchan, Isle of Man

(ii) Order of the Secret Monitor

1	Shield of David	2001	Faversham
2	David & Jonathan	2002	London
3	Sword of David	2005	Cardiff
4	Semper Fidelis	2005	Barnsley
5	Arrow	2007	Bury
6	Seal of Solomon	2007	Bournemouth
7	Fraternal Friendship	2010	Leigh-on-Sea

(iii) Mark Degree (with Royal Ark Mariner where shown R)

1	Keystone (R)	1946	London
2	Lebanon (R)	1947	London
3	Bondstone (R)	1947	Liverpool
4	Meridian (R)	1947	London
5	Sincerity (R)	1948	Manchester

6	Archstone	1948	travelling+Toronto,S,*rev.*2011
7	Progress (R)	1949	Worthing
8	Perseverance (R)	1950	Sunderland
9	Sanctuary (R)	1950	Newcastle
10	Granite	1952	Aberdeen
11	Fellowship (R)	1952	Cardiff
12	Concord (R)	1952	Wolverhampton
13	Fraternity (R)	1953	Westcliff-on-Sea
14	Constancy & Faith (R)	1954	Sheffield
15	St. Mungo	1955	Glasgow
16	Whitestone (R)	1955	Leeds
17	Joppa (R)	1957	Gillingham
18	Serenity (R)	1962	Ryde, I. of Wight
19	Quarry	1962	Richmond
20	Corinthian (R)	1962	Liverpool S
21	Zaradatha	1963	Belfast
22	Tyrian (R)	1964	Brighton S
23	Ionic	1966	Southport
24	Fylde Coast (R)	1966	Lytham St. Annes
25	Gwynedd (R)	1967	Llandudno
26	Yarwood (R)	1967	Birmingham
27	Gebal (R)	1969	Faversham
28	Lightstone (R)	1971	Scarborough
29	Cheshire (R)	1971	Chester
30	Rosetta Stone (R)	1974	Todmorden
31	Severn (R)	1976	Atcham
32	Sandstone (R)	1976	Runcorn
33	Cedar (R)	1977	Bournemouth
34	Charnwood (R)	1978	Leicester
35	Hall (R)	1978	Upholland S
36	Mallet & Chisel (R)	1979	Margate
37	Celtic (R)	1979	Exeter
38	Flintstone (R)	1979	Flint
39	South Gate (R)	1979	London N11
40	Carreg Wen (R)	1980	Swansea
41	Hestenga	1980	St. Leonards
42	Loyalty	1980	Crewe
43	Mannanan	1981	Douglas, I. of M.

44	Ashlar (R)	1981	Maidstone	
45	Les Isles de la Manche	1981	Guernsey	S
46	Northumbria (R)	1981	Alnwick	
47	Humber Bridge	1982	Scunthorpe	
48	Sheva	1983	Bootle	S
49	St. Clare (R)	1983	Warrington	
50	Iceni (R)	1984	Colchester	
51	Tamar	1984	Plymouth	
52	Dunedin	1985	Edinburgh	
53	Chorley (R)	1986	Chorley	
54	Tylehurst (R)	1987	Reading	
55	Matopos (R)	1991	Bulawayo	
56	Austral	1992	S. Australia	
57	Pilgrim's Way (R)	1992	Thetford	
58	Msasa	1997	Harare, Zimbabwe	
59	Mount Horeb	1997	Kloof, Natal	

(iv) Chapter

1	Premier	1929	Worthing	
2	Logos	1930	London	A+4
3	Zodiac	1930	London	
4	Zerah	1944	London	A+2
5	Joyous	1945	Liverpool	
6	Perseverance	1948	Sunderland	
7	Meridian	1950	London	
8	Sincerity	1953	Manchester	
9	Golden Square	1955	Birmingham	
10	Catenarian	1961	Cardiff	
11	St. William's	1961	York	
12	Zion	1961	Bradford	
13	Signet of Truth	1962	Southport	A+30
14	Medway	1962	Gillingham	
15	Zenith	1963	Southsea	
16	Corinthian	1963	Liverpool	S
17	Lucy O'Hea	1963	Liverpool	S
18	Concord	1963	Wolverhampton	
19	Triad	1964	Enfield	S

20	Circle & Triangle	1964	London	
21	Sanctuary	1964	Newcastle	
22	Fylde Coast	1964	Blackpool	
23	Valiant	1964	Manchester	
24	Golden Triangle	1966	Toronto	S
25	St. Andrew's	1966	Plymouth	
26	Chapter of Light	1967	Chester	
27	Gwynedd	1969	Llandudno	
28	Corban	1969	Christchurch	A+39
29	St. Clare	1969	Wigan	
30	Pentagon	1970	Wigan	A+13
31	Thorngate	1971	Margate	
32	Priory	1972	Leigh-on-Sea	
33	De Montfort	1973	Leicester	
34	Acropolis	1974	Salisbury, Rhodesia	
35	Radiant Light	1974	Bulawayo	
36	Seal of Solomon	1974	Runcorn	
37	Splendour of Light	1974	Shrewsbury	
38	Constancy & Faith	1974	Barnsley	
39	Fiat Lux	1975	Bournemouth	A+28
40	Halcyon	1975	Eastbourne	
41	Llandaff	1976	Cardiff	
42	Irree-yn-Laa	1976	Douglas, I. of M.	S
43	Bethania	1976	Flint	
44	Loyal Jubilee	1977	Crewe	
45	Faversham Abbey	1980	Faversham	
46	Bon Accord	1980	Aberdeen	S
47	Iceni	1993	Essex	
48	Holyrood	1994	Edinburgh	
49	Circle of Light	1997	Kloof, Natal	
50	Portcullis	1999	Wallingford	
51	Eastern Light	2007	Attleborough	

(v) Order of the Red Cross of Constantine and the Holy Sepulchre

1	Pillar of Light	1952	London *(Holy Sepulchre)*
2	St. Helena	1952	London
3	Cross Fleury	1952	London

4	St. Cuthman	1954	Worthing
5	St. Margaret	1958	Cardiff
6	Torch Bearer	1959	York
7	St. Ann	1959	Liverpool
8	Sincerity	1959	Manchester
9	Paternoster	1964	Salisbury, Rhodesia
10	Labarum	1965	Bradford
11	Rose & Lily	1972	Sunderland
12	Trinity	1972	Flint
13	* * *		
14	Fleur-de-Lys	1973	Bournemouth
15	Mystic Light	1975	Faversham
16	St. Elizabeth	1979	Runcorn
17	Gwynedd	1981	Llandudno S
18	St. Hilary	1984	Wallasey
19	St. Cuthbert	1990	Lytham St. Annes
20	Lux Sabrinensis	1992	Atcham
21	Celestial Cross	1992	Leigh-on-Sea
22	Isca	1993	Exeter
23	St. Andrew	1996	Glasgow
24	Byzantium	1997	Bulawayo
25	Inspiration	2000	Wouldham
26	Trinity in Unity	2009	Wallingford

(vi) Allied Masonic Degrees

1	Euphrates Council	1954	London
2	Veritas Council	1994	Faversham

(vii) Royal and Select Masters

2	Light Invisible Cryptic Council	1949	London
3	Hidden Mysteries Cryptic Council	1949	Liverpool
4	Aries Cryptic Council	1949/1991	Faversham
5	Ninth Arch	2012	Bournemouth

(viii) Templar Grand Conclave

1	Faith & Friendship	1945	Bournemouth
2	Avalon	1949	London
3	Cambrensis	1968	Cardiff
4	Holy Lance	1992	Flint
5	Coeur de Lion	1994	Faversham
6	Excalibur	1996	Barnsley
7	Peace & Harmony	1997	Bulawayo
8	Crusader	1999	Leigh-on-Sea
9	Venerable Bede	2000	Sunderland
10	Jaques de Molay	2002	Liverpool

(ix) Commemorative Order of St. Thomas of Acon

1	Londinium Chapel	2006	London
2	Becket Chapel	2006	Faversham

(x) Knight Templar Priests

1	Alpha Tabernacle	1999	London
2	Beta	2000	Faversham
3	Gamma	2003	Cardiff
4	Delta	2003	Flint
5	Epsilon	2010	Bournemouth
6	Zeta	2012	Barnsley

(xi) Ancient and Accepted Rite

Rose Croix

1	Mystic Cup Chapter	1950	London
2	Rose & the Flame	1952	Flint
3	Crown of Thorns	1994	Faversham
4	Living Circle	2000	Bournemouth

5	Eternal Wisdom	2002	Leigh-on-Sea
6	Holy Sanctuary	2004	Sunderland
7	Circle of Light	2009	Barnsley
8	Pax Vobiscum	2010	Cardiff

30th Degree

Camp of the Black & White Eagle No.1 *revived* 1992 London, Faversham

31st Degree

Grand Inspector Inquisitor Commander 2004 London, Faversham

32nd Degree

Sublime Prince of the Royal Secret 2006 London, Faversham

33rd Degree

Sovereign Grand Inspector General 2006 London

(xii) Royal Order of Scotland

1955, *revived* 1991 London

Appendix III - **Senior Grand Lodge Officers 1908 to 2007**

	G.Master	D.G.M.	A.G.M.	S.G.W.	J.G.W.
1908	W.F.Cobb	J.W.Sidley	*	A.J.Faulding	F.Faulding
1909	W.F.Cobb	J.W.Sidley	*	A.J.Faulding	F.Faulding
1910	W.F.Cobb	J.W.Sidley	*	A.J.Faulding	F.Faulding
1911	W.F.Cobb	M.L.Halsey	*	F.Faulding	F.W.Lacey
1912	M.Halsey	P.Birchall	*	F.W.Lacey	M.Mackenzie
1913	M.Halsey	P.Birchall	*	M.Mackenzie	J.A.Johns
1914	M.Halsey	P.Birchall	*	J.A.Johns	C.E.Hughes
1915	M.Halsey	P.Birchall	*	C.E.Hughes	G.I.Lloyd
1916	M.Halsey	P.Birchall	*	G.I.Lloyd	G.D.Anderson
1917	M.Halsey	P.Birchall	*	J.J.Lewis	J.B.Carrington
1918	M.Halsey	P.Birchall	*	J.B.Carrington	F.J.Hawkins
1919	M.Halsey	P.Birchall	*	F.J.Hawkins	A.Theophilus
1920	M.Halsey	P.Birchall	*	A.Theophilus	C.Boyd
1921	M.Halsey	P.Birchall	*	M.E.Cook	M.McClatchie
1922	M.Halsey	P.Birchall	*	M.McClatchie	A.Harrison
1923	M.Halsey	P.Birchall	*	A.Harrison	P.I.Alt
1924	M.Halsey	P.Birchall	*	A.Theophilus	F.M.Ayrton
1925	M.Halsey	P.Birchall	*	F.M.Ayrton	A.M.Hope
1926	M.Halsey	P.Birchall	*	A.M.Hope	H.B.Winter
1927	M.Halsey	P.Birchall	*	H.B.Winter	L.J.Pearson
1928	A.Litten	P.Birchall	*	L.J.Pearson	M.D.Pennant
1929	A.Litten	P.Birchall	*	M.D.Pennant	H.Worthington
1930	A.Litten	P.Birchall	*	A.Gascoigne	M.Litten
1931	A.Litten	P.Birchall	*	M.Litten	A.M.Collet
1932	A.Litten	P.Birchall	*	A.M.Collet	H.M.Strange
1933	A.Litten	P.Birchall	*	A.M.Collet	F.Leveridge
1934	A.Litten	P.Birchall	*	F.Leveridge	M.Cresswell
1935	A.Litten	L.Parker-Jervis	*	H.M.Strange	C.Shepherd
1936	A.Litten	L.Parker-Jervis	*	C.Shepherd	A.I.Young
1937	A.Litten	L.Parker-Jervis	*	A.I.Young	L.Perkins
1938	L.O'Hea	L.Parker-Jervis	*	L.Perkins	E.M.Suggate

G.Chaplain	G.Treasurer	G.Registrar	G.Secretary	G.D.C.	
*	F.W.Schon	E.Greenfield	P.Birchall	*	1908
*	E.Greenfield		P.Birchall	M.Symonds	1909
*	E.Greenfield		P.Birchall	M.L.Halsey	1910
Rev.F.W.Gilby	E.Greenfield	H.K.Haslam	P.Birchall	M.Symonds	1911
Rev.F.W.Gilby	J.B.Carrington	A.D.Litten	P.Slingsby	J.Boswell-Reid	1912
Rev.F.W.Gilby	J.B.Carrington	B.I.French	P.Slingsby	A.D.Litten	1913
Rev.F.W.Gilby	A.D.Litten	B.I.French	P.Slingsby	J.J.Lewis	1914
Rev.F.W.Gilby	A.D.Litten	B.I.French	P.Slingsby	J.B.Carrington	1915
Rev.F.W.Gilby	A.D.Litten	B.I.French	P.Slingsby	F.J.Hawkins	1916
Rev.F.W.Gilby	A.D.Litten	B.I.French	P.Slingsby	A.Theophilus	1917
*	A.D.Litten	B.I.French	P.Slingsby	M.E.Cook	1918
*	A.D.Litten	B.I.French	P.Slingsby	C.Boyd	1919
*	A.D.Litten	B.I.French	P.Slingsby	M.E.Cook	1920
*	A.D.Litten	M.Mackenzie	P.Slingsby	P.I.Alt	1921
*	A.D.Litten	M.Mackenzie	P.Slingsby	P.I.Alt	1922
*	A.D.Litten	F.E.Turner	P.Slingsby	F.Ayrton	1923
*	A.D.Litten	F.E.Turner	P.Slingsby	A.M.Hope	1924
*	A.D.Litten	F.E.Turner	P.Slingsby	H.B.Winter	1925
*	A.D.Litten	F.E.Turner	P.Slingsby	L.J.Pearson	1926
*	A.D.Litten	F.E.Turner	P.Slingsby	M.D.Pennant	1927
*	B.Ireland	L.O'Hea	P.Slingsby	H.Worthington	1928
*	B.Ireland	L.O'Hea	P.Slingsby	A.Gascoigne	1929
*	B.Ireland	L.O'Hea	P.Slingsby	A.M.Collet	1930
*	B.Ireland	L.O'Hea	P.Slingsby	H.M.Strange	1931
*	C.R.Logan	L.O'Hea	P.Slingsby	F.Leveridge	1932
*	C.R.Logan	L.Parker-Jervis	P.Slingsby	M.Cresswell	1933
*	C.R.Logan	L.Parker-Jervis	P.Slingsby	C.D.Shepherd	1934
*	C.R.Logan	A.Gascoigne	F.Leveridge	A.I.Young	1935
*	L.E.Smith	A.Gascoigne	F.Leveridge	L.Perkins	1936
G.I.Lloyd	L.E.Smith	A.Gascoigne	F.Leveridge	E.M.Suggate	1937
A.M.Collet	L.E.Smith	A.Gascoigne	F.Leveridge	F.E.Turner	1938

	G.M.	D.G.M.	A.G.M.	S.G.W.	J.G.W.
1939	L.O'Hea	L.Parker-Jervis	*	E.M.Suggate	E.How
1940	L.O'Hea	L.Parker-Jervis	*	E.How	A.R.Hillyer
1941	L.O'Hea	L.Parker-Jervis	*	A.R.Hillyer	R.Ashley
1942	L.O'Hea	L.Parker-Jervis	*	R.Ashley	A.J.Parker
1943	L.O'Hea	*	*	A.J.Parker	B.H.Riddel
1944	L.O'Hea	M.G.M.Hope	*	B.H.Riddel	B.A.Bennett
1945	L.O'Hea	M.G.M.Hope	*	B.A.Bennett	E.Fisher
1946	L.O'Hea	M.G.M.Hope	*	E.Fisher	E.F.Lock
1947	L.O'Hea	M.G.M.Hope	*	E.F.Lock	L.E.Smith
1948	M.G.M.Hope	D.A.Taylor	*	L.E.Smith	B.A.Poore
1949	M.G.M.Hope	D.A.Taylor	*	B.A.Poore	K.Street
1950	M.G.M.Hope	D.A.Taylor	*	K.Street	F.C.Swash
1951	M.G.M.Hope	D.A.Taylor	M.R.Low	F.C.Swash	A.Gotch
1952	M.G.M.Hope	D.A.Taylor	M.R.Low	A.Gotch	M.I.Read
1953	M.G.M.Hope	D.A.Taylor	M.R.Low	A.Gotch	M.I.Read
1954	M.G.M.Hope	D.A.Taylor	M.R.Low	M.I.Read	F.H.Hawes
1955	M.G.M.Hope	D.A.Taylor	M.R.Low	F.H.Hawes	N.de Pass
1956	M.G.M.Hope	D.A.Taylor	M.R.Low	H.Eckenstein	N.de Pass
1957	M.G.M.Hope	D.A.Taylor	M.R.Low	N.de Pass	C.Cooper
1958	M.G.M.Hope	D.A.Taylor	M.R.Low	N.de Pass	C.Cooper
1959	M.G.M.Hope	D.A.Taylor	M.R.Low	C.Cooper	B.H.Wilson
1960	M.G.M.Hope	D.A.Taylor	M.R.Low	C.Cooper	B.H.Wilson
1961	M.G.M.Hope	D.A.Taylor	M.R.Low	C.Cooper	B.H.Wilson
1962	M.G.M.Hope	D.A.Taylor	Low/Cooper	B.H.Wilson	E.V.Smith
1963	M.G.M.Hope	D.A.Taylor	Low/Cooper	B.H.Wilson	E.V.Smith
1964	M.R.Low	D.A.Taylor	C.Cooper	F.Owen	E.V.Smith
1965	M.R.Low	D.A.Taylor	C.Cooper	F.Owen	E.V.Smith
1966	M.R.Low	D.A.Taylor	C.Cooper	E.V.Smith	D.H.Stanuell
1967	M.R.Low	D.A.Taylor	C.Cooper	E.V.Smith	D.H.Stanuell
1968	M.R.Low	D.A.Taylor	C.Cooper	D.H.Stanuell	E.M.Elvey
1969	M.R.Low	D.A.Taylor	Mullen/Lloyd	H.E.Buchmann	E.M.Elvey
1970	M.R.Low	D.A.Taylor	Mullen/Lloyd	H.E.Buchmann	N.E.Thorn
1971	M.R.Low	D.A.Taylor	Mullen/Lloyd	H.E.Buchmann	N.E.Thorn
1972	M.R.Low	D.A.Taylor	Mullen/Lloyd	H.E.Buchmann	N.E.Thorn

G.Chaplain	G.Treasurer	G.Registrar	G.Secretary	G.D.C.	
*	L.E.Smith	A.Gascoigne	F.Leveridge	M.I.Read	1939
*	M.R.Low	A.Gascoigne	F.Leveridge	M.I.Read	1940
L.E.Smith	M.R.Low	A.Gascoigne	F.Leveridge	M.I.Read	1941
L.E.Smith	M.R.Low	A.Gascoigne	F.Leveridge	M.I.Read	1942
L.E.Smith	M.R.Low	A.Gascoigne	F.Leveridge	M.I.Read	1943
L.E.Smith	M.R.Low	A.Gascoigne	F.Leveridge	M.I.Read	1944
L.E.Smith	M.R.Low	A.Gascoigne	F.Leveridge	M.I.Read	1945
L.E.Smith	M.R.Low	A.Gascoigne	F.Leveridge	M.I.Read	1946
F.M.Grant	M.R.Low	A.Gascoigne	F.Leveridge	M.I.Read	1947
F.M.Grant	M.R.Low	F.C.Swash	F.Leveridge	M.I.Read	1948
M.M.Bird	M.R.Low	F.C.Swash	F.Leveridge	M.I.Read	1949
M.M.Bird	M.R.Low	A.Gotch	M.V.Ellis	M.I.Read	1950
C.M.Pearson	E.Henderson	W.G.Ashby	M.V.Ellis	M.I.Read	1951
C.M.Pearson	E.Henderson	W.G.Ashby	M.V.Ellis	B.H.Wilson	1952
Pearson/Coast	E.Henderson	N.de Pass	M.V.Ellis	B.H.Wilson	1953
Pearson/Coast	E.Henderson	N.de Pass	M.V.Ellis	B.H.Wilson	1954
Pearson/Coast	E.Henderson	C.Cooper	M.V.Ellis	B.H.Wilson	1955
Coast/Focke	E.Henderson	C.Cooper	M.V.Ellis	B.H.Wilson	1956
Coast/Focke		C.Cooper	M.V.Ellis	Wilson/Allison	1957
Coast/Owen	I.M.Gould	H.Crosby	M.V.Ellis	Wilson/Allison	1958
F.Owen	I.M.Gould	A.Lewis	M.V.Ellis	Allison/Tasch	1959
Owen/Thorn	D.H.Stanuell	A.Lewis	M.V.Ellis	Allison/Tasch	1960
Focke/Thorn	D.H.Stanuell	E.V.Smith	M.V.Ellis	Allison/Prior	1961
Focke/Deed	D.H.Stanuell	Thorn/Allison	M.V.Ellis	W.Prior	1962
Focke/Deed	D.H.Stanuell	Thorn/Allison	M.V.Ellis	W.Prior	1963
Focke/Deed	D.G.Jones	Thorn/Allison	M.V.Ellis	W.Prior	1964
Focke/Deed	M.B.Webber	H.Buchmann	E.M.Stokes	W.Prior	1965
Deed/Mosse	M.B.Webber	H.Buchmann	E.M.Stokes	W.Prior	1966
Deed/Mosse	M.B.Webber	H.Buchmann	E.M.Stokes	W.Prior	1967
B.E.Mosse	E.E.Chaplin	H.Buchmann	E.M.Stokes	W.Prior	1968
B.E.Mosse	E.E.Chaplin	F.Hall	E.M.Stokes	W.Prior	1969
K.M.Saunders	E.E.Chaplin	F.Hall	E.M.Stokes	W.Prior	1970
K.M.Saunders	E.E.Chaplin	F.Hall	*	W.Prior	1971
K.M.Saunders	E.E.Chaplin	F.Hall	I.N.Campbell	W.Prior	1972

	G.M.	D.G.M.	A.G.M.	S.G.W.	J.G.W.
1973	M.R.Low	Prior/Mullen	Lloyd/Hall	H.E.Buchmann	M.Sowerby
1974	M.R.Low	Prior/Mullen	Lloyd/Hall	H.E.Buchmann	M.Sowerby
1975	M.R.Low	W.Prior	Lloyd/Hall	H.E.Buchmann	M.Sowerby
1976	F.Hall	W.Prior	O.M.Lloyd	D.Hoadley	D.E.Smyth
1977	F.Hall	O.M.Lloyd	D.Hoadley	L.J.Isam	D.E.Smyth
1978	F.Hall	O.M.Lloyd	D.Hoadley	L.J.Isam	D.E.Smyth
1979	F.Hall	O.M.Lloyd	D.Hoadley	L.J.Isam	I.M.Roberts
1980	F.Hall	O.M.Lloyd	D.Hoadley	D.E.Smyth	I.M.Roberts
1981	F.Hall	O.M.Lloyd	D.Hoadley	D.E.Smyth	I.M.Roberts
1982	F.Hall	O.M.Lloyd	D.Hoadley	D.E.Smyth	E.Shepherd
1983	F.Hall	O.M.Lloyd	D.Hoadley	E.Shepherd	B.Whitehouse
1984	F.Hall	O.M.Lloyd	D.Hoadley	E.Shepherd	B.Whitehouse
1985	F.Hall	D.Hoadley	E.Shepherd	B.Whitehouse	D.Cudmore
1986	F.Hall	D.Hoadley	E.Shepherd	D.Cudmore	A.Aldred
1987	F.Hall	D.Hoadley	E.Shepherd	D.Cudmore	A.Aldred
1988	F.Hall	E.Shepherd	M.Kennedy	J.Abbott	A.Aldred
1989	B.Fleming-Taylor	E.Shepherd	M.Kennedy	J.Abbott	M.Masters
1990	B.Fleming-Taylor	E.Shepherd	M.Kennedy	J.Abbott	M.Masters
1991	B.Fleming-Taylor	E.Shepherd	M.Kennedy	M.Masters	V.Nield
1992	B.Fleming-Taylor	E.Shepherd	M.Kennedy	M.Masters	V.Nield
1993	B.Fleming-Taylor	E.Shepherd	M.Kennedy	M.Masters	V.Nield
1994	B.Fleming-Taylor	E.Shepherd	L.Chapman	M.Masters	V.Nield
1995	B.Fleming-Taylor	M.Masters	B.Whittingham	V.Nield	B.Wildman
1996	B.Fleming-Taylor	M.Masters	B.Whittingham	V.Nield	B.Wildman
1997	B.Fleming-Taylor	M.Masters	B.Whittingham	V.Nield	B.Wildman
1998	B.Fleming-Taylor	M.Masters	B.Whittingham	B.Wildman	B.George
1999	B.Fleming-Taylor	M.Masters	B.Whittingham	B.Wildman	B.George
2000	B.Fleming-Taylor	M.Masters	W'ham/Wildman	B.George	E.J.Keitch
2001	B.Fleming-Taylor	M.Masters	B.Wildman	B.George	E.J.Keitch
2002	B.Fleming-Taylor	M.Masters	B.Wildman	B.George	E.J.Keitch
2003	B.Fleming-Taylor	M.Masters	B.Wildman	B.George	E.J.Keitch
2004	B.Fleming-Taylor	M.Masters	B.Wildman	B.George	E.J.Keitch
2005	B.Fleming-Taylor	M.Masters	B.Wildman	B.George	E.J.Keitch
2006	B.Fleming-Taylor	M.Masters	Wildman/Penn	B.George	E.J.Keitch
2007	B.Fleming-Taylor	M.Masters	Wildman/Penn	B.George	E.J.Keitch

G.Chaplain	G.Treasurer	G.Registrar	G.Secretary	G.D.C.	
K.M.Saunders	E.E.Chaplin	B.Jones	I.N.Campbell	Williams/Rutherford	1973
K.M.Saunders	E.E.Chaplin	L.Chapman	I.N.Campbell	Marshall/Williams	1974
K.M.Saunders	E.E.Chaplin	L.Chapman	I.N.Campbell	Roberts/Williams	1975
K.M.Saunders	E.E.Chaplin	L.Chapman	I.N.Campbell	Roberts/Williams	1976
K.M.Saunders	E.E.Chaplin	L.Chapman	I.N.Campbell	Roberts/Williams	1977
K.M.Saunders	E.E.Chaplin	L.Chapman	*	Roberts/Williams	1978
D.E.Smyth	E.E.Chaplin	L.Chapman	*	R.Williams	1979
E.V.Smith	E.E.Chaplin	L.Chapman	*	D.E.Disspain	1980
E.V.Smith	E.E.Chaplin	L.Chapman	*	D.E.Disspain	1981
E.V.Smith	E.E.Chaplin	L.Chapman	*	D.E.Disspain	1982
E.V.Smith	E.E.Chaplin	L.Chapman	*	D.E.Disspain	1983
E.V.Smith	E.E.Chaplin	L.Chapman	*	D.E.Disspain	1984
E.V.Smith	E.E.Chaplin	*	J.Goss	D.E.Disspain	1985
E.V.Smith	E.E.Chaplin	*	V.M.Clare	D.E.Disspain	1986
E.V.Smith	E.E.Chaplin	*	V.M.Clare	B.Pickett	1987
V.Nield	E.E.Chaplin	B.Fleming-Taylor	*	B.Pickett	1988
V.Nield	E.E.Chaplin	*	E.Parker	B.Pickett	1989
V.Nield	E.E.Chaplin	L.Chapman	E.Parker	B.Pickett	1990
E.V.Smith	H.I.Naldrett	J.Abbott	E.Parker	B.Pickett	1991
E.V.Smith	H.I.Naldrett	J.Abbott	E.Parker	B.Pickett	1992
E.Hayward	H.I.Naldrett	J.Abbott	E.Parker	B.Pickett	1993
E.Hayward	H.I.Naldrett	J.Abbott	E.Parker	B.Pickett	1994
E.Hayward	H.I.Naldrett	J.Abbott	E.Parker	Z.Penn	1995
E.Hayward	H.I.Naldrett	J.Abbott	E.Parker	Z.Penn	1996
E.Hayward	H.I.Naldrett	J.Abbott	E.Parker	Z.Penn	1997
E.Hayward	H.I.Naldrett	J.Abbott	E.Parker	Z.Penn	1998
E.Hayward	H.I.Naldrett	J.Abbott	J.S.Brown	Z.Penn	1999
E.Hayward	H.I.Naldrett	J.Abbott	J.S.Brown	Z.Penn	2000
E.Hayward	H.I.Naldrett	J.Ion	J.S.Brown	Z.Penn	2001
E.Hayward	H.I.Naldrett	J.Ion	J.S.Brown	Z.Penn	1002
E.Sherwood	H.I.Naldrett	A.Pilcher-Dayton	J.S.Brown	Z.Penn	2003
E.Sherwood	H.I.Naldrett	A.Pilcher-Dayton	J.S.Brown	Z.Penn	2004
E.Sherwood	H.I.Naldrett	A.Pilcher-Dayton	J.S.Brown	Z.Penn	2005
E.Sherwood	H.I.Naldrett	A.Pilcher-Dayton	J.S.Brown	J.Briggs	2006
E.Sherwood	H.I.Naldrett	A.Pilcher-Dayton	J.S.Brown	J.Briggs	2007

Appendix IV

Areas with their own Temples

(i) Liverpool - Devonshire Road

(Although this building is no longer in the possession of the Order, it functioned for over fifty years as a dedicated Temple, and as such merits inclusion here).

On the 21st January 1933 the sixth daughter Lodge of the travelling Lodge Mercury No.11 was consecrated by the Most Worshipful The Grand Master, M.W.Bro. Adelaide D. Litten, and R.W.Bro. Lucy O'Hea was installed as Master. The Lodge was named Joyous in memory of a bright and joyous spirit, the daughter of Lucy O'Hea, who died young.

The Lodge meetings were held in various places in Liverpool, but the members decided they wanted a home of their own. The property at 19 Devonshire Road was acquired in July 1934 with a first mortgage vested in the names of four Joyous Lodge members - Mrs. O'Hea, Mrs. Turner, Mrs. Peck and Mrs. Sydney Wright. This was because the titledeeds could not be vested in the name of the Lodge, as the Masonic Constitutions do not give either the Order or Private Lodges power to

hold freehold property. A second mortgage of £500 was granted by R.W.Bro. O'Hea to these three Lodge Joyous members.

The necessary alterations were carried out to the house and the furnishing of it proved a great incentive to the Lodge members. R.W.Bro. O'Hea provided a quantity of furniture for the communal rooms. The house and Temple were dedicated for the sole use of the Order of Women Freemasons on Sunday October 14th 1934, and the ceremony was followed by the dedication of the Lodge Banner. From then on the Lodge members worked hard to raise funds for repaying the mortgages (the first £100 being paid off at the end of the first year) as well as supporting local outside and Masonic charities.

With the outbreak of the Second World War in 1939 the normal activities of the Lodge were inevitably curtailed. Nevertheless in 1941, 1942 and 1944 the Grand Master, accompanied by the Grand Secretary, attended Installation ceremonies, giving much encouragement to the Lodge and the house in those difficult days.

On 17th March 1945 Lodge Inspiration No.24 was consecrated, in May 1945 Joyous Chapter No.5, and in May 1946 Bondstone Mark Lodge No.3, and these all met at Devonshire Road. By the end of 1948 the first mortgage was repaid. Two more Lodges had been formed to meet in Devonshire Road - Lodge Lucy O'Hea No.99, Lodge of The Three Lights No.101 - both in 1958. These were followed by St. Ann Conclave No.7 in 1959, Corinthian Mark Lodge No.20 in 1962 and Lucy O'Hea Chapter No.17 in 1963.

In 1967 it became increasingly obvious that although the Trustees had worked hard to maintain the building, more support and funding was needed, particularly as dry rot had been discovered. Accordingly, through the kind concern and intervention by the Past Grand Master, M.W.Bro. Muirhead Hope, an agreement was entered into by the then Trustees that a committee should be formed to take over the general management of the house, consistent with the existing provisions, consisting of two members of each Lodge, Chapter and Conclave meeting there, and the Past Grand Master.

R.W.Bro. O'Hea generously discharged the remaining mortgage and transferred the safekeeping of the house by a Declaration of Trust, relieving the previous Trustees. It was requested that the building should never be called a club and no dancing or drinking would be allowed. In later years the no-drinking rule was relaxed to the extent that, at Installation Dinners only, Lodges were permitted sherry and wine for the toasts.

Over the years there have been changes to the Trustees due to death and retirement. The number was always four and from 1962 until it was sold one of the four Trustees was the reigning Grand Master. In the early days, parts of the house were let as flats to members of the Order. As they left, gradually those rooms were taken over for practice and dressing rooms. The house stood in approximately one-fifth of an acre of ground, backing on to a beautiful park. We had a Temple, Library, kitchen and Tyler's Room - in all, we had thirty rooms and parking space in front for at least fourteen cars, with a large garden at the rear.

However, in time the house in Devonshire Road unfortunately became a non-viable proposition and eventually had to be disposed of. The final meeting took place in May 1988. However, let us keep in mind that the impact of Lodge Joyous No.18 and the Devonshire Road Temple was instrumental, both directly and indirectly, in the formation of Lodges in Liverpool, Lancashire, Cheshire, Wirral, Shropshire and North Wales.

V.Wor.Bro. P.J. Gregg, P.G.D.C.,
Grand Inspector, Liverpool.

(ii) Sussex - Worthing - Porchway House

(see pages 132-3 and 190-192)

Porchway House in Rowlands Road, West Worthing, West Sussex was bought by the Adelaide Litten Trust Fund in 1952. It was opened by the Grand Master, M.W.Bro. Mary Gordon Muirhead Hope on 7th June 1952 and the following day consecrated as a Residential and Rest Home by R.W.Bro. Maud Litten, P.G.W. on the first anniversary of the death of her sister, M.W.Bro. Adelaide Litten, Past Grand Master. On

the same day the large music room belonging to the house was dedicated as a Masonic Temple. Initially it was let to Lodge Progress No.19 which met at Worthing. After the dedication, Lodge Progress opened a Lodge in the new Temple. A remark by a male Mason at the Opening of the house made the point that we had achieved something that U.G.L.E. had never done so far - opened a home with a Temple attached, so that the residents could continue to enjoy their Freemasonry.

Later in 1977 the grounds of *Porchway House* were used to build the Doris Jones Memorial Home, a nursing home for the Brethren. At the same time the Temple in the house was extended out into the garden. This extension came into use with the meetings of the newly-consecrated Doris Jones Memorial Lodge No.300 in 1978.

The Temple at *Porchway House* continues to be used for the two week-end meetings every year of the Doris Jones Memorial Lodge and for the meetings of Lodge Progress/Sussex Downs No.19/90, Progress Mark No.7, Premier Chapter No.1 and St. Cuthman Conclave No.4.

(iii) Midland Counties - Birmingham - Yarwood Hall

In December 1960 the Most Worshipful The Grand Master, M.W.Bro. Mary Gordon Muirhead Hope, graciously chaired a general meeting of the combined Birmingham Lodges to discuss the possibility of purchasing a property suitable as a permanent home for women's

Freemasonry in the district. Hitherto, Lodge meetings had been held in various hotel rooms in the city centre.

With monies from Lodge Arbitrium No.60, Lodge Orion No.56, Lodge Peace and Harmony No.59, Golden Square Chapter No.9 and a £1,000 interest-free loan from Grand Lodge, that possibility became reality in May 1961 when the land and premises at Yarwood Hall, Smirrells Road, Hall Green, Birmingham were purchased and the Women Freemasons Temple Trust was created.

Intensive fund-raising then became necessary in order to adapt and equip the building. In October 1961 it was dedicated as a Masonic Temple by the Grand Master, M.W.Bro. Mary Gordon Muirhead Hope. Since that time we have had the pleasure of receiving other high-ranking and important Brethren to our Temple. In recent years we have had the honour of welcoming the Most Worshipful The Grand Master, M.W.Bro. Brenda Irene Fleming-Taylor, on three occasions.

Fund-raising still continues to be of major concern for, as one would expect with an older building, maintenance is a constant drain on our limited resources. In addition to those Lodges already mentioned, the Hall is used by Lodge Peace and Harmony No.58, Lodge Alliance

(Installed Masters) No.232, Lodge St. Alphege No.283 and Yarwood Mark Lodge No.26. The Brethren of all the Lodges and other Degrees are members of the Temple Trust.

In 1983 it was found that the roof was in danger of collapse and that much of the building was infested with woodworm. Major building work necessitated raising more loans and donations and the Hall could not be used for some months. We have recently been involved in extensive repairs and redecoration following the collapse of the ceiling in the east end of the Lodge.

Due to the foresight of our Founder Brethren we are able to enjoy the luxury of our own Temple and it is incumbent on the current membership to uphold the memory of those courageous ladies by working tirelessly to maintain our 'home'. As W.Bro. Elsie Bailey of Lodge Orion No.56 wrote at the time of the repairs in 1984 -

> *May the roof above us never fall in*
> *and may those who gather below never fall out.*

V.W.Bro. M. Attwood, D.G.Reg., G.M's.G.S.,
Lodge Arbitrium No.60,
Trustee, Women Freemasons Temple Trust.

(iv) Northern Counties - Sunderland - 18 Tunstall Road

The building now known as the Sunderland Temple was built as a Church of the Latter Day Saints (the Mormons), and we still have near the East a small indentation in the carpet where the bath used for total immersion was situated.

The two Lodges that were instrumental in buying this building were Lodge Perseverance No.15 and Lodge St Mary's No.42. After holding their meetings in many buildings around the area both Lodges were desperately looking for a building they could purchase as a joint venture. A member of Lodge St Mary's, W.Bro. Dorothy Macbeth, P.A.G.Purs. and her husband were estate agents and they heard about the building in Tunstall Road. The Latter Day Saints wanted to purchase some land in Sunderland, and after much negotiation and lots of hard work by the Brethren, the Church was purchased in 1965 for the sum of £1,675, which was a lot of money then, and the two Lodges had to pay seven guineas for every meeting they held, including Lodges of Instruction.

The Brick Fund was started - every member was asked to buy a brick and to put their name on it on a painting of the Temple - and this became the Building Fund.

The Grand Master at the time, M.W.Bro. Mildred Rhoda Low, and her team of Officers dedicated the Temple on the 6th August 1966. In the same year the two Lodges moved in to hold their meetings, W.Bro. Macbeth being the first to occupy the Chair of King Solomon.

The Master's Chair and pedestals have been donated by various members over the years and we are very grateful to them all for their foresight and generosity. The seating consisted of tip-up cinema seats - you can just imagine the noise as Brethren were required to stand up and sit down - but at least this ensured that they stayed awake during the meetings. The only toilet at the time was outside in the yard, which was a bit chilly in the winter months. It was also cold inside as the only heating at that time was an open fire - what would Health and Safety say about that?

In 1975 new heaters were purchased and in the course of time central heating was installed and this has recently been upgraded. In 1981 we were able to buy a new Lodge carpet for £120; this is still in excellent condition and is a focal point on entering the Temple. Over the years Brethren have donated various items of furniture in memory of their loved ones. New chairs have been bought and the interior redecorated. The building has proved very popular over the years and we now accommodate five Craft Lodges and most of the Higher Degrees, and also hold many social events.

V.W.Bro. J. Briggs, G.D.C.,
with grateful thanks to W.Bro. D. Macbeth, P.A.G.Purs.and
W.Bro. B. Wilkinson

(v) Essex - Leigh-on-Sea - Fraternity Hall

Lodge Fraternity No.12 was the first provincial Lodge of our Order - the first fruit of the work of Lodge Mercury No.11, the travelling Lodge - and was consecrated in July 1930.

Over the years the Lodge had many homes, including a Boots' café and four hotels in Southend. In the early years before the Second World War the Brethren were very keen to have their own Temple and so a Building Fund was started and many social functions held to raise money for it. It takes a long time for a Penny Building Fund to grow, and after the War land prices and building costs grew much faster. Much later, in 1957, Lodge Thorpe No.95 was founded - which meant that two Lodges were able to contribute to the slow growth of the Fund.

Then an event in December 1963 changed the situation dramatically. The *S.S. Lakonia* was destroyed by fire off the coast of Madeira and two Fraternity members were on board for a Christmas cruise - W.Bro. Flossie Walker, her husband and another member. They spent five and a half hours in an open lifeboat before being rescued and unfortunately the second member did not survive.

W.Bro. Walker's husband was anxious to make his feelings of relief and gratitude tangible and he offered his wife anything she wanted as a thank-offering for their escape. She remembered both the long-hoped-for Temple and that her husband had purchased a plot of land on Eastwood Road North, Leigh-on-Sea. This was a sizeable piece of land behind some shops he had built, where gypsies grazed their

horses, and she asked if she could have it. When her husband gave her the land she donated it for the erection of a Temple for the two Lodges.

The original design by the son of another Lodge member proved too expensive and had to be modified. Mr. Walker built the Hall at cost price, and in a memorable ceremony in August 1966 three hundred visitors were able to see the dream come true. The Grand Master, M.W.Bro. Mildred Rhoda Low, assisted by the Deputy Grand Master, R.W.Bro. Dorothy Taylor and other Grand Lodge Officers, dedicated the building for Masonic use. The memorial glass container and the stone were lowered into a cavity in the north east part of the building by W.Bro. Walker, who had also laid the first brick and who gave our Temple its name - Fraternity Hall.

In the same way that every stone, tile, chair and cushion represents someone's effort and thought, later money was raised with a Brick Fund to have a wall built at the front of the Temple to protect it, and the building has been constantly maintained and improved through tireless fund-raising. In 2000, on the 70th anniversary of the Consecration of Lodge Fraternity No.12, a new large dining room extension was built. Called the Millennium Room, it was opened by the Grand Master, M.W.Bro. Brenda I. Fleming-Taylor.

In 2002 the kitchen was completely transformed through the kindness of W.Bro. A. Anderson, A.G.Std.Br. of Lodge Endurance No.218 and her husband, W.Bro. L. Scott, S.G.D. who gave an industrial dishwasher, members of Lodge Obedience No.346 who provided a cooker, and many generous donations from members of the Lodges using the Hall. The balance was covered by the Building Fund. The kitchen was officially opened by the  M.W. The Grand Master at the Installation Meeting of Lodge Endurance No.218 in September 2002.

In addition to Lodges Fraternity and Thorpe, Fraternity Hall is now the home of the Essex Lodge of Installed Masters No.348, Fraternity Mark No.13, Priory Chapter No.32, Celestial Cross Conclave No.21, Crusader Preceptory No.8 and Eternal Wisdom Rose Croix Chapter No.5.

In 1994 the five Craft Lodges in south east Essex, experiencing many problems with their venues, formed the Essex Masonic Property Company to raise money towards the acquisition of a Masonic Temple in their part of the county. The company has a Board of Directors and issues shares for purchase. Capital is accruing and the efforts are on-going.

V.W.Bro. D. Bunting, P.G.Reg., G.I. Essex, G.M's.G.S.
V.W.Bro. E. Mylward, P.G.D.C., W.Bro. O. Blunden, P.G.Purs.

(v) South Wales - Cardiff - Hawthorn Temple

Women's Freemasonry in South Wales began with the consecration of Lodge Fellowship No.20. The Brethren of this Lodge played an important part in the expansion of the Order in south Wales and the West.

The council of Lodge Fellowship decided that Freemasonry in Cardiff had outgrown its current home. There were then three Craft Lodges -

St. David No.76, Cartref No.140 and Dyffryn No.147, as well as several Higher Degrees, a Lodge of Installed Masters, a Lodge of Instruction and a study circle, all of which met at the same premises.

Quite early in its existence the Lodge had set up a Building Fund, which had reached the sum of £500. This sum remained intact, despite the expenses involved in maintaining Fellowship House, and this was to form the nucleus of a fund which it was hoped would eventually be used to build a Masonic Temple. Such a building would no longer be the sole responsibility of Lodge Fellowship, and would look to the help and support of all the Cardiff Craft Lodges and the other Lodges within the South Wales and the West area.

Early in 1968 a premises committee was formed from the four Craft Lodges to explore every possibility of buying or renting premises which might suitable for adaptation to use as a Masonic Temple. Numerous premises were inspected by the committee, while the Brethren set to work to increase the Building Fund. In October 1968 it was decided to make an offer for a disused church in Llandaff North. The Grand Master was consulted and a legal advisor was engaged. Eventually an offer of £3,500 was accepted.

The church proved unsuitable for adaptation and was demolished. Planning permission to build afresh was successfully applied for and the work started in earnest. The plans included a Temple with ante room, cloakrooms and kitchen in a one storey building at a cost of £19,750. Demolition and architect's fees brought the total cost to £24,220. The Brethren set to work to raise money by gifts, loans and fund-raising efforts - every Lodge in the South Wales and West Area contributed to swell the funds.

By April 1975 the work was completed and a Masonic Temple stood on the site of the old church. The key was handed over to R.W.Bro. Olwen Lloyd, chairman of the Finance and Premises committee. The Brethren were delighted with their new home, which was given the name of Hawthorn Hall as it was situated in Hawthorn Road West. The Hall was now under the trusteeship of the four Cardiff Craft Lodges.

In July 1975 the new Temple was dedicated by R.W.Bro. Olwen Lloyd, P.D.G.M., G.M's.G.S., assisted by the Grand Wardens, other Grand Lodge Officers and the reigning Masters of the four Cardiff Craft Lodges. This was a proud and memorable day for all the members of the Cardiff Lodges, but particularly for Lodge Fellowship, the senior Lodge and the pioneers of Freemasonry for women in Wales. The beautiful and impressive ceremony will always be remembered with pride by those privileged to be present. The importance of this day was fully appreciated as the beginning of another era - the era of Hawthorn Hall, a beautiful Masonic Temple.

Each of the four Craft Lodges has appointed a Trustee and these Trustees are responsible to their Lodges for the management of Hawthorn Hall. Later the consecration of Lodge Sŵn-y-Gân No.312 meant that eventually another Trustee was added to the original four.

A Finance Committee was formed to advise and instruct the Trustees on financial affairs and to concentrate on the management and control of the finances of Hawthorn Hall. The House Committee was formed to oversee domestic affairs and minor repairs.

Since the original building, an extension has been built to provide a larger kitchen, a dining room and a storage room with cupboards for each Craft Lodge and Higher Degree. Several improvements have been made including double glazing, central heating, furniture and carpets as well as a sophisticated security system. Within the curtilage of the premises there is parking for twelve cars and the whole site is contained within a steel fence and gates.

It is to be regretted that so few of the original Founders are still with us to appreciate the fruits of their labours and of their foresight - to enjoy, as we do, the pleasure which Hawthorn Hall gives us.

V.W.Bro. V. Griffiths, P.J.GD. , G.M's.G.S.
Photograph by W.Bro. J. Hooper, P.J.GD.

(vi) Southern Counties - Bournemouth - Harcourt Temple

In the late 1960s, the three Lodges meeting in the Bournemouth area - Lodge Sirius No.31, Priory Lodge of Christchurch No.141 and Lodge Friendship No.169 - were experiencing problems with their venues. In early 1969 the Worshipful Master of Lodge Friendship, W.Bro. E. M. Goodacre, proposed that the Lodge should set out to accumulate funds to eventually buy its own Temple. Later the other two Lodges expressed an interest in working together for this purpose. A joint meeting of the three Lodges was held and a representative Committee elected, chaired by W.Bro. Goodacre. The fund was called the Harcourt Hall Building Fund.

Many different buildings were viewed, and eventually a suitable hall was found, at a price of £4,000. It was decided to go ahead with the purchase in October 1969 and the deposit was loaned by a Brother and her husband. Approval was sought from the M.W.The Grand Master, M.W.Bro. Mildred Rhoda Low, and, although a loan from the Order was refused, the Brethren were given permission to go ahead on their own.

W.Bro. Goodacre circularised all the members of the three Lodges to ask for donations, interest-free loans of £100 for five years or loans at a low rate of interest. Enough money was raised to allow completion to take place in late November. In the meantime, Brethren's husbands organised the carpentry, electrics, decoration and so on to make the Hall ready for use. The Lodges moved in during January 1970 and named it Harcourt Hall. Duplicate sets of furniture and effects from the other Lodges were also sold to raise funds.

Unfortunately dry rot was soon discovered in the building, necessitating further expenditure for treatment and making-good. Again application for financial help was made to Grand Lodge, but refused. The first Worshipful Master of Lodge Friendship, V.W.Bro. L. Butterworth, stepped in and lent £2,000 at 5% interest.

A company was formed called Harcourt Temple Limited to run the building, of which the shareholders were - and still are - the three Craft Lodges using it. The proposed rent was to be £10.50 per meeting for the first year, which later became £220 p.a. to cover rates, gas, electricity, cleaning, bank charges and other expenses. Many social events were held in the Temple itself to raise funds, which involved much hard work in dismantling and putting back the Lodge equipment.

On 9th September 1973 the Temple was dedicated by the Most Worshipful The Grand Master, M.W.Bro. Mildred Rhoda Low in a very beautiful ceremony. There was a procession of all the Officers of the three Craft Lodges, followed by the Consecrating Officers, R.W.Bro Frances Hall (later Grand Master) as Senior Warden, R.W. Bro. Anne Daley (then Grand Inspector for South Western Counties) as Junior Warden, assisted by other Grand Lodge Officers who occupied the Chairs. The Most Worshipful The Grand Master assumed the Chair and was saluted. There was an opening hymn and an address by the Grand Master and this was followed by a lovely solo sung by W.Bro. Mary Goodacre. The Invocation was pronounced by the Grand Master and a memorial glass was lowered into the floor in front of the Master's pedestal. This glass contains coins of the realm for that date and other contemporary items. Then came a reading from Isaiah,

Chapter 66, and the memorial stone was tried by the G.J.W., proved by the G.S.W., and tested by the Most Worshipful The Grand Master, who then blessed it and lowered it into the cavity. Corn, wine and oil were then poured on the stone. After this the Grand Wardens presented charcoal and a trowel and the cover was placed over the stone and again blessed by the Grand Master.

Salt was then scattered over the Lodge Floor, there were more readings from the Bible and the Temple was censed three times. The solemn Act of Dedication took place, then the closing hymn. The Blessing was invoked and the Most Worshipful The Grand Master closed the Lodge.

The loans and other monies were repaid in 1975, and the Temple was at last owned by the Brethren - to become the heritage of all Bournemouth Brethren in the future.

V.W.Bro. Jean Rogers, P.D.G.Reg.

(vii)   North Wales - Oakenholt, Flint - Bethania Temple

Bethania Temple stands on the banks of the Dee Estuary where the tide regularly ebbs and flows, and is home to three Craft Lodges and eight Higher Degrees.

The Order of Women Freemasons was introduced into north-east Wales in 1963 when Mrs. Mary Cameron Jones and Mrs. Lily Bevan (who had both been initiated into Lodge King Solomon No.13), with the assistance of Grand Lodge Officers, founded Lodge Bryn Golau No.165 in Flint. The first meetings were held in Flint's Memorial Hall, and the Lodge went from strength to strength with an ever-increasing number of candidates. In those halcyon days, double ceremonies were held in order to accommodate the Initiation of so many new members.

It soon became apparent that a new venue was desperately needed and in 1969 the old Bethania Chapel, constructed in 1883, was purchased by a group of far-sighted Masons headed by W.Bros. Lily Bevan (whose untimely death precluded her seeing her work come to fruition), Mary Cameron Jones and the redoubtable Sarah Edith 'Minnie' Flynn. A Board of Trustees, W.Bros. Mary Cameron Jones, Minnie Flynn, Sally Maybe and Wilhelmina Parkinson, was appointed to hold the building on behalf of the members.

The building was in dire need of repair and alterations to fit it for Masonic use, so the Bethania Building Fund was established to administer the generous donations and loans provided by Lodge members and to raise money to finance the building works. An additional floor level was inserted to provide a beautiful Temple, retiring room and storage facilities on the upper level, and a large meeting room for festive boards and social events, committee room, kitchen and toilet facilities on the ground floor.

On Sunday 4th June 1972 the building was dedicated, in a sumptuous ceremony, by the Grand Master, M.W.Bro. Mildred Rhoda Low, who, aided by R.W.Bro. Olwen Lloyd, the Assistant Grand Master, laid the foundation stone and consecrated the Temple with corn, wine and oil. The presiding Master was, very appropriately, W.Bro 'Minnie' Flynn.

With the ever-increasing membership of Lodge Bryn Golau, a daughter Lodge, Bethania No.284, was consecrated in 1973. The two Lodges have subsequently amalgamated, and the Temple is now also home to Lodge Anwyl No.256 (Mold) and Clwyd Lodge of Installed Masters No.324.

The guiding light, until her passing in 2005 to the Grand Lodge above, was the indomitable V.W.Bro. Mary Cameron-Jones. Through her foresight, dedication and perseverance, and the assistance of our Grand Inspector, R.W.Bro. Stella Margaret Williams, the Higher Degrees were brought to North Wales and Bethania Temple is now home to Flintstone Mark and Ark Mariner Lodges No.38, Bethania Chapter

No.43, Trinity Conclave No.12, Holy Lance Encampment No.4, Delta Tabernacle No. 4 and Rose and Flame Rose Croix Chapter No.2.

The building has been graced by the visit of the Grand Master, M.W.Bro. Brenda Irene Fleming-Taylor, on the occasions of anniversary celebrations of both Lodge Bryn Golau/Bethania and Lodge Anwyl, and by R.W.Bro. Monica Oktabcova for the consecration of the Higher Degrees.

The cost of maintaining the Temple is of course major, and the Bethania Fund Raising Committee exists to organise events and raise money for running repairs and ongoing acquisitions and embellishments for the comfort of Brethren and visitors. The current Trustees acknowledge here the financial aid given by the generous donations of individuals and the North Wales Lodges, which enables the work to continue. Bethania Temple is an enclave of comfort and solace to members and their families in times of need, and of joy and rejoicing in times of celebration. Our Founders can be rightly proud that within these peaceful walls their children and their children's children have enjoyed every satisfaction and delight.

W.Bro. Judith A. Corbelli, J.G.D.

(vi) Midland Counties - Leicester - Millicent Morris Memorial Hall

Millicent Morris died in 1966 and left her insignia of the Order of the Commander of the British Empire to the Order of Women Freemasons and her Masonic regalia to any member of Lodge Crusader No.108 who wished to enter the Higher Degrees. After bequests to relatives and friends Mrs. Morris left the remainder of her estate to Lodge Crusader No.108 in order to help with the purchase of their own Temple, as she had had so much happiness, love and affection from members of the Order.

Our building was originally a tin church on an allotment in East Park Road, Leicester which we know was in existence in 1906. We have no information as to when it was dismantled and re-sited in Dore Road but we do know that it was used as a community building prior to it being purchased by Lodge Crusader in 1970.

The Temple Trust, with a Board of Trustees drawn from the members of the Lodge, was formed to run the building, and the Brethren worked hard to make it into a suitable place for their meetings. Over the years members and their husbands have painted and cleaned and kept the building going with the help of the necessary tradesmen.

In 2001 the Brick/Share Fund was started with the idea of purchasing a larger building but it was soon realised this was way beyond us. The Fund today helps with the maintenance of the existing building.

A legacy left to us by the late W.Bro. Dorothy Bradley has enabled us to have a cladding put on the building, central heating installed, chairs, a new ceiling, pedestals and carpet surround in the Temple, also a new kitchen and table and chairs for the dining room. It would be lovely to have larger premises, but we do have a building to be proud of.

Bro. Pauline Gibbs,
Secretary to the Temple Trust and Maintenance Fund

(viii) Yorkshire - Barnsley - St. Barnabas Temple

The St. Barnabas Mission - now re-named St. Barnabas Hall - was purchased by Barnsley Lodge No.234 (later re-named St. Barnabas Lodge) in 1972.

The first Grand Inspector for Yorkshire, R.W.Bro. Agnes Parkinson, P.J.G.W., G.M's.G.S., who was invited to view it, remarked that the Brethren did not know what they were taking on, whilst R.W.Bro. M. H. Lancaster, P.J.G.W., G.M's.G.S immediately felt that it was undeniably the right place - it was so beautiful with its arched ceiling and high windows and would make a lovely Temple.

In the East the stained glass windows depicting the dove and the square and compasses would form a wonderful background for our ceremonies. The majestic organ was also in excellent condition, so the deposit was paid and the contract signed in April 1973. Buying a church was found to be a very slow process and whilst we were allowed to use it in the meantime the sale was not completed until January 1974. St. Barnabas Church was built in 1933 so the structure is comparatively modern. The beautiful arched ceiling and high windows make it very suitable as a Temple.

The Temple, ample in area, was initially used for both ceremonial and social occasions whilst the schoolroom, which was not so elegant, was let for the storage of building materials to help with the cost of the upkeep of the Temple. New toilets were built and also a kitchen. The first Installation dinner was held in the Temple on Sunday 2nd July 1972 when W.Bro. Muriel Biltcliffe became the new Worshipful Master.

After some years it was decided to keep the Temple as a place set apart from the social activities. It was decided to open the schoolroom - this was an additional and daunting task as further heavy expenditure was necessary and a loan of £10,000 was obtained. This was to be the new dining area, fitted with ample kitchen space, and a very fine bar (acquired from the Queen's Hotel in the centre of town which was to be re-furbished) which proved another steady source of income for the upkeep of the building. By May 1981 Lodge Argosy No.27 (Bradford) were able to celebrate their Installation dinner in the newly-opened premises.

The Temple could now be dedicated and this ceremony was carried out by the M. W. The Grand Master, M.W. Bro. Frances Hall, assisted by R.W.Bro. Doris Hoadley O.B.E., A.G.M., G.M's.G.S. on Saturday 17th April 1982.

Many Yorkshire Lodges hold their Installation ceremonies at St. Barnabas Hall, and Consecration ceremonies have been - and still are - held in the Temple. Many of the side Degrees in Yorkshire also use the Temple, having ample room to store all their furniture and equipment. Carol Services have been held at Christmas for many years in the Temple.

A feature of the Temple is the illuminated letter G - a black letter on a white ground - which is mounted in a large glass star in a framework of copper with yellow, orange, and blue points to the rays. This is a tribute to the memory of R.W.Bro. Agnes Parkinson who was first Grand Inspector for Yorkshire.

The upkeep of the building is an enormous task. Three regular, seasonal, buffet lunches are held during the year, which are very popular and are sustained through the generosity of all members who provide, prepare and serve food. A Gala Day is organised annually and is supported by other Yorkshire Lodges, to whom we are most indebted for their financial help and support.

It is not possible to single out any individual act of service or kindness in support of our Yorkshire Temple - each member has particular attributes and talents to offer. We should all look up to one of the windows in the Temple that contains the emblem of a golden crown, which represents the 'Final Achievements' - the material and spiritual crown of our endeavours.

W.Bro. Sylvia Hughes, P.A.G.Std.Br.

(xi) Cheshire - Runcorn - Grouville Hall

Grouville Hall is the Masonic Centre for the north of Cheshire and was purchased by Lodge Mercia No.193 in 1976. The Hall was built in 1904 and was at first a private school owned by a Miss Baker and her sister Mrs. Ditchfield. The sisters had both been brought up in Jersey and they named the Hall Grouville Hall after the parish and the bay there. On the outside wall of the building there was a plaque engraved with the name Grouville Hall and the members decided that they would like to keep the original name.

For many years the Lodge had met in five different venues and a lot of hard work was done by members to keep these meeting places up to standard. In 1976, with the help of many husbands and friends, we

heard about Grouville Hall. The Hall was purchased by donations from all the members and loans of varying sizes from Founders, which were all in turn paid back.

The first meeting at Grouville Hall was held by Dispensation and was the 70th meeting of the Lodge. The Lodge consisted of members of other Lodges from Liverpool, Widnes and surrounding areas - a very happy and dedicated band of Masons. The Hall consists of a large room, now the Lodge room, together with a dining room, kitchen and smaller rooms for members to use.

When the other Lodges in the area found premises difficult to find, they were welcomed with open arms by the members of Lodge Mercia No.193. They are our Mother Lodge, Pilgrim No.153, Lodge Minerva No.249, Lodge Cornucopia No.268 and Lodge Grouville No.298 who all meet happily together and support each other at meetings and social events.

We also have the Higher Degrees meeting in the Hall - Lodge Norton Priory No.325 (Installed Masters), Sandstone Mark and R.A.M No.32, Seal of Solomon Chapter No.36 and St. Elizabeth Conclave No.16. This means that the Hall is used almost to capacity. The Hall is also used sometimes by other Cheshire Lodges when they have difficulty with their normal venues.

The Cheshire members realise how lucky they are to own their own Temple. It is hard work for the three Trustees, and all the members appreciate their hard work on our behalf. We thank them so much, but even more so our Founder members for their foresight in buying the Temple for the use of the Order of Women Freemasons in North Cheshire.

R.W.Bro. Beryl Daniels, P.G.W., care of Cheshire,
W.Bro. L.H. Howard, P.S.G.D.

(x) West Lancashire - Lytham St. Annes - Northolme

The Order of Women Freemasons has a residential home for members called *Northolme* at Lytham St. Annes in West Lancashire. Hidden down the garden at the back of the home is the Temple. It is unassuming in appearance, being a one-storey brick building with a plain wooden door at the side for entrance. However, the history of how it came into being from a stable-cum-garage forms an interesting story of vision and dedication.

Lodge of St. Anne No.91 was consecrated by the Most Worshipful The Grand Master, M.W.Bro. Mary Gordon Muirhead Hope in 1957 at the Queens Hotel, Lytham and for the first ten years Installation and Regular meetings were held there. After this period accommodation became a constant problem, rooms becoming too expensive and hotels imposing more and more restrictions. The Brethren longed for their own Temple and with the acquisition of *Northolme* by the Adelaide Litten Trust in 1971 the possibility of converting the building at the rear end of the garden began to be considered. R.W.Bro. V. Nield, P.G.W, G.M's.G.S. was the leading figure in bringing into being the plan presented to Grand Lodge. Eventually, permission was granted in 1981 by the Most Worshipful The Grand Master, M.W.Bro. Frances Hall. Donations and loans were raised and the building conversion commenced.

Plans were drawn up to convert the garage into the Lodge room, cloakroom and toilet facilities. In due course they were executed and the Temple took shape. Inside the Temple the walls were decorated simply with dark blue curtains at the windows and a floor covering of dark blue carpet. As meetings had previously always been held in various hotels, the only seating owned by Lodge of St. Anne No.91 was their beautiful Master's Chair and two Wardens' chairs, so pale gold chairs were purchased by individual Brethren for use by members and visitors at the meetings.

The first meeting was held in the Temple on the 4th October 1982 by the Lodge of St. Anne No.91. On the 9th April 1983 the Temple was dedicated by the Most Worshipful The Grand Master, M.W.Bro. Frances Hall.

Over the years many improvements have been carried out to the structure and interior of the building. A new black and white chequered carpet has been fitted and hand-crafted pedestals made for

the Master, Wardens, Secretary and Treasurer. The walls are now adorned in the East with the banners of Lodge of St. Anne No.91 and Northolme Lodge of Installed Masters No.341, together with photographs of the present and previous Grand Masters.

During the years the Temple has been honoured by the presence of the Most Worshipful The Grand Master, M.W.Bro. Brenda Irene Fleming-Taylor at the 40th Anniversary of the Lodge of St. Anne No.91 and the dedication of the Banner of Northolme Lodge of Installed Masters No.341 and recently by RW.Bro. Zuzanka Penn, Assistant Grand Master, G.M's.G.S. at the 50th Anniversary of Lodge St. Anne No.91.

Alongside Lodge of St. Anne No.91 and Northolme Lodge of Installed Masters No.341, Fylde Coast Mark Lodge (RA.M.) No.24, Fylde Coast Chapter No.22 and St. Cuthbert Conclave No.19 regularly meet at the Temple, ensuring it is fully used throughout the year. Brethren visiting *Northolme* for short stays often attend meetings held in the Temple and their presence is always welcomed.

Walking down the garden path at *Northolme* to attend a meeting always gives a feeling of leaving the busy world behind. Entering the Temple, peace and harmony is sensed immediately and joyful preparation made to participate in a beautiful Masonic ceremony. The Brethren will always be grateful to the Adelaide Litten Trust for allowing the conversion of the garage at the rear of *Northolme*, and for their continued support and help in maintaining it; also to the many Brethren whose kind generosity enables the Temple to be kept in pristine condition.

W.Bro. Elaine Townsend, P.S.G.D.
W.Bro. Muriel Ingham, P.A.G.Std.Br.

(xi) East Kent

In 1982 a group of members at Faversham Abbey Lodge No.215 started a Building Fund at a time when the Lodge was experiencing difficulties in finding a suitable meeting place.

The Temple at Wouldham.

It was soon realised that the Lodge would not make very fast progress on its own and that various other Lodges, having similar difficulties, were also trying to raise money for their own Building Funds. From this grew the idea that if the Brethren of Kent banded together, a joint county-wide effort would have more chance of success. The Kent Masonic Property Co. Ltd. was incorporated on 29th September 1983, with its main purpose to combine the efforts of all and to buy and manage properties for the use of women Freemasons in Kent.

In May 1988 the company bought the building at 71 High Street, Wouldham which had previously been a church hall. Wouldham is close to the River Medway and the towns of Rochester, Chatham and Gillingham. This property is now used permanently by six Craft Lodges for their regular and instruction meetings. The building is also used by two Mark Lodges, one Chapter and one Red Cross of Constantine Conclave.

The temple at Upper Brents in Faversham was purchased in August 1993 as a derelict factory and had to be almost completely rebuilt. It is now the regular meeting place

The Temple at Upper Brents, Faversham.

for four Craft Lodges and most of the Higher Degrees. Faversham is further east than the Medway and close to the northern coast of Kent.

The Temple at St. Saviour's Hall, Westgate.

Our third property, St. Saviour's Hall in Westgate - also previously a church hall - was purchased in February 2001. Westgate is a seaside town near Margate, almost at the north-eastern tip of Kent. The three Kent Temples are therefore geographically spaced throughout the East Kent Area. This Temple is used by three Craft Lodges, one Mark and one Chapter. In addition, this building is used by a men's Craft Lodge and two Chapters. We think this might be the first time that a men's Lodge has rented premises owned by women! The East Kent Lodge of Installed Masters No.354 meets at the three Kent venues in turn.

Now that we have three permanent Temples we are carrying out a programme of refurbishment and so the fund-raising continues. As the Kent Masonic Property Company is a limited company, most of its funding is by share capital. Both individual members and Lodges may buy shares (currently at £3 each) and these shareholders appoint a Board of Directors to manage the company. Every encouragement is given to members to buy shares in the company. In this way they can have a say in who is appointed to the Board of Directors and vote on any resolutions put forward at general meetings. A member has one vote for each share held.

R.W.Bro. Z. Penn, A.G.M., G.M's.G.S.

List of Illustrations

All reasonable efforts have been made to trace the provenance of illustrations, and acknowledgment is given where the source is known.

Page

73   Banner of Lodge Verity No.7. *O.W.F. - Photo: Robyn Wright.*
74a   Dinner of Lodge Harmony No.4 and Lodge Fidelity No.8 in 1931. *O.W.F.*
74b   Banner of Lodge Fidelity No.8. *O.W.F. - Photo: Robyn Wright.*
75   Banner of Lodge Loyalty No.9. *O.W.F. - Photo: Robyn Wright.*
76   Gravestone of Marion Lindsay Halsey, Withyham. *O.W.F. - Photo: Author.*
77   Banner of Lodge Marion Halsey No.10. *O.W.F. - Photo: Robyn Wright.*
78   Adelaide Litten. *O.W.F.*
81   East end of the Grand Temple. *O.W.F.*
83   Adelaide Litten. *O.W.F.*
85   Banner of Lodge Mercury No.11. *O.W.F. - Photo: Robyn Wright.*
87   The Mercury jewel. *O.W.F. – Photo: Robert Brice.*
88   Brooch of Queen Mary's Needlework Guild. *Photo courtesy of Queen Mary's Clothing Guild.*
89   The Babies' Hospital, Deptford. *Photo by permission of the Albany Institute (Deptford Fund).*
92a   Emblem of Logos Chapter No.2. *O.W.F.*
92b   Emblem of Zodiac Chapter No.3. *O.W.F.*
99   Peter Walter Slingsby, G. Secretary 1912-1935. *O.W.F.*
100   Peter Birchall, D.G.M. 1912-1935. *O.W.F.*
102   R.W.Bro. Florence Leveridge, Grand Secretary from 1935-1950. *O.W.F.*
104   W.Bro. Dorothea Irving as Trilby. *www.collectorspost.com*
107   Lucy Bertram O'Hea, Grand Master 1938-1948. *O.W.F.*
108   Banner of Lodge Joyous No.18. *O.W.F.*
111   Lilac Parker-Jervis, Deputy Grand Master. *O.W.F.*
113   Banner of Lodge Fellowship No.20. *O.W.F.*
116   Lucy, Lady Markham. *O.W.F.*
119   Mary Gordon Muirhead Hope. *O.W.F.*
121   R.W.Bro. D.A.Taylor, D.G.M. 1948-1968. *O.W.F.*
123   London Grand Rank apron and jewel. *O.W.F. - Photos: Robyn Wright.*
125   The sword Constancy and Faith. *O.W.F.*
127   Banner of Lodge Stability & Peace No.5. *O.W.F. - Photo: Robyn Wright.*
128   Emblem of the Ancient Free and Accepted Masons. *O.W.F.*

Acknowledgements

Picture credits are given in the List of Illustrations.

Many people have helped me with information and material during the years of writing this book, to all of whom I give my grateful thanks. My apologies to any who are not mentioned by name – they are no less appreciated.

Thanks are due to the Grand Master, M.W.Bro. Brenda I. Fleming-Taylor and the Order of Women Freemasons for access to the Minute Books of Grand Lodge from 1908 to date and various Minute Books of the Board of General Purposes.

To the Grand Master for writing the Preface.

To the Grand Secretary, R.W.Bro. Joan S. Brown, P.G.W., G.M's.G.S. and the Grand Treasurer, R.W.Bro. Hilda Naldrett, P.A.G.M., G.M's.G.S.

To the Adelaide Litten Charitable Trust for permission to reproduce material from the Diamond Jubilee commemorative book.

To Lodges Golden Rule No.1, Emulation No.2, Lodge of Unity No.3, Lodge Stone of Foundation (I.M.) No.22, Lodge Argosy No.27 and Lodge of Freedom No.144.

To:
The late R.W.Bro. Lilian Chapman, P.A.G.M., G.M's.G.S.; W.Bro. Vivienne Crone, P.G.Std.Br.; V.W.Bro. Olive Dean, P.D.G.Reg.; Anthony Geikie-Cobb; the Guildhall Library, London; Margaret Harrison of the Geddes Archive, University of Strathclyde; the Honourable Fraternity of Ancient Freemasons (the Grand Secretary); the Imperial War Museum Library; Rev. Adrian Leak, St. Michael and All Angels, Withyham, East Sussex; Lewisham Local History Library; the late W.Bro. Doreen E.P. Monk, P.D.G.Swd.Br.; the late R.W.Bro. Elizabeth Parker, P.G.W., G.M's.G.S.; W.Bro. Joanna Pigott; Dr. Andrew Prescott and the Centre for Research into Freemasonry, University of Sheffield; V.Ill.Bro. Brian Roberts and the British Federation of the International Order Co-Freemasonry *Le Droit Humain*; Major Frederick H. Smyth for material belonging to the late

R.W.Bro. Doris E. Smyth, P.A.G.M., G.M's.G.S. donated to the O.W.F. Archive; Stephenson Harwood & Co.; Janet Kerschner and the Theosophical Society in America Archives; Trinity College, Dublin Library and Archive; Diane Clements, Martin Cherry, Mark Dennis and Susan Snell of the Library and Museum of Freemasonry, U.G.L.E.; R.W.Bro. Mary Wilkes, P.G.W., G.M's.G.S.; the Women's Library, London; W.Bro. Mollie Wright, P.G.Std.Br.; W.Bro. Robyn Wright, L.G.R. and Tony Wright.

A.P-D.

Abbreviations

A.F. & A.M.	Ancient Free and Accepted Masons
A.G.D.C.	Assistant Grand Director of Ceremonies
A.G.M.	Assistant Grand Master
A.G.Std.Br.	Assistant Grand Standard Bearer
A.L.C.T.	Adelaide Litten Charitable Trust
A.L.T.F.	Adelaide Litten Trust Fund
B.O.G.P.	Board of General Purposes
Bro.	Brother
B.R.F.	Building Restoration Fund
C.B.E.	Commander of the Order of the British Empire
D.G.M.	Deputy Grand Master
D.G.Swd.Br.	Deputy Grand Sword Bearer
G.	Grand
G.A.O.T.U.	Great Architect of the Universe
G.D.C.	Grand Director of Ceremonies
G.L.	Grand Lodge
G.M's.G.S.	Grand Master's Grand Star
G.J.W.	Grand Junior Warden
G.Reg./Registrar	Grand Registrar
G.S.W.	Grand Senior Warden
H.	Haggai (Chapter office)
H.F.A.F.	Honourable Fraternity of Ancient Freemasons
H.F.A.M.	Honourable Fraternity of Antient Masonry
H.M. Borstal	Her Majesty's Borstal Institution
H.R.A.	Holy Royal Arch (Chapter)
H.R.D.M.	Heredom
I.M.	Installed Masters (Lodge)
I.R.A.	Irish Republican Army

J.	Joshua (Chapter office)
J.G.D.	Junior Grand Deacon
J.W.	Junior Warden
L.G.R.	London Grand Rank
M.B.E.	Member of the Order of the British Empire
M.Ex.Comp.	Most Excellent Companion (Chapter)
M.W.Bro.	Most Worshipful Brother (Grand Master)
O.B.E.	Officer of the Order of the British Empire
O.W.F.	Order of Women Freemasons
P.A.G.M.	Past Assistant Grand Master
P.A.G.Purs.	Past Assistant Grand Pursuivant
P.D.G.M.	Past Deputy Grand Master
P.G.D.C.	Past Grand Director of Ceremonies
P.D.G.Reg.	Past Deputy Grand Registrar
P.G.Reg./Registrar	Past Grand Registrar
P.G.W.	Past Grand Warden
P.J.G.D.	Past Junior Grand Deacon
P.J.G.W.	Past Junior Grand Warden
P.S.G.W.	Past Senior Grand Warden
Q.M.A.A.C.	Queen Mary's Army Auxiliary Corps
R.A.	Royal Arch (Chapter)
R.W.Bro.	Right Worshipful Brother
S.G.D.	Senior Grand Deacon
S.G.W.	Senior Grand Warden
S.M.I.B.	So Mote It Be *[at the end of prayers]*
S.R.N.	State Registered Nurse
S.W.	Senior Warden
T.G.A.O.T.U.	The Great Architect of the Universe
U.G.L.E.	United Grand Lodge of England
V.Ill.Bro.	Very Illustrious Brother
V.Puiss.Bro.	Very Puissant Brother
V.S.L.	Volume of the Sacred Law
V.W.Bro.	Very Worshipful Brother
W.A.A.C.	Women's Army Auxiliary Corps
W.Bro.	Worshipful Brother
W.M.	Worshipful Master
Z.	Zerubbabel (Chapter office)

Index

References in italics relate to illustrations. Specific Lodges belong to the O.W.F. unless stated otherwise. Individual Lodges in the Higher Degrees are entered under the Order or Degree. Overseas Lodges are entered under the country.